RESHAPING LABOUR: ORGANISATION, WORK AND POLITICS — Edinburgh in the Great War and After

In a few short years during and just after the Great War, the Labour Party and the trade unions established themselves firmly at the centre of the British political and industrial scene. But at the same time, the politics and organisation of both Labour and unions were reshaped.

This is a grass-roots study of a key period in the building of Labour's political and industrial base. It is a study of how unions and Labour were organised and motivated to seize their moments of destiny — and of how a new political and industrial movement was limited by the commonsense of the age in which it was born. It is a study of shifting support for various Labour and Communist political and industrial strategies — of the pressures and struggles which reshaped the movement, stamping on it the character we know today. And it is a study of how labour — at work and in the community — responded to war, to prosperity, to depression.

Drawing on Gramsci, and on other work in sociology and industrial relations, it breaks new ground in the study of the formation of Labour politics — in both theory and material.

John Holford is Tutor Organiser at the Workers' Educational Association, Dartford.

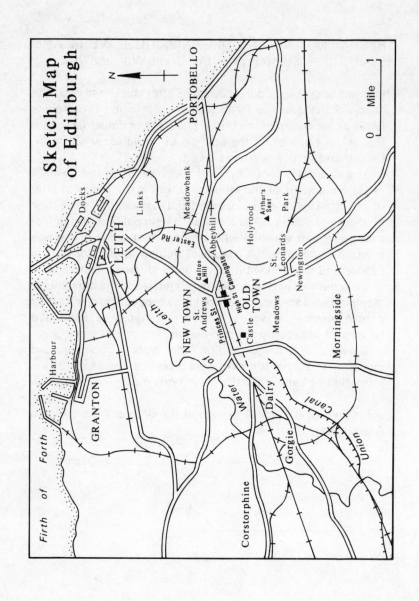

Sketch Map of Edinburgh

N

Firth of Forth

Docks

Harbour

GRANTON

LEITH

Links

Meadowbank

PORTOBELLO

Easter Rd

Water

of

Leith

NEW TOWN

St. Andrews

Princes St

Calton Hill

Abbeyhill

High St Canongate

Castle

OLD TOWN

Holyrood

Arthur's Seat

Park

St. Leonards

Newington

Meadows

Corstorphine

Dalry

Gorgie

Canal

Union

Morningside

0   Mile   1

RESHAPING LABOUR:

Organisation, Work and Politics~ Edinburgh in the Great War and After

John Holford

CROOM HELM
London • New York • Sydney

© 1988 John Holford
Croom Helm Ltd, Provident House, Burrell Row,
Beckenham, Kent, BR3 1AT

Croom Helm Australia, 44-50 Waterloo Road,
North Ryde, 2113, New South Wales

Published in the USA by
Croom Helm
in association with Methuen, Inc.
29 West 35th Street
New York, NY 10001

British Library Cataloguing in Publication Data

Holford, John
    Reshaping labour: organisation, work and
    politics — Edinburgh in the Great War and
    after.
    1. Labor and laboring classes — Great
    Britain — History — 20th century
    2. Socialism — Great Britain — History
    — 20th century
    I. Title
    335'.1'0941   HD8390
    ISBN 0-7099-4755-0

Library of Congress Cataloging-in-Publication Data

Holford, John.
    Reshaping labour — organisation, work, and politics: Edinburgh in
the Great War and after/John Holford.
        p. cm.
    Includes index.
    ISBN 0-7099-4755-0
    1. Labor and laboring classes — Scotland — Edinburgh (Lothian) —
History — 20th century. 2. Labor and laboring classes — Scotland —
Edinburgh (Lothian) — Political activity — History — 20th century.
3. Industrial relations — Scotland — Edinburgh (Lothian) —
History — 20th century. 4. World War, 1914–1918 — Economic aspects —
Scotland — Edinburgh (Lothian) I. Title.
HD8400.E342H64   1988
331'.09413'4 — dc 19   87-30513

Printed and bound in Great Britain by
Biddles Ltd, Guildford and King's Lynn

CONTENTS

Contents

TABLES AND FIGURES

TABLES

Tables and Figures

FIGURES

ABBREVIATIONS

AEU	Amalgamated Engineering Union
AR	Annual Report
ASE	Amalgamated Society of Engineers
ASLE(&)F	Associated Society of Locomotive Engineers and Firemen
BSISLP	British Section of the International Socialist Labour Party
BSP	British Socialist Party
CP(GB)	Communist Party (of Great Britain)
DLP	Divisional Labour Party
Edin.	Edinburgh
E&EA (EofS); E&AE(EofS)A	Engineering and Allied Employers Association (East of Scotland)
EC	Executive Committee
ESAE&I; ESAE&IA	East of Scotland Association of Engineers and Ironfounders
ILP	Independent Labour Party
JP	Justice of the Peace
LP	Labour Party
NAC	National Administrative Council
NAUL	National Amalgamated Union of Labour
NCLC	National Council of Labour Colleges
NEC	National Executive Committee
NSP	National Socialist Party
NUC	National Union of Clerks
NUR	National Union of Railwaymen
NUW(C)M	National Unemployed Workers (Committee) Movement
PLP	Parliamentary Labour Pary
RILU	Red International of Labour Unions
SBU	Scottish Brassmoulders Union
SDF	Social Democratic Federation
SLC	Scottish Labour College
SLHA	Scottish Labour Housing Association
SLP	Socialist Labour Party
SSF	Scottish Socialist Federation
STA	Scottish Typographical Association
STUC	Scottish Trades Union Congress
TC	Trades Council (Edinburgh unless otherwise stated)
TDA	Tenants Defence Association
TDL	Tenants Defence League

T&LC	Trades and Labour Council (Edinburgh unless otherwise stated)
TUC	Trades Union Congress
WEA	Workers' Educational Association

General Note: Save in quotations (where the spelling and punctuation of the original are retained), and in tables, the names of organisations (unions, etc.) are spelled with capital letters to distinguish them from the categories of people who compose them. Thus 'Clerks' refers to the National Union of Clerks, 'clerks' to the occupation; 'Labour' (the Labour Party) and 'labour'; and so forth. By extension, 'Rubber Workers' refers to the No.292 branch of the NAUL.

PREFACE

For my Mother and Father

This book is based on research carried out over many years.
I should like to thank all those labour and trade union
organisations which have kindly allowed me to make use of
their records, together with the staff of the libraries in
which the records are stored. I am particularly grateful for
the hospitality I received from the Edinburgh Trades Council
and its then Secretary, John Henry. The book would never
have been written without the support and encouragement
of Gianfranco Poggi, who supervised the thesis on which it is
based; it would have been the weaker without his criticism. I
am also grateful for the constructive and valuable
comments made by Henry Drucker and Robert Gray in
examining the thesis. My greatest debt, however, is to my
wife Hilary, not merely for bearing with my obsession
throughout, but for encouraging me in the hard times, and
for her unstinting practical and critical support. The arrival
of our daughter Naomi has brightened recent months. She
deserved more of me; I am happy I shall now have more time
to share with them.

Dartford   J.A.K.H.

Chapter One

INTRODUCTORY

A human mass does not 'distinguish' itself, does not
become independent in its own right without, in the
widest sense, organising itself; and there is no
organisation without intellectuals, that is without
organisers and leaders ...[1]

During the Great War, and a few brief years which followed,
the politics of labour in Britain were transformed. When the
guns began to fire in August 1914, just 42 Labour Members
sat in the House of Commons. Ten years later there were
191; one was Prime Minister. In 1918 the Labour Party
adopted a new Constitution and Programme which led - over
a decade or so - to a wholesale revision of its political
organisation.

Largely in consequence, that colossus of late Victorian
and Edwardian labour politics, the Independent Labour
Party, had by the 1930s dwindled into relative insignif-
icance. Still further left, the formation of the Communist
Party in 1921 brought together many of Britain's Marxist
and revolutionary groups and currents, and in time gave
them a genuinely new identity, replacing the spectre of
Syndicalism. Trade union membership grew at an unprecedented rate, more than doubling to over six millions between
1914 and 1920. When this growth began to be reversed in the
early 1920s, a major regrouping and restructuring of unions
took place: amalgamations were commonplace, and in many
cases - above all, in the TUC's - unions' management
structures were thoroughly revised.

The pattern into which the labour movement was
moulded during those years - the institutions and methods,
outlooks and alliances, cemented over little more than a
decade - has persisted through the succeeding half century
and more. By the later 1920s labour politics were dominated
by a well-entrenched coalition based on an electoral, parliamentary, strategy; trade unions accepted that their role was
essentially confined to collective bargaining - that they

1

would involve themselves in politics only through the Labour Party. Yet it was not inevitable that labour should develop these traits - still so characteristic of the movement. Labour's transformation occurred in the midst of - and, in large measure, in response to - fundamental social, economic and political changes, of which the Great War itself, the onset of economic depression from the early 1920s, and the extension of the franchise in 1918, are but among the most prominent. Within this environment of rapid change, various elements of labour contended (not always consciously) for mastery.

The present work is a study in how labour was reshaped during a period stretching roughly from the midst of the Great War to the mid-1920s. In outline, our argument runs thus. During and immediately after the Great War, the working class movement in Britain made significant advances. In part these were based on changes in economic, social and political structures, which increased the strength of the resources available to workers. But fundamental to the advances, and particularly to their character, were three developments. First, the experience of war altered the terminology of nationalism; the meaning of the 'nation' was inevitably expanded (as working people fought and died in France), and the purchase of the working class on the language of 'nation' increased. There was a distancing of this language from the ruling class, which found more difficulty in mobilising around notions - the national interest, patriotism, and so forth - associated with nationalism: conversely, the working class was more able to mobilise in its own interest around such principles.

Second, the war involved a substantial erosion of the legitimacy of 'profit'. Much of the linguistic apparatus of capital, which can normally be treated as virtually synonymous with profitability, developed relatively independent meanings: 'organisation', 'efficiency', associated now increasingly with national interest rather than profit (and with a national interest more open to working class interpretation), came to be used in attempts to mobilise for the war effort. This was a managerial language through which there was greater - though still highly circumscribed - room for the legitimation of self-interested working class action. Third, this language, associated with and bolstered by the apparatus of wartime planning, inevitably lent some legitimacy to versions of socialism, and thus to the development of the labour movement.

But just as the strength of these notions opened up opportunities for the labour movement, so they strongly influenced the movement's own development. The language of planning, efficiency, organisation, and so forth, provided the essential meaning system through which other radically significant influences were interpreted. The Russian Revolution of October 1917, for example, which might have been seen from the perspective of workers' control and democracy, became an instance of efficient class organisation and planning. These notions also grounded many of the important changes in the structure of the labour movement during our period, especially up to 1921 or 1922. Restructurings of the Labour Party, of the trade union movement, and of Marxist organisations, were all significantly motivated by the strength of this language among the working class.

The extent of the working class advance was not sufficient to overturn the essential power structure; and from 1920 onward a number of economic factors began to shift the balance of power away from labour. The strength of many notions generated by the war was eroding, making working class mobilisation more difficult; whilst economic developments brought the language of 'efficiency' once more into a close liaison with 'profit' (at least in industrial usage), and made managers' (industrial relations) tasks less arduous. At the same time, the counter-attack against labour could, in general, not be based upon the same principles as had been used before the war, so that (especially outside industry) labour was able to achieve significant mobilisation. The counter-attack centred on notions of constitutionalism and democracy: this had the effect of strengthening an important element of the labour movement and encouraging it to concentrate on a parliamentary strategy. Broadly, therefore, labour was again brought under some control, but only by virtue of allowing it important areas of legitimate advance.

Interwoven with this argument are a number of related themes. Two deserve mention at this stage. Firstly, we develop an argument concerning notions of organisation and their impact on labour. We suggest that the strength of the language of 'organisation' was associated with severely limited images of organisation: this meant that the entire labour movement could concur, in the years just after the war, on organisational 'advances' which were later to be used most effectively in strengthening the right within the movement (at the left's expense). Secondly, we examine the

3

shifting pattern of allegiances within the labour movement; we argue that alliances and coalitions were based around key sets of understandings, and that the immediate post-war years were a key period of reassessment of these. By the mid-1920s, a network of alliances had grown up within the movement, with important institutional support, which (in most conditions) ensured the dominance of parliamentary and reformist politics.

Our argument is based on a study of the working class in Edinburgh. The local focus was adopted chiefly as an effective method of addressing questions about the nature of class domination, about the role of labour in the processes of domination and subjection, about how the labour movement developed within this context. Detailed local research helps us to discover how political and industrial institutions and strategies relate to the experience of class, producing forms of action - or inaction. Every local study is, of course, particular and partial, and our conclusions must be viewed in this light. (Nor is this a general history of labour in Edinburgh, even within its brief timespan: several important aspects, such as the role of women in the labour movement, and the influence of religion, receive little attention.)[2] Yet even national studies must make assumptions about local behaviour, and it is as well that we should be able to measure them against local experiences. And - partly because Edinburgh was neither noted for its militancy, nor indeed otherwise outstanding - we shall uncover evidence about how labour developed which we cannot ignore.

As the years around the Great War represent a turning point for labour politics, so they mark a shift in the chief focus of historians of labour - or at least, of those who have been influenced by the Marxist tradition. For the Victorian period, concern has centred on why the working class ceased, at least after Chartism, not merely to be revolutionary in a straightforward Marxist sense, but even to develop class-based political institutions independent of Liberalism. After the Great War, with the advance of the Labour Party, the attention of historians has tended to shift from the nature of the working class to what had now emerged as the working class party.[3] So while historians of nineteenth-century labour have attempted to explain working class political behaviour by reference to the nature of the class itself, as created and sustained in economy and social structure (many of their debates centring on the concept of the 'labour aristocracy'), those working on the period after 1918 have sought explanations in the nature of the political institutions of labour themselves.[4]

Of course, the character of the Labour Party and the movement's other institutions must be an element in an account of working class political behaviour; but to make these the major factors explaining working class consciousness and action comes close to circularity. Yet studies of labour politics in the 1920s often come close to doing just this; they are strong on the nature of political organisations, but short of sustained discussion of the sources of class consciousness. Though they concentrate on different aspects (the Labour Party, union leaders, the Communist Party, the state, and so forth), they generally lack an adequate account of the nature and generation of class consciousness - a fact which is related to their concentration on national political developments. This means that the subject of each study becomes implicitly the fundamental factor (or, as sociologists have it, the 'independent variable') which must account for working class political behaviour. In consequence, they tend to oversimplify the crucial - but highly complex - relationship between organisational factors and political mobilisation.[5]

This is therefore a sociological, as well as an historical, study. Our arguments draw heavily on two currents of social theory. On the one hand, many of our understandings rest within the Marxist tradition, and particularly within the contribution associated with Antonio Gramsci. On the other hand, much of our argument draws on more recent contributions to the sociology of organisations and industry.

Working class consciousness, we suggest, can most profitably be viewed as highly fragmented: consisting of widely varying, and often mutually inconsistent, beliefs and assumptions about aspects of the world. Among workers, some are adopted from the ruling class and dominant institutions, and form the basis for generally expressed attitudes (these are roughly what Gramsci terms 'verbal consciousness'); others are generated by working class institutions themselves, but tend therefore to be specific to their class or group situation ('practical consciousness').[6] The structure of the working class intensifies this fragmentation of consciousness, for each group within the class develops its own (more or less) different practical consciousness. Political action is thus most effective when a motive for action (what we term a 'legitimising principle')[7] is shared by a wide spectrum of groups; but it is also deeply influenced by the relative strength - both institutional and ideological - of opposing classes, groups, or organisations. Parties (and trade unions and similar bodies) develop and deploy legitimising principles so as to encourage action to certain ends. Very often, this requires the deployment of principles which appeal to the leading institutions of other social groups; or to other leading institutions within their own group. This theory forms the basis of our study, although it is necessary, from time to time, to elaborate on it in various ways.

Gramsci remarks that in the study of political movements, 'currents of opinion are normally taken as already constituted around a group or a dominant personality'.[8] If we view the early twentieth-century labour movement, however, not primarily as an ancestor of the creature which we know today, but in its own right, we are faced with many currents of opinion which were clearly not 'already constituted', but very much in the process of formation. Yet trade unions and political parties at every level were self-consciously organised institutions. Broadly, organisation theorists present organisations as institutions which, marked by an essential stability in goals and internal relationships, can be distinguished, more or less precisely, from other social institutions. But the organisations of the early labour movement were often far from developed; from the historian's point of view, they arise and disappear with frightening rapidity, defying the categories of the organisation theorists. In short, the labour movement in the years with which we are concerned was malleable: legion currents of opinion vied for support; one important element of constructing a current of opinion, and generating support, was organisation.

Organisations, however, once created, do not simply persist. They must be continually recreated, sustained.[9] The relationship between organisation and currents of opinion (in Gramsci's sense) is therefore reciprocal: just as organisation helps to solidify a political movement, so an organisation requires a certain ideological coherence if it is to remain in being. For men and women will not generally associate with an organisation with which they do not - in the broadest sense - agree. Our study of the reformation of labour politics during and after the Great War therefore involves studying not merely the development of organisations, but the evolution of the ideological currents within which those organisations have their being.

In the chapters which follow we construct our case thus. First (in Chapters 2 and 3), we explore the social and economic context of class and class relations in Edinburgh. In Chapters 4-6 we examine the development of industrial organisation, and how organisation was perceived, before looking in more detail at how and why trade union strength flowed and ebbed. Finally, in Chapters 7-9, we turn to the development of labour politics in Edinburgh.

NOTES

1. A. Gramsci, Selections from the Prison Notebooks (London, 1971), p.334.
2. Although neither of these were aspects which I particularly sought to explore, I happened upon a good deal of information touching on the role of women; this is a question which deserves further investigation. On the other hand (especially in view of Edinburgh's substantial Irish population, and the meteoric rise of the Protestant Party in Edinburgh politics in the 1930s), the absence of issues with identifiable religious or ethnic dimensions in Edinburgh labour politics or trades unionism before the later 1920s is remarkable.
3. Classically, G.D.H. Cole found his History of the Labour Party from 1914 (London, 1948) an adequate sequel to British Working Class Politics 1832-1914 (London, 1941).
4. The major examples touching on our period are R. Miliband, Parliamentary Socialism (London, 1973); D. Coates, The Labour Party and the Struggle for Socialism (Cambridge, 1975); L. Panitch, 'Ideology and Integration: the Case of the British Labour Party, Political Studies, vol. 19 (1971), pp.184-200.
5. See, e.g., the extremely valuable contributions on state strategy in K. Middlemas, Politics in Industrial Society (London, 1979), esp. pp.120-213, and J. Foster, 'British Imperialism and the Labour Aristocracy' in J. Skelley (ed.), The General Strike 1926 (London, 1976), pp.3-57.
6. See Gramsci, Prison Notebooks, esp. pp.323-43.
7. This term is borrowed from P.J. Armstrong, J.F.B. Goodman and J.D. Hyman, Ideology and Shop Floor Industrial Relations (London, 1981), esp. pp.32-56.
8. Gramsci, Prison Notebooks, p.194.
9. For an impressive contribution in this area, see M. Burawoy, Manufacturing Consent (Chicago, 1979).

Chapter Two

EDINBURGH AFTER THE GREAT WAR

A war of position is not, in reality, constituted by the actual trenches, but by the whole organisational and industrial system of the territory which lies to the rear of the army in the field.[1]

THE GROWTH OF THE CITY

In 1919, Edinburgh was still largely a Victorian artefact. Even by the turn of the century, the city had passed its period of most rapid growth. Between 1851 and 1901 its population had grown by 86 per cent: slightly less than that of more heavily industrialised Scottish cities, such as Glasgow and Dundee, but reflecting the same factors - industrial development and rural depopulation.[2] By 1901 over 300,000 people lived within the municipal burgh (over 380,000 if Leith was included); but thereafter the population stabilised, and growth over the following three decades was exceedingly modest when compared with the Victorian pattern (see Table 2.1).

Along with the population's growth had gone marked changes in its spatial distribution and social composition. In the eighteenth-century Old Town 'social ranks were not segregated by street or quarter but simply by the level of tenement they occupied'.[3] Early in the nineteenth century the construction of the New Town - planned for the wealthy - reduced 'unpleasant contact between the classes',[4] and this trend was intensified during the latter half of the century by the building of suburban estates to the south of the city for the developing bourgeoisie. These - rather than the working class areas - were serviced by a local railway network which was largely complete within fifteen years of the opening of the first suburban line in 1884.[5]

At the same time, and especially during the 1870s and 1880s, the construction of working class housing began: it followed the pattern of class segregation now set. Uniformly working class areas were created, grouped around railways and industry in such districts as Dalry, Gorgie, Abbeyhill,

Easter Road; and with the bourgeois emigration from the Old Town, it too became more uniformly working class.[6] This pattern of social segregation was set by the turn of the century and altered little before the war, although the years 1900-14 saw a profound slump in house building in Edinburgh - and it was working class housing, heavily dependent on small, local capital and quick sales, that suffered most.[7]

Table 2.1: Edinburgh's Population 1891-1931

	1891	1901	1911	1921	1931
Population	338,114	384,732	385,016	393,456	405,399
Inter-censal population increase (per cent):					
Edinburgh	14.8	13.8	0.1	2.2	3.0
Dundee	9.2	3.9	0.7	5.1	4.3
Glasgow	15.8	10.2	-4.7	72.5	-0.7

Notes: Parliamentary burghs. 'Edinburgh' includes Leith and Portobello, but excludes Musselburgh (part of East Edinburgh parliamentary division from 1918).

Source: Census of Scotland 1931.

Concealed between the census years, the war saw a substantial - if temporary - influx of workers into the city, as Rosyth became a major dockyard and base for the Grand Fleet, as lesser units of the fleet were based in Forth harbours such as Granton, and as wartime production took off generally. While figures are obscure, the immigration placed acute pressure on housing, and apparently led to the Admiralty's planning a new town at Rosyth.[8] As a result, not only did housing conditions deteriorate: there was an erosion of the trend toward greater social segregation. And in fact the post-war housing programmes, which led to the creation of new suburban working class areas and re-established the long-term trend, made little impact until the later 1920s.

9

The housing in the working class areas was a mixture of the former dwellings of the wealthier townspeople, and newer - often jerry-built - speculative tenement blocks custom-built for the working class.[9] The former,

> divided and sub-divided until a five or six apartment house has become five or six dwellings and six or eight houses entering from one stair have become thirty or forty, with a population often over one hundred persons,[10]

had lost their former glory; the latter had no pretensions to lose. Within these areas, the problems of Victorian urban deprivation persisted: overcrowding, inadequate sanitation, poor and deteriorating states of repair. Along with these, as several surveys and the annual reports of the Medical Officers of Health and Chief Sanitary Inspectors regularly emphasised - went higher death, infant mortality, and morbidity rates. In 1919, for example, seven of the city's sixteen wards had population densities greater than 78 per acre; of the remainder, only one had a density greater than 37. In St. Leonards, the figure was 243 per acre - and in certain areas, over 600.[11]

A parish minister caught the flavour of life in such conditions:

> within sight of the South Bridge, ... an old tenement is the dwelling of about 70 persons. It has four flats of one-room and two-room houses, with seven tenants in each flat. ... [T]he walls of passages are decayed. The stairs are filthy and littered. In not a single apartment is there water, gas, a press, or a meat safe. ... In each lobby is one sink and one water-closet; there are three or four families in each lobby. Men coming home from a day's work wash at the cold tap in view of anyone passing.[12]

Another minister described conditions for the 80 or 90 residents of a tenement built around 1860. 'The whole building is in a state of disrepair, the walls of the rooms cracked and dirty, and the ceilings ready to fall.' 'Bugs' had 'a firm lodgement in the cracked walls and ceilings and in the floors'; even fumigation apparently gave relief only for 'a week or so, the livestock temporarily emigrating to a neighbouring house, only to return when they were at liberty to do so'.[13]

Writing at the end of the 1920s, Edinburgh's Chief Sanitary Inspector described efforts to improve housing since the 1890s as 'meagre in the extreme': 'they have only touched the fringe of the problem and have failed to alter the position very much for the slum dweller'.[14] Both during and after the war there was a rise in the number of households living in just one or two rooms, although the infant mortality rate (see Table 2.2) does show some improvement during the post war decade - suggesting that despite continuing housing shortages and overcrowding, improvements in diet, welfare facilities and so forth, had some effect.

Table 2.2: Infant Mortality in Edinburgh 1914-30: Rates per Thousand Births

	1914	1919	1922	1925	1928	1930
Edinburgh (a)	110	117	85	94	70	78
Edinburgh (b)			91	96	75	82
Wards:						
Canongate	117	127	109	113	61	108
Colinton	..	..	20	75	12	74
Dalry	115	114	72	80	71	64
Leith Central	..	..	128	107	86	58
Leith North	..	..	140	128	100	93
Merchiston	83	87	30	58	40	47
Morningside	33	82	65	86	31	13
St Andrews	125	134	91	144	91	108
St Giles	151	150	141	146	111	106
St Leonards	140	160	92	119	88	102

Notes: (a) Pre-1920 boundaries
          (b) Post-1920 boundaries, viz, including Leith, and Liberton, Colinton, Corstorphine, and Cramond wards.

Source: Edinburgh Public Health Department Annual Reports.

Post-war Edinburgh was, then, in social-geographical terms, polarised between a bourgeoisie resident in the New Town and the southern suburbs, and a working class occupying housing on land of relatively low value hard by the industrial areas. The main working class areas thus formed a band running from Leith in the north-east, through Easter Road, Abbeyhill and Meadowbank in the east, and then onward through the Old Town to Gorgie and Dalry in the west.[15] It was mainly between these (inner-city) areas that Edinburgh's tramways, a steam-driven cable network - and with 36 miles of track at the end of the war, the fourth largest in the world - plied their trade.[16] Perhaps because they were required by law to provide cheap fares for the 'labouring classes' travelling to and from work,[17] the trams seem to have held the affections of the city's working class during our period, despite growing competition from motor buses[18] - although the Corporation's determination that buses should terminate at the foot of the Mound, Edinburgh's 'speakers' corner', where socialists of all persuasions regaled the public, may have played a part.[19]

With the trams and buses, the speed of journeys within the city increased. It was now, for instance, quite easy while living in Leith to work daily in Dalry, or to travel to an evening meeting in the Old Town.[20] Such a meeting could be summoned rapidly by post - the trades council's secretary could summon an evening meeting of his executive committee by posting cards the same morning.[21] Largely as a result, the distinctions between Edinburgh and Leith became artificial, and their political institutions merged: the town councils in 1920, the trades councils and Labour parties in 1921.

THE BOURGEOISIE AND ITS POLITICS

For the benefit of delegates to the Labour Party's 1936 National Conference, Arthur Woodburn, a prominent product of Edinburgh's labour movement, wrote a brief 'anti-history' of his native city. He argued that four key social groups had created 'Edinburgh and its atmosphere ... of tradition, authority and middle-class culture': the Church, the Law, Medicine, and Commerce.[22] In many ways, his view is mirrored in the census records (see Table 2.3). The proportion of Edinburgh's population occupied in administration, the professions, and personal services was considerable. The capital housed a large civil service. The remarkable proportion of lawyers reflected their role in the capital's legal, commercial and financial institutions. For Edinburgh was also, according to Woodburn, 'probably the largest centre of industrial capital in the world in relation to its size'[23] - and certainly during the early 1920s 'some of the world's largest Investment Trusts,... several banks', and at least ten major insurance companies had head offices in the city.[24] Leith, a major port with by far the largest overseas trade on Scotland's east coast (and in the early 1920s rivalling Glasgow in the value of its imports) also sustained a substantial commercial class. And to service these were doctors and many of the lower status professions, such as nurses and teachers.

Table 2.3: Administration, Commerce, Professions and Personal Service as Percentages of Occupied Populations 1921

	Edinburgh	Glasgow
Commerce and finance	11.82	10.84
Public administration and defence	4.08	1.83
Professional occupations	7.29	3.59
Personal service	12.34	7.23
of which:		
Ministers, clergymen	0.28	0.12
Lawyers	0.47	0.09
Physicians and surgeons	0.30	0.15
Sick nurses	1.00	0.63
Teachers	2.17	1.26
Civil service	1.85	0.49
Commercial travellers	0.85	0.86
Finance and insurance	0.63	0.46
Domestic servants	7.38	3.15

Source: Census occupation tables, 1921.

Edinburgh's system of private education played an important role in the formation of its bourgeoisie. At its core were the Merchant Company schools. Formed from the seventeenth century to educate the daughters and sons of the city's merchants, they had been reorganised after 1870 to service the children of the new middle class: 'the education provided ... appealed to the needs and desires of that class in Scotland.'[25] By our period the various private schools provided a schooling which was both committed to the establishment and maintenance of a class and its values and within this class, universally available.

During the nineteenth century the tensions between various elements of Edinburgh's bourgeoisie had been marked, generating a reputation for snobbery. 'Of course we have a good share of snobbery here,' wrote the Trades and Labour Council's Secretary in 1927,[26] whilst an Edinburgh sociologist wrote in 1936:

> The West End of Edinburgh, though only too ready
> to welcome the casual stranger, acts rather differ-
> ently to those who live within the city. Here in
> fact, social classes are sharply defined, status may
> almost be said to exist.[27]

Yet there do appear to have been changes. The standard of living of the most wealthy seems to have suffered, and there is some suggestion that the compartmentalisation of the various sections - the law, medicine, banking, and so on - began to break down after the Great War.[28] Moreover, Edinburgh's bourgeoisie was very open to influences from beyond the city. The legal profession fulfilled national functions; the medical had if anything a wider frame of reference. And the city's financial institutions were relating more and more to international, rather than local or even Scottish, areas for investment.

This cosmopolitan establishment played a central role in maintaining the key institutions which gave Edinburgh its peculiar atmosphere or culture; it had little time, however, for the city's day-to-day management. Two major (though not mutually exclusive) groups dominated the Town Council. In 1925, 57 per cent of councillors were owners of property (housing, land, or commercial) other than just their own homes; whilst 53 per cent were businessmen. Of the latter, it seems that many were of the petite bourgeoisie, shop-keepers and the like, whose horizons would rarely have been raised wider than the city. In contrast, the professions were a relatively small (and declining) grouping on the Council; and many of these appear to have been members of lower-status professions, such as estate agents. But while the property interest was declining (and made up increasingly of managers, rather than owners of property), the proportion of businessmen was growing.

Local affairs were, then, increasingly being conducted by men (there were very few women) of local orientation, whose concern was for the efficient administration of the city: although they borrowed from the intellectual elite a sense of Edinburgh's history and greatness, they interpreted this in the light of axioms of good government and efficiency which owed as much to principles of sound business administration as to any coherent political philosophy. Indeed, a major claim of the Town Council's ruling groups was that they were 'non-political'; a claim which was powerful enough to justify a restructuring of bourgeois municipal politics in 1928 (when the Progressive Association was formed from a number of loose-knit groups of Tories, Liberals and independents).[29] The immediate mobilising issue in this was the growth of Labour representation on the council, with its greater discipline and more clearly articulated policies - bringing, as the Progressives saw it, politics into local government. Paradoxically, of course, this more intense sense of the localism and non-political nature of city administration occurred just during the period when central government was requiring local councils to become far more the agents of - increasingly contentious - national policies, in such areas as housing, unemployment, and the relief of poverty.[30]

If Edinburgh's bourgeoisie was variegated and compartmentalised, it was also a source of recruits to socialism. They came from a wide range of backgrounds. From the professions there were lawyers such as Michael Marcus, teachers such as Andrew Young, clergymen such as William Marwick; John Young and D.B. McKay were dentists; no doubt there were doctors and nurses. Gerald Crawford was a mechanical engineer, as well as a musician and composer. Others were small businessmen. Thomas Drummond Shiels was a photographer, offering 'Best Work - Moderate Prices' from his premises at 70 and 72 Lauriston Place.[31] Adam Millar was a Gorgie draper. Thomas Paris was 'sole partner' in Hossack and Paris ('Labour and General Printing of Every Description') of 4 Chapel Street and 68 Bristo Street.[32] Some came from more marginal occupations. Willie Graham was a clerk and shorthand typist, before becoming a journalist in Selkirk; subsequently he worked his way through Edinburgh University.

Though few in number among a predominantly working class labour movement, these bourgeois socialists played a disproportionately prominent role in the city's labour politics. Their influence was far from confined to the Fabian Society, intellectual and bourgeois though this was.[33] Thomas Paris gives a clue to the reason in a 1927 letter to Gerald Crawford. Listing the duties required of a

Representative on the Education Authority, and the time
they demand, he adds: 'Of course, I can run out and in close
up to the meeting hours, and so save considerable time in
the aggregate. But a representative in employment would
require to "get off" forenoon or afternoon ...'[34] So the six
Labour Town Councillors sitting at the end of the war, for
instance, included John Young, Crawford, and Graham.
Graham became the city's first Labour MP. Marcus, Andrew
Young, and Drummond Shiels followed him to Westminster
during the 1920s. It was a common complaint, especially
from the left, that 'the movement is too prone to welcome
lawyers, doctors, and men of education and rank',[35] 'all the
petty drapers, drapers' wives, lawyers and doctors who have
wormed their way into the position of being working-class
representatives'.[36]

THE WORKING CLASS
Edinburgh's working class had been formed in a city marked
by a wide variety of largely smaller-scale and labour-
intensive industry. 'The relationships of industrial employment did not figure prominently in local affairs.'[37] In
contrast to a number of other cities, political leadership did
not come from industrialists; and although the proportion of
the working population employed in relatively large-scale
concerns (such as rubber manufacture, brewing, engineering)
seems to have grown, the capital's industrial units remained
small in national terms. The largest single employer, for
example, was St Cuthbert's Co-operative Association, whose
workers were mostly employed in its small branches; the
largest industrial employer (the North British Rubber Co)
had a workforce of rather less than 5,000 at its largest
during the period 1923-34. The next largest employer (a
bread and biscuit maker) employed just over 1,000 insured
workers in 1931; the largest employers in other sectors were
smaller still. The largest in printing employed 621; in
engineering, 549; in shipbuilding, 515; in drink and brewing,
588; in paper-making, 580; in oil, grease and soap manufacture, 721.[38]

A comparison with the industrial structure of Glasgow
at the same time provides a gauge of how distinctive
Edinburgh's was (see Table 2.4). Edinburgh had a far greater
proportion employed in the professions and personal service.
In many industrial groups (transport and communications,
mining and quarrying, food, drink and tobacco, for instance)
there was little to choose between the two cities. But

Table 2.4: Industrial Distribution of Working Populations of Edinburgh and Glasgow 1921 (Per Cent)

		Edinburgh	Glasgow
I	Fishing	0.45	0.01
II	Agriculture	1.57	0.34
III	Mining, Quarrying	1.97	1.57
IV	Bricks, Glass, Pottery	0.54	0.72
V	Chemicals, Dyes	1.07	1.09
VI	Metals, Machines	9.63	27.42
VII	Textiles, Textile Goods	1.33	3.54
VIII	Skins, Leather Goods	0.40	0.49
IX	Clothing	3.09	5.07
X	Food, Drink, Tobacco	5.26	5.19
XI	Woodworking	2.07	2.48
XII	Paper, Printing	5.61	2.79
XIII	Building, Decorating	3.97	3.47
XIV	Other Manufacturing	3.07	1.28
XV	Gas, Water, Electricity	0.90	1.43
XVI	Transport, Communication	9.65	10.32
XVII	Commerce, Finance	19.70	16.59
XVIII	Public Administration	9.94	6.39
XIX	Professions	7.98	2.89
XX	Entertainments, Sport	0.77	0.64
XXI	Personal Service	10.93	6.21
XXII	Other Industries	0.09	0.06
	Total	99.99	99.99
	(Total Industrial Population	201,224	488,599)

Source: Calculated from Census of Scotland, Industry Tables.

Glasgow had roughly twice the proportion of its working population working in clothing and textiles; while the most substantial difference came in the broad engineering industry - what the census categorised as 'manufacture of metals, machines, etc.' This meant that Edinburgh had no major concentration of its working population in a single manufacturing sector, with which to offset the employment in commerce, finance and the professions. More significantly, engineering was an industry central to innovation in industrial organisation and technology in our period; and it also constituted the infrastructure of an industrial economy. Edinburgh thus built up neither a network of highly inter-connected and inter-dependent enterprises, nor a working class with close experience or understanding of other major enterprises in the city - for mobility between jobs in different industries is inevitably relatively limited. There was a further dimension of fragmentation. Nineteenth-century Edinburgh had developed a reputation for craft and good workmanship, when its bourgeoisie had constituted an unusually large luxury market encouraging small-scale, craft production.[39] After the Great War, the reputation was little more than an ideological relic, but it did reflect the strong dependence of Edinburgh's (relatively under-capitalised) industry upon skilled labour.

In Edinburgh then, the bourgeoisie, though conspicuous was not clearly and directly associated with employment and exploitation; the working class was highly fragmented - stratified within each industry to be sure, but divided also between many industries, and within each many firms and workplaces. As one local managing director wrote, in Edinburgh 'frequently ... a working class family of father and several sons and daughters represents half a dozen completely different trades'.[40] So although one important study found a 'strong degree of workplace-resil ence associa-tion' in the city's working class areas,[41] these were not the 'occupational communities' which unproblematically generate attitudes of 'proletarian traditionalism'.[42]

EDINBURGH'S ECONOMY IN WAR AND AFTER
The outbreak of war in 1914 brought an initial dislocation to the Scottish economy, so largely dependent upon exports and international trade. There were redundancies, for instance, in Edinburgh's paper industry, as manufacturers feared for their supplies of imported timber and esparto grass. A fund of £20,000 was raised for the capital's unemployed. But as the months passed, the war brought many benefits. Govern-ment spending sustained a high level of demand, even if it brought inflation. In the war materiel sector, investment was encouraged. Major competitors had been eliminated from overseas and home markets, leading to demand for substitutes where imports were no longer available. Demand for labour quickly outstripped standard sources of supply, encouraging the recruitment of women. Of course, there were also adverse factors, not least those of raw material

supply; and many of these benefits would not survive the war - being the gains of protection and high government spending. But the economic winds of war blew warm and strong.[43]

The post-war boom lasted until perhaps the summer of 1920. It was based on a number of factors. The government, partly because it could not instantaneously rid itself of responsibilities taken on during the war, partly as insurance against Bolshevism and revolution, maintained public expenditure at an unprecedentedly high peacetime level. Demand in certain staple industries - shipbuilding especially, and hence coal, iron, steel - remained high into 1920, chiefly because the disruption caused by war created an apparent shipping shortage in 1919 greater by far than the real shortfall in tonnage.[44] It seems likely that the general extent of dislocation in markets, especially abroad, was not immediately appreciated, and that business expectations remained unjustifiably high for a short period;[45] probably also British traders held an advantage in the short term, as the dislocation to competitors' trade - especially Germany's - was still greater. Edinburgh shared in its transient prosperity: incomes, imports and exports all rose; hours of work fell. But the boom soon passed.

A valuable insight into the dimensions of the slump in Edinburgh can be found in data about Leith's overseas trade (see Figure 2.5). Both imports and exports passing through the port reflected the post-war boom. Imports slumped in 1921, falling by one-third; they fell again the following year, before beginning a slow, faltering, 'recovery'. This largely reflected the poor performance of Scottish agriculture, for Leith specialised in the facilities called for in handling foodstuffs (especially grain and dairy products), which were transported by rail throughout Scotland and the north of England.[46] (Foodstuffs gave Leith's import trade a stronger base than a reliance on the volatile, and often low-level, trade in raw materials for industry, as comparison with other Scottish ports demonstrates.) In exports, the depression came sooner and bit deeper. Again, the explanation is partly to be found in the structure of Leith's trade. The great bulk of its exports was coal, from the Lothian and central Scottish fields.[47] Before the war, this had been shipped in large quantities to Baltic destinations: this trade was lost in 1914, and with civil war in Russia (not to mention British hostility to the Bolshevik government), and the collapse of the German economy in 1923, the loss

Figure 2.5: Overseas Trade of Three Scottish Ports 1919-27

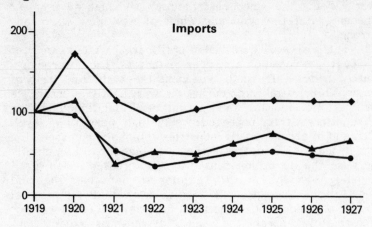

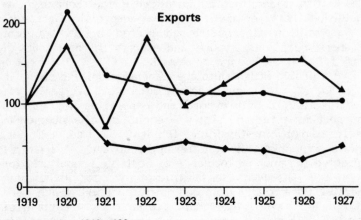

Current prices; 1919 = 100

Leith
Dundee
Glasgow

Source: Calculated from M.W. Flinn, 'The Overseas
Trade of Scottish Ports 1900-60', Scottish
Journal of Political Economy, vol.13 (1966),
pp.231-2.

was not recovered.[48]

The reductions in government expenditure, spurred on by the Beaverbrook and Northcliffe press campaigns against waste - 'squandermania' - affected general purchasing power. The Out-of-Work Donation was phased out by 1921; unemployment insurance was not an adequate substitute. The Addison housing programme was guillotined - a severe blow to the labour-intensive building industry. By 1922 all 'non-established' workers at Rosyth dockyard (to which thousands had been drawn during the war) had been paid off, and most of the 'established' transferred to bases in England; many had commuted daily on special trains from Edinburgh, whose economy thus suffered.[49] Across a wide spectrum of industry, factory owners - who may have carped at Ministry of Munitions direction during the war, especially when required to manufacture products outside their normal range - began to appreciate the advantages of assured markets.

The depression of 1921 deepened during 1922; thereafter recovery came only slowly and fitfully, as Leith's trade figures suggest. Unemployment in Edinburgh (excluding Leith) fell through 1923 to a low point of 8 per cent in 1924, rising thereafter; in Leith, it fell through 1923 and 1924, to a low point of 17 per cent in 1925, before rising again. (See Chapter 3 for more details on unemployment.) Yet throughout these years the total number of those counted as 'effectively employed' was rising: the problem was that the (insured) working population was at times rising faster (see Table 2.6). And - as Chapter 3 also shows - there is some evidence that, after a decline between 1921 and 1923, real wages (if not necessarily real incomes) edged upwards through the mid-twenties, though this was due to falling prices rather than rising money wages.

With its diverse industrial structure, these economic trends were not reflected uniformly throughout Edinburgh. While, for example, some of the city's industries were those which expanded most in the inter-war period,[50] Leith (with its dependence on shipbuilding and ship-repairing, 'suffered much like a Clydeside town'.[51] But with this proviso, the signs are that Edinburgh's economic experience in wartime and the earlier 1920s was, in direction if not in degree, that of the nation as a whole. After growth tied to war production, the boom lasted at best two years; the slump was at its worst through 1921 and 1922; thereafter, trade experienced a slow, faltering upturn - 'recovery' is too strong a word.

Table 2.6: Working Population and Employment in Edinburgh

	1923	1925	1927
Population of Working Age	291,309	294,964	298,618
Insured Persons (a)	120,930	124,830	126,150
Effectively Employed (b)	107,873	111,700	114,681
Unemployed ((a)-(b))	13,057	13,130	11,469
Unemployed (per cent)	10.8	10.5	9.1

Source: N. Milnes, A Study of Industrial Edinburgh and the Surrounding Area 1923-34 (London, 1936), pp.93-4, and calculations thence.

NOTES

1. A. Gramsci, Selections from the Prison Notebooks (London, 1971), p.234.
2. R.Q. Gray, The Labour Aristocracy in Victorian Edinburgh (Oxford, 1976), p.10.
3. B. Elliott and D. McCrone, 'Urban Development in Edinburgh: a Contribution to the Political Economy of Place', Scottish Journal of Sociology, vol.4 (1980), p.1.
4. T. Adams, 'Town Planning and Housing', supplement to Architectural Review (May 1910), pp.311-16, quoted in H. Richardson, J. Vipond, and R. Furbey, Housing and Urban Spatial Structure: A Case Study (Farnborough, Hants., 1975).
5. Richardson et al., Urban Spatial Structure, p.25.
6. Ibid., pp.9-10.
7. Elliott and McCrone, 'Urban Development', pp.10-12.
8. TC AR 1917, p.2. According to the Royal Commission on the Housing of the Industrial Population of Scotland (Cd. 8731, 1917, p.345), war work caused 'a very considerable influx of workers. The housing accommodation is not only taxed to its very utmost, it is overtaxed and overcrowded'.
9. By 1900 there were also about 1,400 houses built for workers by the Edinburgh Co-operative Building Society; but often they were too expensive for many workers. See G. Gordon, 'The Status Areas of Edinburgh; a Historical Analysis', unpublished Ph.D. thesis, Edinburgh University, 1971, pp.94-5.
10. A.W. Ritchie (Chief Sanitary Inspector of Edin.),

Housing: Improvement and Clearance Schemes in Populous Areas (Edin., n.d. [c. 1930]), p.2.
11. Edin. Public Health Department AR 1919; A Joint Committee of the Presbytery of Edinburgh and of the United Free Church Presbytery of Edinburgh, The Housing of the Poor in Edinburgh (Edin., 1922), p.6.
12. Presbyteries' Joint-Committee, Housing of the Poor, p.10: emphasis in original.
13. Ibid.
14. Ritchie, Housing, p.4.
15. Gordon, 'Status Areas', p.172; Richardson et al., Urban Spatial Structure, pp.24-5.
16. D. Hunter, Edinburgh's Transport (Huddersfield, 1964), p.92; M.F. Huq, 'The Urban Geography of the Heart of a City: with Special Reference to Edinburgh', unpublished Ph.D. thesis, Edinburgh University, 1960, ch. 6.
17. D. Keir (ed.), The Third Statistical Account of Scotland. The City of Edinburgh (Glasgow, 1966), pp.410-11.
18. Huq, 'Urban Geography', ch. 7.
19. See T&LC minutes, 17 September 1918, 21 June, 19 August 1921.
20. Cp the engineering employers' refusal, after 1923, to pay accommodation allowances to outworkers in nearby towns. During negotiations, an employers' representative asked 'is it such a dreadful hardship to sit in a [tram] car with your morning paper[?] I suppose you do take time to read[?]' To which sallies an AEU negotiator responded: 'You cannot read in the Edinburgh cars; it is impossible'. ESAE&I and AEU, 'Local Conference Proceedings: in re Outworking Allowances, Edinburgh District', 22 January 1923, pp.6-7.
21. But few trade unionists had telephones until Edinburgh installed an automatic exchange in 1926. Judging from numbers printed in T&LC ARs (which acted as a trade union directory for the area), the number of T&LC officials (and trade union organisers and secretaries) with telephones grew thus: 1922/3, 0 (0); 1923/4, 0 (1); 1924/5, 0 (1); 1925/6, 1 (17), 1926/7, 2 (18); 1927/8, 7 (23); 1928/9, 5 (23). (The T&LC figures include, in each year, the T&LC's legal adviser, a solicitor, at his office, and for 1926-8, the T&LC's Secretary.)
22. A. Woodburn, 'Edinburgh and Social Progress', in The Labour Party Annual Conference Edinburgh 1936, souvenir brochure and programme (Edinburgh, 1936), pp.13-18. Woodburn was by then the LP's Scottish Secretary; he was Secretary of State for Scotland, 1947-50.

23. Ibid., p.17.
24. J. Reid, The New Illustrated Guide to Edinburgh Historical and Antiquarian (Edin., n.d. [c. 1921]), p.121; Keir, City of Edinburgh, pp.580-2.
25. J. Stewart, The Organisation of Education in Edinburgh (Edin., 1925), p.41.
26. G.W. Crawford, 'Foreword' to Edin. T&LC, Souvenir of the Trades Union Congress at the Synod Hall, Edinburgh (Edin., 1927), p.6.
27. N. Milnes, A Study of Industrial Edinburgh and the Surrounding Area 1923-1934, vol. 1 (London, 1936), pp.4-5.
28. Cp the comments of Lord Cameron in Keir, City of Edinburgh, pp.453-6.
29. From about 1920 onward these groups had been co-operating, by mutual tacit agreement, on an anti-socialist basis: see Chapter 9 below.
30. The preceding two paragraphs draw on B. Elliott, D. McCrone and V. Skelton, 'Property and Politics: Edinburgh 1875-1975', unpublished paper, Edinburgh University, n.d. (c. 1978).
31. TC AR 1920, p.8.
32. Ibid., p.55.
33. Edin. Fabian Society minutes survive from 9 October 1926. Membership varied between 50 and 70, and attendance at meetings between 30 and 80, in the later 1920s.
34. Letter, Thomas Paris to Gerald Crawford, 14 May 1927, in the possession of Edinburgh Trades Council.
35. William Rutherford in Labour Standard, 8 January 1927.
36. The Red Flag, vol. 1, no. 1 (February 1927), p. 9.
37. Gray, Labour Aristocracy, p.21.
38. Milnes, Industrial Edinburgh, p.114.
39. Ibid., p. 15; Sir W.J. Thompson, 'Edinburgh as an Industrial Centre' in Scottish Chamber of Commerce, Trade and Commerce between Scotland and the Empire (Glasgow, 1934), p.11.
40. J. Waterston, 'Labour in Edinburgh' in T. Stephenson (ed.), Industrial Edinburgh (Edin., 1921), p.92. Many families also included mothers!
41. Gordon, 'Status Areas', p.174.
42. A partial exception was the concentration of railway and brewery workers in the Meadowbank-Abbeyhill-Canongate area.
43. See C. Harvie, No Gods and Precious Few Heroes, Scotland 1914-1980 (London, 1980), esp. pp. 10-15; B. Lenman, An Economic History of Modern Scotland 1660-

1976 (London, 1977), esp. pp. 208-14.
44. Lenman, Economic History, p.212.
45. A.L. Bowley, Some Economic Consequences of the Great War (London, 1930), pp.94-6.
46. M.W. Flinn, 'The Overseas Trade of Scottish Ports, 1900-1960', Scottish Journal of Political Economy, vol.13 (1966), p.226.
47. Scottish Chamber of Commerce, Trade and Commerce, p.32.
48. See Harvie, No Gods, pp.13-14, 25-6; Bowley, Economic Consequences, pp.95-7. F. Douglas, Zero Hour for the Forth (Edin., n.d. [c. 1940]), argues strongly that British intervention in Russia was a vital factor.
49. Douglas, Zero Hour, p.11.
50. C.E.V. Leser and A.H. Silvey, 'Scottish Industries during the Inter-War Period', Manchester School, vol. 18 (1950), p.165.
51. Keir, City of Edinburgh, p.603.

Chapter Three

STANDARDS OF LIVING AND THE WORKING CLASS

> Slums and slum-dwellers are the products of a
> system which perpetuates poverty, adds daily to
> the number of poor, and makes it the easiest thing
> in the world for the poor to remain poor.[1]

The 'cost of living' index issued by the Board of Trade after
1914 to 'measure the percentage increase in the cost of
maintaining a minimum or subsistence standard of living
among working class households'[2] was mistrusted within the
labour movement. The Edinburgh Trades and Labour Council
described it as 'obsolete and unreliable' in 1923, although it
did not doubt that the index should be based on a <u>minimum</u>
expenditure level - asserting only that it should relate 'to
those commodities which form the cost of subsistence of the
workers'.[3] Such a dispute over detail underlay the Trades
Council's decision to publish annually a detailed 'Household
Budget' - the 'Minimum for Man and Wife and Two Young
Children'[4] - from 1914 until 1920.[5] These figures (see Table
3.1) confirm that Edinburgh shared the general wartime and
immediate post-war experience of inflation.

If these figures illustrate some of the pressures behind
post-war militancy, they give us little grasp of the actual
standard of living of Edinburgh's working class families. The
elements of the Trades Council's minimum household budget
(set out in Table 3.2) do not make up a generous allowance.
No 'expenditure for Tobacco, Beer, Papers, Amusements,
Holidays, Renewal of Furniture, etc.'[6] is included; neither is
work-related expenditure such as fares. A working class
view of a minimally adequate weekly shopping basket is
helpful, but even the Trades Council's calculations should be
treated with caution. Its budget assumed a family of two
adults and two children to be typical: a survey carried out in
1931 among Edinburgh households where the 'chief occupations' included

> Asphalters, railwaymen, motor-drivers, Corpora-
> tion employees, building trades operatives,

labourers, shop assistants and porters, coopers, laundry workers, office-cleaners, carters, messengers, dockers, fishermen, miners, vanmen, apprentices of all descriptions, etc., etc.[7]
found 5.8 members of each family on average, with the mean varying in different streets between 4.3 and 8.2.[8] The censuses suggest that the mean number of children per family in Scotland at this time was in the region of four, and that the number was significantly greater where the husband was a manual worker (and still more where he was an unskilled manual worker).[9] The line between bare adequacy and poverty was narrow indeed: the same family income could lead to both.

Table 3.1: Cost of Living Indices 1914-27

	Official	Edinburgh Trades Council: 'Restricted'	'Full'
1914	100	100	100
1915	125	127	n.a.
1916	144	158	n.a.
1917	179	206	n.a.
1918	205	215	n.a.
1919	221	208	192
1920	269	258	234
1921	199	[Not available after 1920]	
1922	180		
1923	177		
1924	180		
1925	176		
1926	174		
1927	166		

Definitions: 'Official': Cost of Living index issued by Board of Trade and Ministry of Labour. For definitions of Trades Council indices, see Table 3.2.

Sources: Calculated from A.H. Halsey (ed.), Trends in British Society since 1900 (London, 1972), p.122; TC ARs 1916-20.

Table 3.2: Edinburgh Trades Council's Minimum Household Budget, with Prices Applicable on 19 June 1920

	s	d		s	d
¼ stone meal	1	6	Vegetables	1	6
4 lbs sugar	4	8	Currants & raisins		7½
½ lb tea	1	4	¼ lb corned beef		5
½ lb margarine		7½	1 lb fish		9
½ lb butter	1	6	Teabread		5½
1 stone potatoes	2	8	6 2lb loaves	3	3
1 jar marmalade	2	1½	1 cwt coal	2	7½
1 lb barley and peas		6	4 bunches firewood		5
½ lb lentils		3½	Soap and		
Rice, tapioca, etc	1	0	washing powders	1	7
1¾ lb self-raising flour		8	Sundries	2	10
½ lb cheese		10			
½ lb bacon	1	3	('Restricted total' 44		6)
½ dozen eggs	1	9			
Milk	2	4	Rent and rates	6	0
Butcher Meat	7	0	Light		10
			Boots and clothing 20		4
			('Full total'	71	8)

Note: 'Restricted total' was used in 1916-18; 'full total' in 1919-20.

Source: T&LC AR 1920, p.6.

For those in employment, working class incomes seem to have followed, broadly, national trends. Money wages rose during the war. 'In several trades ... wages have been doubled,' the Trades Council recorded in 1919, but 'in the trades and occupations which are not so well organised ... the workers have been unable to maintain a proper standard of life.'[10] Rates were highly volatile during 1919-22, but thereafter stabilised, and in several cases remained unaltered until the later 1920s. Some of these wage movements are represented in Table 3.3. The figures are available because, each year, the Trades Council questioned its affiliates about (inter alia) the wages and conditions

Table 3.3: Money Wage Rates in Certain Edinburgh Trades 1914–27

	1914 s	1914 d	1918a s	1918a d	1919 s	1919 d	1920 s	1920 d	1921 s	1921 d	1922 s	1922 d	1923 s	1923 d	1925 s	1925 d	1927 s	1927 d
Electricians	41	2	n.a.		78	11½	86	2	86	2	78	0	66	7	72	6	72	5½
Painters	39	7	54	2	77	0	81	7	102	8	77	0	69	8	73	6	73	4
Engineers	38	0	59	4	76	0	88	6	88	6	56	3b	56	3	56	3	56	3½
Sheet Metal Workers (in motor works)	34	0	58	0	68	6	88	1½	88	1½	72	6	57	0	57	0	57	0
									105	9	85	6	62	0	66	6	67	0
Compositors	35	0	56	0	66	0	90	6	95	6	83	0	75	6	77	6	77	6
Bakers	34	0	53	0	69	0	84	0	96	6	79	0	69	0	76	6	75	0
Rubber Workers:																		
(max)	36	0	58	0		c	70	8	70	8	n.a.		56	0	56	0		d
(min)	24	0	44	6		c	61	10	61	10	n.a.		42	0	42	0		d
Shop Assistants:																		
(men)	24	0	32	0e	60	0	75	0	77	6	68	0	62	6	62	6	65	0
(women)	18	0	23	6f	45	0	50	0	51	6	45	0	40	0	40	0	40	0
Printing Warehouse Assistants and Packers	20	0	39	0	49	0	n.a.		n.a.		n.a.		n.a.		58	6	58	0

Table 3.3 continued

	1914		1918a		1919		1920		1921		1922		1923		1925		1927	
	s	d	s	d	s	d	s	d	s	d	s	d	s	d	s	d	s	d
Laundry Workers:																		
(max)	12	0	18	0	30	0	35	0	35	0	28	0	28	0	28	0	28	0
(min)	5	0	10	0	10	0	12	0	12	0	10	0	10	0	10	0	10	0
Building Trade Labourers	28	0g	n.a.		n.a.		n.a.		n.a.		n.a.		n.a.		55	11	55	11
Foundry Labourers	n.a.		n.a.		n.a.		n.a.		n.a.		n.a.		n.a.		41	6	41	6
(Unemployment Insurance Rates:																		
(adult man)	7	0	7	0	7	0	11	0	h		15	0	15	0	18	0	18	0
(adult woman)	7	0	7	0	7	0	11	0	h		12	0	12	0	15	0	15	0
(dependent wife)	-		-		-		-		-		5	0	5	0	5	0	5	0
(child under 16)	-		-		-		-		-		1	0	1	0	1	0	1	0
(boy 16-18)	3	6	3	6	3	6	5	6	10	0	10	0	10	0	7	6	7	6
(girl 16-18)	3	6	3	6	3	6	5	6	8	0	8	0	8	0	6	0	6	0)

Notes: (a) 1918 figures exclude any 'war bonus', where this is mentioned. (b) 'At 25 September 1922'. (c) A single figure of 56s 10d is given for Rubber Workers in 1919. (d) '1914 plus extra cost of living'. (e) A range of 28s to 36s is given. (f) A range of 21s 6d to 25s 6d is given. (g) A range of 25s to 31s is given. (h) Rates changed four times between November 1920 and November 1921.

Source: TC and T&LC ARs, 1918-27.

applicable to their trades.[11] Of course, many branches responded only fitfully: it was easier for branch secretaries to complete the form where a single, uniform rate existed in the district, and this applied more to skilled ('trades') unions, rather than to those organising many grades and occupations. We therefore have quite full information on many trades (electricians, engineers, bookbinders, compositors, bricklayers, bakers, and so forth), but the data about the semi-skilled and unskilled are patchy. (This is especially true of unorganised, or non-union, sectors: a small indication of what may lie hidden is provided by the laundry workers, whose unionisation was recent - and weak.)

Table 3.4: Wage Differentials in Building and Printing: Edinburgh 1914-26

	1914	1919	1921	1926
Building:				
Bricklayers	100		100	100
Painters	93		130	98
Labourers	59-73		n.a.	74
Printing:				
Compositors	100	100		100
Warehouse Assistants and Packers	57	74		75

Source: Calculated from TC and T&LC ARs.

Nevertheless, we have some evidence on the progress of pay differentials. Adequate data are available for two industries: building and printing (see Table 3.4). (In building, Bowley's designation of bricklayers and painters as skilled and semi-skilled respectively has been followed;[12] in printing, 'warehouse assistants and packers' are taken to be unskilled.) They present a picture of narrowing pay differentials as between skill. This is still more marked in the comparison of skilled and unskilled workers' pay between industries (see Table 3.5): whereas in 1914 there was a marked differential between the wages of skilled and semi-skilled workers as a group, and the unskilled, this was no longer the case in the 1920s. Substantial differentials

Table 3.5: Wage Rates as a Percentage of Compositors' Wage Rates: Edinburgh 1914, 1921, 1925

	1914	1921	1925
Over 120:	Bricklayers (121)		
110–119:	Electricians (118); Painters (113)	Sheet Metal Workers in Motor Works (111)	
100–109:	Engineers (109); Compositors (100)	Painters (107); Compositors (100)	Compositors (100)
90–99:	Sheet Metal Workers (97); Rubber Workers (max) (91)	Engineers (93); Sheet Metal Workers (92); Electricians (90)	Bricklayers (97); Painters (95); Electricians (93)
80–89:	Building Trade Labourers (max) (89)	Bricklayers (82); Shop Assistants (men) (81)	Sheet Metal Workers in Motor Works (89); Shop Assistants (men) (81)
70–79:	'Labourers' (74); Brewery Workers (max) (71); Building Trade Labourers (min) (71)	Rubber Workers (max) (74)	Printing Warehouse Assistants and Packers (75); Engineers (73); Sheet Metal Workers (73); Rubber Workers (max) (72); Building Trade Labourers (72); 'Labourers' (1924) (71)
60–69:	Rubber Workers (min) (69); Shop Assistants (men) (69)	Rubber Workers (min) (65); Brewery Workers (max) (62)	
50–59:	Brewery Workers (min) (57); Printing Warehouse Assistants and Packers (57)	Brewery Workers (min) (52)	Rubber Workers (min) (54); Foundry Labourers (53)

Source: Calculated from TC and T&LC ARs, 1918, 1921, 1925.

remained, but these were almost as much among the various skilled and unskilled occupations, as between the skilled and unskilled. (The trades which suffered most were in engineering.) By the mid-1920s, in short, wage rates seem to have been determined as much by the condition of the industry as by the worker's skill.

We can use the Trades Council's own minimum household budget to provide estimates of local 'real' wage rates (see Table 3.6).[13] The trends are much as we might expect: falling real wage rates during the war; significant increases in 1919-21, somewhat eroded during 1922 and 1923, followed by a small improvement. Almost all occupations seem to have improved their real wages by 1927, as compared with 1914, and especially with 1918. The real wages of the unskilled tended to improve faster than those of the skilled; engineers' real wages fell.[14] But more than this, before and immediately after the war, the bulk of unskilled workers operated at below the Trades Council's 'minimum' level; and immediately after the war, even skilled workers were perilously close to it. By the mid-1920s, however, most unskilled male workers seem to have earned more than this minimum, if only marginally so.

Some further qualifications are necessary. Not all wage rates were time rates. Some workers were paid piece rates - and we may suppose that, being more difficult to estimate and summarise, they were often omitted from the Trades Council's compilations. Piecework seems to have been especially prevalent in two categories of work: where the finished product was quite standardised and the production process relatively simple and labour-intensive (such as brushmaking); and where the production process, though highly capitalised, involved the manufacture of large quantities of standardised items (for example, the seasonal production of golf balls and hot-water bottles in rubber works,[15] or in making gas-meters, where there were over 400 separately priced jobs for brass finishers alone).[16] And, of course, piecework was not necessarily a strategy to reduce earnings (although sometimes it was):[17] rather, to encourage productivity, it offered the 'clever craftsman' relatively high rewards at the expense of the 'duffer'.

Earnings over a period of time also depend upon regularity of employment. During the war the Trades Council pointed out that as there had 'been no rise in wages locally to equal half of the financial imposts on the necessaries of life', it was

Table 3.6: 'Real' Wage Rates in Certain Edinburgh Trades 1914–27: Wage Rates Expressed as a Percentage of the Cost of Purchasing the Trades Council's Minimum Household Budget

	1914	1918a	1919	1920	1921	1922	1923	1925	1927
Electricians	154	n.a.	134	120	162	162	141	155	164
Painters	148	99	130	114	193	160	147	157	166
Engineers	143	109	129	124	166	117	119	120	128
Sheet Metal Workers (in motor works)	128	106	116	123	166	150	121	122	129
					199	177	131	142	152
Compositors	131	103	112	126	180	172	160	165	176
Bakers	128	108	117	117	182	164	146	163	170
Rubber Workers (max)	120	106	n.a.	99	133	n.a.	118	119	n.a.
(min)	90	82	n.a.	86	116	n.a.	89	90	n.a.
Shop Assistants (men)	90	79b	102	105	146	141	132	133	147
(women)	68	43b	76	70	97	93	85	85	91
Printing Warehouse Assistants and Packers	75	72	83	n.a.	n.a.	n.a.	n.a.	125	131

Table 3.6 continued

	1914	1918a	1919	1920	1921	1922	1923	1925	1927
Laundry Workers									
(max)	45	33	51	49	66	58	59	60	63
(min)	19	18	17	17	23	21	21	21	23
Building Trade Labourers	105b	n.a.	n.a.	n.a.	n.a.	n.a.	n.a.	119	127
Foundry Labourers	n.a.	n.a.	n.a.	n.a.	n.a.	n.a.	n.a.	86	94
(Unemployment Insurance Rate for Man, Wife, and Two Children under 16:		13	12	15	c	46	47	58	61)
(Out-of-Work Donation, 1919			56						)

Notes: (a) 1918 figures exclude any 'war bonus', where mentioned. (b) Calculated from mid-point of range of wage rates given. (c) Rate changed three times between November 1920 and November 1921. (General) Base year 1920: cost of purchasing TC Minimum Household Budget in other years estimated by using official Cost of Living index.

Sources: Calculations based on Tables 4.1, 4.2, 4.3.

> only the comparative regularity of employment
> now obtaining under the present abnormal condi-
> tions, and the overtime worked in some trades,
> that makes the increased cost bearable.[19]

Wartime full employment and overtime enabled the standard
of living to rise despite falling real wage rates. During 1919
and 1920 the common demand was for a shorter working
week combined with the abolition of overtime and high basic
wages.[20] With the passing of the boom, however, short-time
working was the more common complaint.[21] So whilst those
in full-time employment may have somewhat improved their
position, work was in the 1920s becoming increasingly
uncertain and unpredictable.

In one sense, the extent of employment and under-
employment was determined by what employers were wont
to call 'the state of trade'. In certain industries, this was
seasonal. In building, for instance, 'In spite of all modern
improvements ... the weather is still of paramount importance'.[22] The rubber industry experienced seasonal fluctua-
tions in demand which led to a 20 per cent variation in
women's employment, always the most vulnerable.[23]
Confectionery was also seasonal, as of course were most
holiday-related trades. Although seasonality declined in
some industries, such as printing,[24] and although it may
have appeared insignificant beside more secular trends in
employment, it remains an important qualification standing
against any over-easy assumptions about the working class
standard of living.

Short-time working and seasonal unemployment were
compounded in several industries by casual labour. Leith's
dockers were, of course, casually engaged. So too were
building workers. 'No builder of a lower grade than foreman
can count on continuous employment from one day to
another. Technically, he cannot count on it from one hour to
another ...'[25] But casual employment of this relatively
formalised type was only one point in a spectrum of
managerial prerogative and tactics which included, for
example, the short-term employment of married women to
overcome peaks in demand, and the use of apprentices as
both cheap, and limited-term, labour.

UNEMPLOYMENT

Unemployment was important for the employed as well as
the workless, for especially during the 1920s it was a
widespread threat to workers' security of income. During

1919 and early 1920 unemployment was not seen as significant. It arose, for instance, only at four Trades Council meetings in 1919. The following year it was discussed on ten occasions. By 1921 it had become a major issue, arising at least 35 times - rather more than twice, on average, at each meeting. As the council recorded in the middle of 1922,

> On the average, during the year [1921-22] approximately 15,000 of our people have been on the live Registers of the Labour Exchange alone. Those people, with their dependants constituting about a fifth of the population ...[26]

The official progress of unemployment during the 1920s is shown in Table 2.6. While the relationship of insurance figures to the percentage rate of unemployment is unclear, in terms of simple volume they can only have understated the problem. Various groups were excluded, and a substantial section of the gainfully employed was not insured.[27] The numbers unemployed (see Table 3.7) should therefore be seen as conservative approximations, especially as regards the incidence of unemployment in working class areas of the city.[28]

Unfortunately, the evidence on the duration of unemployment, where it exists at all, is sparse and unreliable.[29] We can thus make little more than rough estimates about what proportion of the city's workers experienced unemployment in the early and mid-1920s. Milnes estimated that between 1923 and 1930, 65.8 per cent of the city's insured population experienced 'intermittent unemployment', and of these over 60 per cent 'would have known but short spells'.[30] By the same token, of course, nearly 40 per cent would have known longer spells; and these (rough and ready) calculations suggest that some experience of unemployment was the rule, rather than the exception, during these years.

Unemployment was, then, sufficiently common to be widely feared. It also created a considerable financial gap between the employed and unemployed sections of the working class (leaving aside those whose unemployment was short term and relatively predictable), and especially between the unemployed and the employed trade unionist - for the compression of inequalities between trade unionists itself emphasised their distance from the workless. Of course, there remained a substantial sector of ill-paid labour, much of it female, of which the laundry workers are indicative.[31] But this sector was very largely non-union - very often it was de-unionised - for as the depression bit deeper, the frontiers of unionisation were rolled back.

If the workless were poor, the long-term unemployed could be poor indeed. During the winter of 1923-4, the Labour Standard's editor met a man

> in the Waverley Station who had been unemployed for 18 months, had lost his wife, and was then in his third week of the 'gap', had had two meals in three days, had wrists that were mere skin and bone.

He also, apparently, carried some poison 'for the simple purpose of killing himself and ending his torture'.[32] The - very limited - income available to the unemployed came from two main sources: unemployment insurance benefit and parish relief under the Poor Law. Both were circumscribed by regulations, often onerous, designed to prevent 'abuse' by 'scroungers'. Insurance benefit rates (shown in Table 3.3) became somewhat more generous, although not when the 'Out-of-Work Donation' - 29s for men, 24s for women, 6s for the first dependent child, 3s for each additional child - introduced by a fearful government in November 1918 is taken into account. This lasted until November 1919 for civilians, but until March 1921 for ex-servicemen and women.[33] But even as the unemployment insurance scales became more generous, so they were more harshly administered. A climate of opinion was created in the press which assumed abuse of the system to be normal, as the Manchester Guardian noted.

> Judging by the correspondence columns of some newspapers ... the unemployed would rather draw the dole than go to work, and ... the one ideal of the poorer classes is to get something for nothing out of the pockets of the richer.[34]

This approach certainly underlies the questions asked by one well-known study,[35] and led to wry comments in the labour press. For instance, the Evening News drew

> a tortuous moral from the fact that a poor house-holder must now spend £30 a year having his garden weeded by casual labour, whereas he could get the work done for £12 before the War. 'The broad lesson,' says the News, 'is that there is now the dole to fall back upon'.

'Why do these people do it?' asked the Labour Standard. Was it 'in the British tradition to kick a man when he is down?' Did they 'ever inflict their sermons on the idle rich'? Or was it 'merely that the existence of the dole raises the cost of the retainers which they require to keep them in a life of ease?'[36]

Such protests were vain. There were continual bouts of 'tightening up' - especially as to whether the applicant was 'genuinely seeking work'. One example shows how government directives and local administration combined to this end. Legislation in 1925 decreed that benefit should be paid for periods for which contributions had not been paid 'only if ... [the Minister] deems it is expedient in the public interest to pay such benefit to the particular applicant concerned'.[37] Especially relevant to so-called 'extended benefit', decisions were to be made by three-member Rota Panel Committees, which included employers' and workers' representatives. According to Unemployment Insurance in Great Britain,

> Since these conditions involve the determination of what is 'reasonable', as distinct from questions of technique, the democratic Rota Panel is a more appropriate adjudicating body than the employment exchange officials.[38]

This view was not shared in the Edinburgh Employment Exchange, for whereas 'Prior to the new regulations ... the applicant only appeared before the Rota Committee, and, if satisfactory, a grant was recommended',

> With the tightening-up process now in force, many applicants have been called before the permanent officials of the Divisional Office. Following this interview they were again called before a Rota Committee, with those gentlemen's written observations.

'The results', according to the Labour Standard, were 'best known to many who are now getting Parish Relief.'[39] The AEU District Secretary claimed that officials had interviewed claimants for extended benefit even 'in certain cases where grants had been recommended by Rota Committees': no Rota Representatives were present and 'claimants were "tricked" into making statements likely to injure their claims', leading to the reversal of decisions in 47 cases out of 75.[40] Certainly the numbers in receipt of Parish Relief (see Table 3.7) varied in a manner which suggests changes in policy.

Those who had been unemployed too long, or had paid too few contributions, or were unfit for or 'not genuinely seeking' work (or, apparently, who had been insufficiently quick-witted in interviews with Ministry officials) were thrown onto the Parish. The Parish Council's outlook was

Table 3.7: Numbers in Receipt of Public Assistance in Edinburgh 1923-8

	1923	1924	1925	1926	1927	1928
Able-Bodied Poor	4,095	3,135	2,284	3,626	3,446	3,810
Disabled Poor	3,064	3,470	3,602	3,549	3,550	3,664

Note: Number on Roll at 15 May each year.

Source: N. Milnes, A Study of Industrial Edinburgh and the Surrounding Area 1923-1934 (London, 1936), p.27.

summed up by its chairman, one Colonel Young, in a speech to its 1925 Annual Dinner:

> It was not the duty nor in the power of any community to find work for anybody ... The poor they would always have with them, but that should not be taken as any encouragement for those who feared nothing so much as their success in getting a job.[41]

The Parish Council operated a means and an attitude test: the fate of those who failed these is described by a Labour parish councillor:

> Recently a number of unemployed workers drawing Parish Relief for themselves and their families, called on me stating that the Assistant Inspector had told them that as they were not genuinely seeking work their Parish Relief had ceased. They would have to go into the Poorhouse and the Parish would look after the wife and family while they were there.[42]

For those who were successful, the Relief scale (see Table 3.8) was less generous than the so-called 'Mond Scale' suggested by the Minister of Health in 1922, but was in national terms not unfavourable.[43] For even an average-sized family, it was more generous than unemployment insurance.

For those able to obtain unemployment insurance benefit, conditions seem to have been best in 1919 (taking the

Table 3.8: Edinburgh Parish Relief Scale 1926

Adult	Adult Living at home	Man and Wife	Each Child	Maximum
15s	7s 6d	22s 6d	3s 6d	40s

Source: Labour Standard, 7 August 1926.

Out-of-Work Donation into account), and then to have improved again from 1921 onward (see Table 3.6). The widespread middle-class assumption that the dole sapped the incentive to work is given little support when the rates are compared with the wages even of unskilled manual trade unionists (see Table 3.9). The pay of laundry workers suggests there may have been a sector of at best semi-organised, semi-casual, unskilled and low-paid employment, where there was little financial incentive to work - unless, of course, two or more members of a family could find employment. Yet a 1930 study of St Andrews ward, a poorer and older area of the New Town, provides clear evidence that - even among the poor - unemployment did make people poorer. Essentially a study of housing conditions (chosen because of its high infant mortality rate, though in this it was broadly comparable with four or five other wards), it included a survey of the weekly earnings of 407 families in 22 streets. In Figure 3.10, we compare for each street, the mean family income with the number of families unemployed. The relationship between unemployment and family income is unmistakable.

WOMEN'S EMPLOYMENT
Between 1919 and 1921 men returning from the war, together with a 50 per cent increase in family formation, largely displaced women in the factories, offices and work-shops.[44] But with unemployment and short-time working, married women began to seek work again to supplement family incomes; there was also a decline in the marriage rate after 1920, which tended to increase the supply of female labour.[45] It is therefore likely that the increase in the number of women in insured employment in Edinburgh (which was rather greater than the rise in male employment) nevertheless understates the increase in the number of women seeking work: 'more women obtain work largely

Table 3.9: Relationship of Wages and Unemployment Insurance Rates: Edinburgh 1920-6

	1920	1923	1926
Compositors	100	100	100
Engineers	98	74	73
Labourers (a)	n.a.	73	72
Laundry Workers			
(max)	37	37	36
(min)	13	13	13
Unemployed:			
- single man	12	20	23
- single woman	12	16	19
- couple	12	26	30
- couple with			
two young children	12	29	35
- boy, 16-18	6	13	10
- girl, 16-18	6	11	8

Note: (a) 'Labourers', 1923; Building Trade Labourers, 1926.

Source: Calculated from TC & T&LC ARs, each year.

because many more seek it'.[46]

So in one respect, the rise in women's employment reflects a falling average standard of living, a response to family poverty and unemployment. But as women became cheaper to employ (compared to men), employers exploited the opportunity.[47] Straightforward displacement of men by women seems to have been unusual; more often, it accompanied changes in technology or product. It was said, for instance, that the replacement of men by women in the rubber industry was due to 'the development of certain branches of the work which are particularly suited to the women workers' - including, apparently, the making of shoes, golf balls and hot water bottles.[48] In the laundries, married women were not normally employed, for their enforced retirement on marriage 'gives those who remain a greater chance of promotion', provided - in married former employees - a pool of trained, casual labour for use in

Figure 3.10: Relationship between Family Income and Unemployment in Certain Streets in St Andrews ward, Edinburgh, c. 1930.

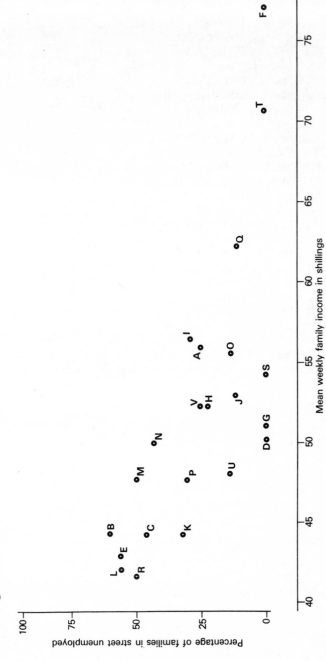

Key to Streets:
A. India Place (88 families visited)
B. Church Street (5)
C. Church Place (17)
D. Church Lane (1)
E. Saunders Street (9)
F. St Bernards Place (10)
G. Darlings Buildings (5)
H. South St James Street (40)
I. North St James Street (14)
J. East St James Street (8)
K. St James Square (19)
L. St James Place (23)
M. Elder Street (4)
N. Clyde Street (7)
O. Broughton Street (30)
P. Leith Street and Terrace (45)
Q. Little King Street (9)
R. Albany Street (2)
S. Duke Street (2)
T. York Place (4)
U. Rose Street (49)
V   Thistle Street (16)

Source: Calculated from I.T. Barclay and E.E. Perry, Behind Princes Street, A Contrast (Edin., 1931), p.32.

'holiday or rush periods',[49] and no doubt helped to depress the average wage level. Elsewhere, women were less well organised by trade unions: on the railways, for instance, 'women carriage cleaners ... were not coming up to the "scratch" ' in 1920, and the NUR arranged meetings to encourage 'better organisation' among them.[50]

WORKERS' HOUSING

Later nineteenth century Edinburgh saw two complementary processes of social segregation. First, many of the bourgeoisie migrated to new suburbs, leaving their former houses to the working-class. Until the 1920s, however, the new areas were not far removed from the older areas, and much of the town centre (especially of the New Town) remained prosperous. R.L. Stevenson observed that

> Social inequality is nowhere more ostentatious than
> at Edinburgh [for] ... to the stroller along Princes
> Street, the High Street callously exhibits its back
> garrets.[51]

Even between the wars the physical distance between the classes was very small.

Second, within the working class a similar process occurred. More prosperous workers were able to move to superior, new housing, although often this was not in geographically distinct areas. The standard and status of accommodation in Victorian Edinburgh was well-understood, and could vary from 'block to block or stair to stair', so that even within socially mixed working-class streets, the 'respectable' stood apart from the 'rough'.[52] This segregation seems to have diminished, at least in intensity, from the late nineteenth century onwards. In two working-class streets built in the 1880s and originally occupied largely by skilled manual and white collar workers, the proportion of these shrank and that of unskilled workers grew.[53] But it was most severely eroded by the war (together with its immediate aftermath), which not only flattened inequalities in income and increased real incomes, but did so especially in relation to housing costs.

In 1915, under pressure from the Clydeside rent strike, Asquith's government introduced a freeze on rents. The Edinburgh Trades Council judged that average working-class rents had not changed in the city in 1920 compared with 1914.[54] Within the working-class budget, therefore, the cost of housing plummeted in relation to other expenditures (see Table 3.11). Although rents were increased during the

Table 3.11: Rent as a Proportion of Edinburgh Trades Council's Minimum Household Budget 1914-20

29 July 1914	19.7 per cent
28 June 1919	10.2 per cent
19 June 1920	8.4 per cent

Note: This was the TC's view of a minimum rent for man, wife and two children aged five and nine.

1920s, they remained controlled, and at the end of the decade remained a much smaller proportion of working-class income and expenditure than before 1914.[55] In short, it became far more difficult for exclusion practices to be based on housing standards, for even good quality working-class housing was within the grasp of a group larger than any former 'labour aristocracy'.

Table 3.12: Marriages and Births in Edinburgh 1914-27

	Marriages		Births
	Number	Rate	
1914	3,165	9.7	6,466
1919	4,690	13.8	5,612
1920	4,483	13.4	7,774
1921	4,610	11.0	9,028
1922	4,057	9.6	8,772
1923	4,164	9.8	8,662
1924	3,963	9.3	8,404
1925	4,065	9.6	7,843
1926	3,823	n.a.	7,926
1927	3,861	n.a.	7,621

Note: Figures 1914-20 relate to Edinburgh proper; those for 1921-7 include Leith, Liberton, Colinton, Corstorphine, and Cramond.

Source: Edin. Public Health Department ARs.

The supply of housing was severely limited. Very little working-class housing was built in the pre-war decade, and none during the war; thereafter the Town Council was less than enthusiastic in taking up the opportunities offered under successive Housing Acts, so that its schemes made little impact in volume terms until the mid-1920s.[56] Private enterprise building was also at a low level, so the process of 'filtration' (by which accommodation was meant to 'filter down' through the social scale as the richer built new houses and those they vacated were sub-divided) had little effect.[57] Yet a substantial rise in family formation and birth figures after the war (see Table 3.12) suggest ever-increasing demand and pressure on space. With but a single exception, those Edinburgh wards normally considered working class experienced greater increases in population density during the war years than did the city as a whole[58] (see Table 3.13) - and in any case their densities were well above the city's mean. Although these figures must be treated with some reservation, the number of households occupying just one or two rooms in the city also rose significantly (by 4.3 per cent and 9.7 per cent respectively) during the war; and continued to rise through the early 1920s, if less rapidly (see Table 3.14). So three indicators point to intensified working-class demand for housing during the war, and at least two suggest that the demand continued to be high throughout the 1920s.

Short supply, an imperfect market, and high demand brought important shifts in the social allocation of housing. In particular, the stratum of skilled manual workers - the Victorian labour aristocracy - lost some of its ability to isolate itself. A parish minister, for instance, reported in 1922 that 'several respectable families' were living in the tenement (mentioned in Chapter 2) of 80 or 90 residents whose vermin were so active and resilient.[59] Yet stratification within the working class was by no means eliminated, despite these pressures. The Presbytery investigators' impression was of the respectable holding out in adversity. They rejected, for instance, the notion that the inhabitants of such stairs were 'unfitted to the responsibility of being tenants', as it was applied 'indiscriminately': 'Characters of this kind are too common, but the local patriotism of the lobby and the stair in better instances repudiates them.' The proportion of 'well-kept' rooms was 'high', 'considering the cramped conditions';[60] and although the lack of privacy made 'any form of intelligent study or practice in the Arts

Table 3.13: Changes in Population Density in Edinburgh 1914-25

	1914	1919	1922	1925
Edinburgh	96.0	100.0	97.0	97.0
Selected Wards				
Calton	95.4	100.0	92.4	90.6
Canongate	97.3	100.0	92.3	90.8
St Stephens	94.2	100.0	100.2	90.6
St Andrews	93.3	100.0	92.0	92.5
St Giles	95.9	100.0	85.3	82.8
Dalry	94.3	100.0	91.2	89.5
George Square	96.0	100.0	88.9	87.1
St Leonards	93.4	100.0	90.3	88.7

Note: Edinburgh figure is for 1914 and 1919 boundaries throughout.

Source: Calculated from Edin. Public Health Department ARs.

or Religion ... very difficult', there were 'occasional breaks in the clouds':

Sometimes the people possess gramophones and a selection of overtures: they generally read the evening paper; and their taste, if it passes beyond china dogs and family photographs, relieves the walls with surprising reproductions of good paintings.[61]

While this also tells us much about the investigators' attitudes, the suggestion is that the attitudes and lifestyles of pre-war working class 'respectability' did not die as quickly as purely economic analysis might suggest.

Finally, by the later 1920s structurally-based segregation within the working class had begun to intensify again, as the corporation housing schemes, with their higher rents, gave renewed significance within the housing market to differentials in working class family income. In 1924 the Medical Officer of Health lamented the unwillingness of working-class families to pay for better facilities:

Table 3.14: Edinburgh Households Occupying One and Two Rooms 1914-25

	One Room		Two Rooms	
	Number	Top 5 Wards (per cent)	Number	Top 5 Wards (per cent)
Edinburgh				
1914	5,771	73.3	19,783	54.4
1919	6,017	72.8	21,705	55.2
1922	6,157	73.0	21,971	55.2
1925	6,059	72.1	22,097	55.3
Leith				
1922	1,222		8,238	
1925	1,243		8,240	

Notes: (a) Edinburgh and Leith according to 1914-19 boundaries. (b) Top 5 Wards: percentage of (respectively) one- and two-bedroomed households found in the five wards with the largest number of such households. In each year, these were found to be the same, viz, for one-roomed households: Canongate, St Andrews, St Giles, George Square, St Leonards; for two-roomed households: Calton, Canongate, Gorgie, Dalry, St Leonards.

Source: Edin. Public Health Department ARs, and calculations thence.

It is apparently a waste of time and energy to attempt to convince many people who live in slums that a £15 house provided with such conveniences as electric light, gas boiler, hot water system, wash house, tub and sink, drying green, and open air all round, is in every possible direction worth £5 more than the dungeon-like slum devoid of almost every comfort that a human habitation should possess.[62] There were, in fact, other disincentives to moving,[63] but the strong suggestion is that those who moved to the new schemes consisted chiefly of the 'respectable' (though it is far from clear that we can treat these simply as skilled workers and their families). In 1928, for instance, sanitary inspectors found that only 30 (out of 600) tenants who moved to the new corporation houses 'continued to show careless inclinations' in their domestic habits.[64] But the re-assertion of important segregation based on income from the later 1920s only serves to stress its relative absence during our crucial period: the post-war years were special, and they stand out in large measure because of the pressures to which existing patterns and trends of working-class fragmentation were exposed.

During the war and the earlier 1920s, the structure of Edinburgh's working class was changing. Pre-war patterns of fragmentation were placed under various - but continuous - pressures: shifting income differentials, rapid but irregular inflation in the overall price level, distortions of the relative cost of major items of family expenditure, rapid changes in the extent and nature of women's involvement in the labour market, and so forth. But no new, single or dominant pattern emerged to replace them. Rather, relics of the old patterns, combined with newly-emerging (and sometimes transient) sources of fragmentation, produced a complex network of intersecting divisions within the working class: and the structural fragmentations thus tended not to generate culturally exclusive groupings. At the same time, the war was a period when the economic and social conditions of working-class life deteriorated; the advances of 1919 and 1920 were short-lived, and thereafter any improvements were small, and to be set against substantial areas of deterioration.

NOTES

1.   Labour Standard, 25 December 1926.
2.   G.S. Bain, R. Bacon and J. Pimlott, 'The Labour Force' in A.H. Halsey (ed.), Trends in British Society since 1900 (London, 1972), p.107.
3.   T&LC minutes, 31 July 1923.
4.   TC AR 1916, p. 19.
5.   Cp the comment by the engineering employers' chairman in negotiations in 1922: 'There was no grumbling on your part about going on the Board of Trade cost of living when wages were going up, but now it is coming down people are taking exception to it although it is worked out in the

same way.' ESAE&I and AEU, 'Conference Proceedings: Proposed Reduction of 12½ per cent on Piecework Prices of Brass Finishers and Brass Moulders, in Gas Meter Making Works', 20 July 1922, p. 5.
6.   T&LC AR 1920, p. 6.
7.   I.T. Barclay and E.E. Perry, Behind Princes Street: A Contrast. Report on Survey of Housing Conditions of 443 Families Situated in St. Andrews Ward, Edinburgh (Edin., 1931), p.33.
8.   Ibid., pp.28-9.
9.   C. Rollett and J. Parker, 'Population and Family' in Halsey (ed.) Trends, pp.55-7.
10. TC AR 1919, p. 5: emphasis added.
11. A fragment of the questionnaire used survives in a TC minute book (its reverse having been used for scrap paper). It requests the following information for 'the compiling of the Annual Report': Union; Branch; Membership; Contracted-in Membership; Secretary; Address; Wages, including Bonuses; Hours per Week; Overtime Rate (here the page is torn off).
12. A.L. Bowley, Some Economic Consequences of the Great War, (London, 1930), p. 149.
13. For the years after 1920, the cost of the TC's minimum household budget has been estimated using the official cost of living index.
14. Cp comments by two AEU negotiators: 'Mr. STUART: ... [with] the starvation wages that you are now offering ... I am quite serious in saying that some of our fellows are looking for anything bar engineering ... What they are looking for are jobs either in pubs or at labouring work.'
'Mr. WRIGHT: I might tell you for my own part that I was getting more some time ago for labouring.' ESAE&I and AEU, 'Local Conference Proceedings: in re Outworking Allowances, Edinburgh District', 22 January 1923, pp.20-1.
15. N. Milnes, A Study of Industrial Edinburgh and the Surrounding Area 1923-1934, vol. 1 (London, 1936), p.251.
16. ESAE&I and Brassfinishers Society, 'Local Conference Proceedings: Piecework Prices - Application for Advance of 20 per cent', 29 October 1920, p.15.
17. Cp Andrew Clarke's tale of events 'in one of the largest pits in East Lothian' (Labour Standard, 25 April 1925). 'The men thinking (foolishly of course) that if they put their backs into it and were able to earn an extra shilling or two - well, the ton rate being so small, the manager would surely never think of reducing it. But alas ... One fine day recently

(or rather, one very black day for them) they were told that on and after a certain date the ton rate would be reduced [from 2s.] ... to 1s 6d.'

18. ESAE&I and Brassfinishers Society, 'Piecework Prices', 20 October 1920, pp.13-14.

19. TC AR 1916, p.6; the same point is made in ibid., 1917, p.8.

20. E.g. NAUL No. 292 branch minutes, 12 January 1919; NUR Edin. No. 1 branch minutes, 2 February 1919.

21. E.g. NUR Edin. No. 1 branch minutes, 11 March 1923, 27 July 1926; Labour Standard, 9 January 1926; ESAE&I and AEU, 'Outworking Allowances', 19 December 1922, pp.15-16.

22. Milnes, Industrial Edinburgh, p.158; see also A.D. Webb, 'The Building Trade' in S. Webb and A. Freeman (eds.), Seasonal Trades (London, 1912), pp.312-93.

23. Milnes, Industrial Edinburgh, pp.251-2: women made up roughly one half of the labour force.

24. J. Child, Industrial Relations in the British Printing Industry (London, 1967), p.234.

25. Milnes, Industrial Edinburgh, p.158.

26. T&LC AR 1922, p. 7: on the relationship between the 'Live Register' and other unemployment statistics, see W.R. Garside, The Measurement of Unemployment. Methods and Sources in Great Britain 1850-1979 (Oxford, 1980), pp.40-45.

27. 'At the 1931 Census nearly $19\frac{1}{2}$ million persons within the insurance age limits were counted as gainfully employed, of whom only $12\frac{1}{2}$ were insured against unemployment.' Garside, Measurement of Unemployment, p. 32: see also pp.29-61.

28. Regarding the 'idle list of 20,000 people', on behalf of a TC and unemployed committees' deputation to the Town Council (Labour Standard, 13 February 1926), 'Mr. Hew Robertson ... contended that the position was worse than appeared, because the industrial section of the community, from whom this 20,000 was drawn was comparatively small'.

29. Garside, Measurement of Unemployment, pp.39, 183-4.

30. Milnes, Industrial Edinburgh, p.64; on the survey on which her calculations are based, see Garside, Measurement of Unemployment, p.184.

31. See Milnes, Industrial Edinburgh, esp. pp.257-9.

32. Labour Standard, 20 June 1925. The 'gap' was a period of five weeks during which no uncovenanted benefit could be claimed.

33. A. Deacon, In Search of the Scrounger. The Administration of Unemployment Insurance in Great Britain

1920-1931 (London, 1976), p.13. W. Hannington, Unemployed Struggles 1919-1936 (London, 1936), p.28, attributes the origins of the NUWCM in large measure to the ending of the Out-of-Work Donation.

34. Manchester Guardian, 7 January 1926.

35. J.J. Astor et al., Unemployment Insurance in Great Britain (London, 1925).

36. Labour Standard, 21 March 1925, referring to the Evening News, 16 March 1925.

37. Astor et al., Unemployment Insurance, p.12.

38. Ibid., pp.13-14.

39. Labour Standard, 21 November 1925.

40. Ibid., 19 December 1925. The AEU District Secretary was also Secretary of the Advisory Committee of Workpeople's Representatives for Edinburgh and Leith.

41. Labour Standard, 21 March 1925.

42. W. Waterston in Labour Standard, 11 December 1926.

43. Labour Standard, 7 August 1926; Astor et al., Unemployment Insurance, p. 34.

44. Bowley, Economic Consequences, pp.57-61.

45. Milnes, Industrial Edinburgh, pp.70-1.

46. Ibid., p.74.

47. See, e.g., ibid., pp.190-1, 256-7.

48. Ibid., p.245.

49. Ibid., p.257.

50. NUR Edin. No. 1 branch minutes, 1 February 1920; see also 15 February 1920.

51. R.L. Stevenson, Picturesque Notes on Edinburgh (London, n.d.), p.18.

52. R.Q. Gray, The Labour Aristocracy in Victorian Edinburgh (Oxford, 1976), p.96.

53. B. Elliott and D. McCrone, 'Urban Development in Edinburgh: A Contribution to the Political Economy of Place', Scottish Journal of Sociology, vol.4 (1980), p.18.

54. TC AR 1920, p.6. The TC made no major complaint about breaches of the 1915 Act.

55. Bowley, Economic Consequences, p.82.

56. Milnes, Industrial Edinburgh, p.176.

57. Cp 'Filtration' in The Red Flag, no. 1 (1927), p.14; R. Tressell, The Ragged Trousered Philanthropists (London, 1959), esp. p.79.

58. According to the Royal Commission on the Housing of the Industrial Population of Scotland (Cd. 8731, 1917, p.345) war work caused 'a very considerable influx of workers. The housing accommodation is not only taxed to its very utmost,

it is overtaxed and overcrowded'.

59. A Joint-Committee of the Presbytery of Edinburgh and of the United Free Church Presbytery of Edinburgh, The Housing of the Poor in Edinburgh (Edin., 1922), p.10.

60. Ibid., p.11.

61. Ibid., p.13.

62. W. Robertson, in Edin. Public Health Department, AR 1924, p.v. The Chief Sanitary Inspector reported (ibid., pp. 73-4) his officials' 'Repeated visits' to tenants in the Canongate-Grassmarket area: 'although a number of tenants were induced to go to Lochend, the majority were very apathetic and a variety of excuses were made. Many averred that the rents were too high, and others that they did not want to leave the district'. Cp Barclay and Perry, Behind Princes Street, p.31: 'The rents charged for new houses (including rates) average 13s. for three-roomed houses, and 15s. for four-roomed houses. These rents are obviously outside the range of the low-paid worker ...'

63. E.g. 'systematic visitation' and 'constant supervision' of Council tenants by 'Women Sanitary Inspectors', using 'encouragement, persuasion, practical advice, and failing these, ... sterner methods' apparently had 'wonderfully good results in improving the habits of the people': see Edin. Public Health Department, AR 1927, pp.81-2; 1928, p.94.

64. Ibid., 1928, p.94. For the Chief Sanitary Inspector's views on workers' 'careless inclinations', see also ibid., 1924, pp.73-4.

Chapter Four

ECONOMIC DEVELOPMENT
AND THE ORGANISATION OF WORK

> This 'rationalisation of industry' is ... only rational
> in the long run if it is <u>not</u> based on the physical,
> and, still less on the nervous exhaustion of the
> workers.
>
> But at the present moment attention is chiefly
> concentrated only on the rationalisation of
> industrial processes, and little or none is given to
> the more rational use of the worker ...[1]

During the later nineteenth and early twentieth centuries,
the Scottish economy was marked by conservative and
individualistic industrial decision-making. The economy was
dominated by heavy industry - heavy engineering, shipbuilding, iron manufacture, coalmining.[2] Eight staple
industries produced 60 per cent of Scottish output in 1913:[3]
much of this went to the empire. Before the war, many of
the major enterprises were in practice family concerns.[4]
Scottish financial concerns, centred in Edinburgh, were
internationally-oriented: concerned more with overseas
investment than domestic profitability.[5] So there was little
restructing of industry or rationalisation in the pre-war
years. Numerous company amalgamations between 1890 and
1914 involved a holding company structure but 'little
reorganisation at the technical or financial level'.[6]
Investment in domestic manufacturing industry was
relatively low; its profitability declined, encouraging
overseas and imperial ventures.[7]
    The conservatism of Scottish industry was confirmed by
the war, which enhanced demand for its traditional
products.[8] Rationalisation and restructuring were imposed -
largely from without; such company amalgamations as did
occur continued to take the 'holding company' form.[9] The
post-war boom - lasting at best into the first half of 1921 -
again offered the prospect of continuing heavy demand in
the industries of Scotland's traditional strength. There was
little apparent need for a thorough-going reassessment of

investment and market strategies. Yet the post-war boom obscured a wartime loss of markets, and perhaps further erosion of competitiveness through quality deterioration.[10]

The recession, which bit deep in Scotland with its narrow industrial base, did bring industrial restructuring.[11] But the assumptions behind the strategic choices remained in the defensive mould set before the war. During the boom, for instance, confident of demand, many shipbuilders sought to secure their steel supplies by purchasing steel producers; their expectations disappointed, they turned to price fixing agreements, negotiations (often fruitless) with continental competitors, only 'when all else failed to seek a solution in various forms of rationalisation'.[12] These were rational responses to low, if unpredictable, demand: uncertainty, induced by recession, encouraged defensiveness but discouraged radical restructuring. To pursue the example of shipbuilding (whose problems were but those of recession writ large), market unpredictability led to the maintenance of excess capacity in labour and plant - as intense competition encouraged rapid delivery times and the ability to fulfil a variety of orders - and thus to a shortage of finance for technological innovation.[13] Save, perhaps, during the war, then, the early twentieth-century Scottish economy discouraged both innovative investment and organisational restructuring.

IMAGES OF ORGANISATION AND
THE ORGANISATION OF MANAGEMENT

By 1914 few doubted that hierarchy and bureaucracy were fundamental to efficient management. This belief went far wider than the devotees of Taylor's 'scientific management': even the most routine management texts assumed it;[14] its ascendancy is most graphically shown in the stark simplicity of the organisation chart.[15] Its importance was explained by two main metaphors - illustrating, if implicitly, the coordinating and controlling functions of management. On the one hand, 'factory organisation is very similar ... to a machine': just as 'Efficiency in a machine is a result of good material, proper design, and careful operation', so in a factory 'there must be definite objectives toward which the separate and combined efforts of all members of the organisation are directed'.[16] On the other hand, with regard to labour control, a works manager's 'requirements of character, initiative, decision, leadership, practical psychology or understanding of men, technical knowledge, etc., are very similar' to those of 'an officer in the British Navy';[17] whilst foremen were seen as 'non-commissioned officers'[18] in essentially military structures.

Now the problem with managerial structures of this kind - roughly what Tom Burns has termed 'mechanistic' systems[19] - is that their effectiveness is limited to relatively stable conditions. Rapid changes in market conditions or workers' behaviour, or technological innovation, can render them highly ineffectual. The achievement of the later Victorian period was in large part the extension of large-scale production, and of a mass market in Britain and overseas, which could sustain unprecedented levels of demand through a wide spectrum of inter-related industries and markets. On this basis a relative stability was attained which allowed such mechanistic management systems to grow and prosper.

The war brought rapid and frequent changes to managers' environments. Government increasingly intervened in matters of supply and demand; demand for labour increased while fewer sought work, and others left to take the King's shilling; the Factory and Workshop Acts were suspended. Government actually managed substantial sections of industry. By 1918 over 3,400,000 people were employed in munitions work, and about 2,250,000 in controlled establishments - in which the Ministry of Munitions exercised many of the central functions of management, determining hours, working rules, and wages.[20] Instability also marked the post-war years. During the boom, not only was labour in a position of almost unprecedented strength, but the structure of markets had to readjust to peacetime conditions, overseas contacts had to be reconstructed; in many cases the end of war production involved a move to substantially different products and markets. And within two years, the boom was gone, leaving managers to confront a world of constantly inadequate demand.

These constant upheavals in the managerial environment placed great strains on existing organisational structures - and, though implicitly, on existing images of management organisation. Such instability calls for non-programmed decision-making, for which mechanistic systems are ill-designed. Organisations can adjust to such circumstances in two main ways. They can move toward adopting what Burns characterises as an 'organic' structure, in which all members of an organisation exercise functions which are not pre-defined, but which must 'be constantly redefined through interaction with others participating in the discharge of common tasks or the solution of common problems'.[21] This requires widespread knowledge of - and commitment to - the objectives and situation of the whole concern; and it implies an emphasis on lateral, rather than merely vertical, interaction within the organisation. It is likely to succeed, however, only where those in authority correctly identify the overall problem facing the organisation, can generate the necessary knowledge, commitment and abilities among its members or employees, and are willing to take the apparent risks involved in doing so.

The alternative response to constant upheaval is more common when notions of hierarchy and bureaucracy are deeply ingrained. Those in authority can 'redefine, in more precise and rigorous terms, the roles and working relationships obtaining within management along orthodox lines of "organisation charts" and "organisation manuals", and ... reinforce the formal structure'.[22] In short, this repsonse involves efforts to 'make the system work', with the strong assumption that informal interaction is in some way improper - yet, perversely, that where it exists, the formal structures must be respecified accordingly. But while such responses can cope with a single moment of change, where change is frequent (and unfamiliar circumstances the norm), formal structures, rules and procedures tend to mushroom. And some of the - formal or informal - institutions generated may be dysfunctional to the mechanistic structure as a whole.[23] An important theme of the chapters which follow is the balance between mechanistic and organic elements in how Edinburgh's industrial organisations responded to the crises of war and the post-war world.

MANAGEMENT STRATEGY AND WORK ORGANISATION

If the organisation of management was limited by the strength of mechanistic images, so too was management's organisation of the entire process of work. Early twentieth-century British management ideology was strongly influenced by American Taylorism, which was widely assumed to be both 'scientific' and the true route to industrial efficiency. Frederick W. Taylor's gospel of detailed central planning of production, breaking down work processes into individual and specific tasks, and close, strictly-disciplined supervision of shop floor workers, found little favour with British employers in practice, however. It required management to gather, store, process and evaluate a vast body of information about production, and thus demanded a heavy investment in 'unproductive' labour (to process information, and to control workers), and in fixed capital (to minimise the need for workers' skills). These promised returns only with mass production, strong demand, and market stability. At the same time, British managers had long relied heavily on the abilities of skilled workers, whose flexibility was a source of strength. So as late as 1916, it was 'still a fact that "Scientific Management" is a wholly American movement', according to one pessimistic survey of Britain's industrial situation: 'we are still more than ten years behind the United States'.[24]

Taylorism provided no panacea for business ills. But, an ideological movement as well as a management strategy, it appeared to do so. Its apparent resonance with the late Victorian and Edwardian trend toward larger-scale production meant that many emerging management techniques were subsumed within it - while others were dismissed as by-ways from the main path of progress. Bonus systems and payment by results, for instance (both increasingly common before the war), were essential to Taylor's system: it was but a short step to seeing them as inadequate and partial without it. Thus, in pre-war management literature, Taylorism and good management could often seem synonymous.[25] Even those with severe reservations about Taylorism, such as Edward Cadbury, argued not that it was ineffectual or limited as a method of management, but that its social implications were unacceptable.[26]

In practice, managers found that, in the interests of production - whether for national or commercial interest - they had often to devolve an important degree of autonomy to their shop floor workers. With the war, for instance, came a restructuring of output, the conscription of labour into the armed forces, and dilution with its sub-division of processes, specialised machinery, upgrading of existing workers, recruitment of new labour. All this required the goodwill and expertise of existing workers, whose bargaining strength had increased. And although 'dilutees' were often required to perform tightly specified tasks (reminiscent of Taylor's written instruction card scheme),[27] many were called upon to attain quite high levels of sophistication.[28]

After the Armistice, British management adopted a number of reforms and innovations, motivated by notions of efficiency and reconstruction. As we shall see, post-war industry was faced with rapid shifts in demand, in labour supply, in wages and hours, in product range. As a result, managers continued to need the commitment and practical expertise of their shop floor workers: to adapt, to produce, to survive. But the language of this British 'thrust for efficiency'[29] was overwhelmingly the language of Taylorism, of direct control. Machinery was efficient; the 'human factor introduces uncertainty in quantity and quality'; unless 'centralisation of production control' could be achieved, there would be 'waste'.[30] Even the welfare movement, which during the war had begun to offer an alternative to scientific management,[31] was by the mid-1920s justifying its policies in identical language: 'Our object is ... to eliminate all useless or ineffective expenditure of energy and all other kinds of waste.'[32]

The hegemony of Taylorism - soon the commonsense of management - was no passing phenomenon. With no viable non-Taylorist theory of management, many important developments have been obscured. Only quite recently have historians begun to appreciate that management by 'responsible autonomy' is no mere relic. This strategy promises to enable managers to 'harness the adaptability of labour power by giving workers leeway and encouraging them to adapt to changing conditions in a manner beneficial to the firm'.[33] It means devolving status, responsibility, authority, to (at least some) workers; it means persuading workers that firm and employees share a common interest; it may mean involving unions in a common endeavour.[34] During the war and post-war years, the reality of management was an admixture of responsible autonomy with more direct control. The next chapter examines how shifting management strategies affected the strength of labour.

NOTES

1. Labour Standard, 8 May 1927.
2. N.K. Buxton, 'Economic Growth in Scotland between the Wars: the Role of Production Structure and Rationalisation', Economic History Review, vol. 33 (1980), esp. pp.547-9.
3. C. Harvie, No Gods and Precious Few Heroes, Scotland 1914-1980, (London, 1981), p.1.
4. J. Scott and M. Hughes, The Anatomy of Scottish Capital. Scottish Companies and Scottish Capital 1900-1979

(London, 1980), pp.49-54.

5.   Ibid., pp.22-37.

6.   Ibid., p.54.

7.   Harvie, No Gods, p.5; T. Dickson (ed.), Scottish Capitalism (London, 1980), esp. pp.245-54.

8.   B. Lenman, An Economic History of Modern Scotland 1660-1976 (London, 1977), p.208.

9.   Scott and Hughes, Anatomy, p.67.

10. Lenman, Economic History, p.211.

11. Scott and Hughes, Anatomy, p.66.

12. P.L. Payne, 'Rationality and Personality: A Study of Mergers in the Scottish Iron and Steel Industry, 1916-1936', Business History, vol. 19 (1977), pp.166-8.

13. A. Slaven, 'A Shipyard in Depression: John Brown's of Clydebank 1919-38', Business History, vol. 19 (1977), pp.193-4.

14. E.g. F. N[asmith], 'Factory Management', in An Encyclopaedia of Industrialism (London, n.d. [c. 1912]), pp.207-23.

15. For contemporary examples, see J.F. Whiteford, Factory Management Wastes: and How to Prevent Them (London, 1919), pp.221-2.

16. Ibid., pp.10-11.

17. W.J. Deeley, Labour Difficulties and Suggested Solutions. A Manual for Technical Students, Cashiers, Foremen, Departmental or Works Managers and Employers, (Manchester, 1918), p.129.

18. John Brown and Co. Ltd., 'Memorandum on the Shortage of Ironworkers at Clydebank', quoted in J. Melling, ' "Non-Commissioned Officers": British Employers and their Supervisory Workers, 1880-1920', Social History, vol. 5 (1980), pp.209-10.

19. T. Burns and G.M. Stalker, The Management of Innovation (London, 1966), esp. pp.119-20.

20. G.R. Rubin, 'The Origins of Industrial Tribunals: Munitions Tribunals during the First World War', Industrial Law Journal, vol. 6 (1977), p.162.

21. T. Burns, 'On the Plurality of Social Systems', in T. Burns (ed.), Industrial Man (Harmondsworth, 1969), p.242.

22. Burns and Stalker, Management of Innovation, p. ix.

23. Ibid., pp. ix-xi.

24. H.B. Gray and S. Turner, Eclipse or Empire? (London, 1916), pp.152-3. For introductions to recent debates on Taylorism and the development of the labour process, cp C.R. Littler, The Development of the Labour Process in

61

Capitalist Societies (London, 1982); M. Burawoy, The Politics of Production (London 1985).

25. Cp, e.g., N[asmith], 'Factory Management', passim; G. Brown, Sabotage (Nottingham, 1977), p.150.

26. E. Cadbury, 'Some Principles of Industrial Organisation', Sociological Review, vol. 7 (1914), esp. p. 117.

27. See J. Maclean, 'The War after the War' (1917) in id., In the Rapids of Revolution (London, 1978), pp.124-36; A.S. Milward, The Economic Effects of the Two World Wars on Britain (London, 1970) esp. pp.33-7, 41.

28. As can be seen from some of the literature produced to help dilutees, e.g. E. Pull, The Munition Workers' Handbook. A Guide for Persons taking up Munition Work (London, 1916) which claimed 'to provide in as small a space as possible all the practical information a person taking up munition work would be required to know, in order to start work in an engineering shop'.

29. The phrase is taken from B. Palmer's work on early twentieth-century US employers' strategies, 'Class Conception and Conflict: The Thrust for Efficiency, Managerial Views of Labor, and the Working Class Rebellion, 1903-22', Review of Radical Political Economics, vol.7, no. 2 (1975), pp.31-49.

30. Whiteford, Factory Management Wastes, p.39, 44-5.

31. Cp E.D. Proud, Welfare Work. Employers' Experiments for Improving Working Conditions in Factories (London, 1916).

32. B.S. Rowntree in the Cocoa Works Magazine, quoted Brown, Sabotage, p.219; see also Rowntree, The Human Factor in Business (London, 1920).

33. A.L. Friedman, Industry and Labour (London, 1979), p.95.

34. Ibid.

Chapter Five

EMPLOYERS' STRATEGIES AND THE CONTROL OF WORK

> the human complex (the collective worker) of an
> enterprise is also a machine which cannot, without
> considerable loss, be taken to pieces too often and
> renewed with single new parts.[1]

This chapter examines the industrial context in which
Edinburgh's trade unionism developed during and after the
Great War. We analyse the development of four of
Edinburgh's industries: engineering, printing, rubber
manufacture, and railway transport. Engineering and
printing illustrate the profoundly varying developments of
job control structures in two long-established industries;
rubber was an industry with a very different economic
situation, and one where unions were established only during
the Great War; and on the railways union recognition was a
very recent development in a highly complex industry. In
1921 engineering and printing were Edinburgh's two largest
manufacturing industries in terms of employment; the
railway was the largest employer in transport; while the
rubber industry in Edinburgh was centred on the largest
factory of any kind in the East of Scotland.

ENGINEERING: STRUCTURE AND TECHNOLOGY
Relative to the economy of Scotland as a whole, the
engineering industry was under-represented in Edinburgh.
Nevertheless, it remained the largest single (manufacturing)
industrial group in the 1921 Census, and by a considerable
margin; while engineers made a substantial contribution to
the labour movement in the city. The bulk of Edinburgh's
engineering firms developed areas of specialisation during
the 1850s and 1860s: in many cases these specialisms were
associated with the manufacture of capital equipment for
other Edinburgh industries. Thus Bertrams, founded in 1821,
was by the 1850s specialising in papermaking machinery;[2] a
separate firm, James Bertram and Sons, was founded in 1845
for the same purpose;[3] Miller and Co., founded in 1867,

specialised in the production of large chilled iron goods, notably rollers used in papermaking;[4] MacKenzie and Moncur, founded in 1900, specialised in large casting, particularly for papermaking machinery.[5] Similar 'servicing' origins are apparent in relation to other local industries: printing, ink and colour manufacturing, brewing, ship-building, rubber-manufacture, mining and so on (by the 1920s, of course, products were sold more widely than Edinburgh). 'With the diversity of requirements represented by these trades', a Professor Oliver wrote in the early 1930s, 'Edinburgh's engineering industry has developed along highly specialised lines where craft, skill, ingenuity and inventive-ness rather than mass production prevail'.[6] This was a division of labour, to be sure, but rather than integrating the entire production process within one factory, and then dividing it internally according to a centrally-determined pattern between different sub-processes and work-groups, here the division was not merely between workers but between limits of capital. The production process was divided between various firms, as elements of it were sub-contracted from one to another.

This pattern persisted into the 1920s. The manufacture of capital equipment was largely carried out in response to individual contracts, on each of which the specifications were likely to vary. The holding of stocks was thus both risky and expensive. One paper-making machine, for instance, might take a year to construct; a relatively large firm like Bertrams might, on average, make two a year.[7] Sub-contracting for components was an important method of spreading risks. It also allowed specialisation, since sub-contracting firms might construct components not only for one firm, but for several (and not always for the same industry). In short, the costs of production and the uncertainty of demand put a premium on low fixed costs. To be sure, this doubtless appealed to a capital market which preferred short-run to long-run investment, and to firms which were small and often family-owned. But it was also itself a form of organising industrial capital, a method of structuring production so as to achieve economies of scale without surrendering flexibility. For these capital-goods industries, market uncertainty, and changes in product, were normal; and the entire industry could be organised accord-ingly. Similar considerations applied in relation to construc-tion engineers, shipbuilders, and those firms ancillary to shipbuilding (such as Brown Bros, who made steering gear and similar components for ships).

There were, of course, exceptions to this industrial structure: but they tend to be of the sort which prove the rule. For instance, between 1899 and 1914, nine types of motor car were manufactured in Edinburgh.[8] Few firms were commercially successful, although in at least one case a motor works was purpose-built: on a seven-acre site by the Granton branch of the Caledonian railway. Yet this site was occupied by three different manufacturers within six years, all of whom closed down (and one of whom went bankrupt): by the outbreak of war it had become a printing works.[9] The reasons were twofold: firstly, Scotland's heavy engineering had not led to the development of a network of component or sub-assembly producers appropriate to the motor industry (in contrast, say, to developments in the midlands of England). Most components for Scottish-built cars were imported from England or France, with consequently high transport costs. Secondly, the pre-war market for motor vehicles was not a Scottish one: there were roughly three times as many new vehicle registrations per head in London as in Scotland.[10] Economies of scale were thus achieved only at the price of an inflexibility which, with a shortfall in demand, left these companies dangerously exposed.

The manufacture of heavy capital goods placed a premium on flexibility of labour as well as of capital: this implied a relatively heavy dependence on the skills of the craftsman, and the more so as few of the firms were large enough to justify substantial managerial and research costs. Perhaps the extreme case of employers' explicit reliance on workers' responsibility is outworking, which was common in the city: 'There is barely a shop in Edinburgh but which sends men out working, while extremely few in Glasgow do', declared an ASE negotiator:[11] and it was common ground that, in the words of the local engineering employers' chairman, 'In most cases, with any normal firms, the outworker is a man who is known and there is trust given on both sides'.[12] Outworkers[13] were governed by local agreements on conditions and allowances, but might be required to travel anywhere in Great Britain and Ireland to execute their tasks, and would do so unsupervised. But this is only the extreme case: within the workshops engineering craftsmen continued to exercise a considerable degree of what James Hinton calls 'craft control'.[14] H.N. Blyth's account of his apprenticeship at Brown Bros during the war is evocative of this: the men whose role is pre-eminent are not, despite their formal authority, the foremen, but rather 'the journeymen'.[15] The majority of Edinburgh's engineering employers were thus bound to adopt strategies which emphasised the 'responsible autonomy' of their workers: 'direct control' on any scale was neither economic nor, in many cases, even possible. Thus it was that payment by results was relatively rare in the industry in Edinburgh: the only clear example lies in the gas meter sector.[16]

ENGINEERING IN WAR AND PEACE

In Edinburgh, whilst there was rationalisation and war production, it was often not mass production. Whilst there was a greater standardisation of product, in many cases this was the production of standardised batches, rather than continuous production over a long period of identical products. Brown Bros, for instance, moved in a two-year period from starting and reversing engines, to triple expansion engines, to searchlight gears, to tanks.[17] Productivity needed to be achieved quickly in each case, and could not rely on the construction of elaborate or specialised assembly lines. Thus employers (and government) rested heavily on the ability of skilled workers to adapt production processes: clearly this meant a devolution of responsibility and decision-making, which tended to strengthen the pre-existing tendency to organic management structures. After 1919 firms in general returned to their pre-war product structure: general lessons, about management, rationalisation, and so on might be carried over, but the contexts of peace and war were very different.

Nevertheless, associated with the demands of war, there was a drive to greater productivity, greater 'efficiency', less 'waste'.[18] There seems to have been a conscious effort on the part of certain elements of the state, among others, to demonstrate that the 'lesson of the war' - the importance of 'all working together for a common purpose' from which any diversion of energy was a waste - was equally valid in peacetime.[19] But after the war, and particularly after 1921, the drive was bolstered by the increasing crisis in engineering. Edinburgh did not escape this. 'No skilled tradesmen has had a worse time during the last five years than the engineer', the Labour Standard recorded in 1926.[20] Engineers' pay, of course, declined steeply relative to other trades; and whilst the only major closure during our period was of the North British Railway's St Margarets Locomotive Erecting shop at Meadowbank,[21] the poor state

66

of trade was a constant employers' complaint.[22]

The drive for efficiency was thus not limited to a single form, even within engineering. During the war employers became conscious of the strength of their workforces, and anxious to integrate them with a common definition of purpose for their enterprises. In wartime such a definition was more readily available, more self-evident, and perhaps less questioned: recalling his wartime workmates at Brown Bros, Blyth averred

> I never saw any slackness in that works. A few men held that the war was unnecessary because German employers could not possibly be worse than British ones and anyway the capitalist system was so rotten that it did not matter who held power. These malcontents had next to no influence or following.[23]

But the attempt to integrate at the ideological or attitudinal level was bolstered by a willingness to make material concessions. Wages rose 100 per cent for engineers between 1914 and 1919. And employers were also prepared to make - perhaps had to make - concessions with potentially more lasting implications: especially in relation to workplace union organisation. In a remarkable local conference held in January 1918, for instance, district officials of the ASE raised the question of shop-steward organisation: they did so, however, in order to ensure the development went along the right lines:

> The whole thing, as far as we are concerned, resolves itself into this: we don't want any unofficial shop stewards started in the district. You quite understand our position. The official shop steward is under the direction of the district committee. That is the official body, and to have any unofficial body started would not be very desirable in this district at any rate, whatever may be said at Coventry.[24]

But, in practice, the local employers were recognising shop stewards already, and seemed reluctant to jeopardise their in-plant working relationships for the sake of union structures. 'Of course,' the employers' chairman remarked, 'at the present time the greater part of the firms [in Edinburgh] recognise a man as a shop steward.'[25] The question which concerned them suggests they were finding resistance difficult: 'how far will it go? That is really the point we should like to know.'[26] There was no reply.

Employers' Strategies and the Control of Work

As elsewhere, so in Edinburgh: the increasing complexity of payments systems during the war was a major factor in the development of shop-steward organisation in engineering.[27] The employers' account of their recognition of shop stewards focuses on piece-work as providing the issue around which stewards came to their attention;[28] whilst there was one example quoted, from a firm which manufactured heavy capital equipment, which lends support to this view from the opposite direction. 'We never knew until a few weeks ago that we had such a thing as a shop-steward about the place', the firm's representative said. 'You have had shop stewards there for the last 16 years,' retorted the union negotiator.[29] This exchange indicates, first, that shop stewards were a well-established part of the engineering union world;[30] second, that where a firm relied on 'craft control', the role of the shop steward could be a quiescent one; and third, that the war posed all kinds of new questions for shop stewards.[31]

While the post-war boom lasted, there was little incentive for employers to press for greater efficiency. With unions relatively strong, with demand high, with old markets to be reconquered, the opportunity cost of losing production through industrial disputes was high. There were also just many other things to do; not least organising the changeover from war production, in which workers' goodwill was an important asset. The achievement of 'efficiency' remained, in theory, an important managerial objective, and there was no slackening in the efforts to swing public opinion to the view that the common objective of workers and management should be the elimination of waste.[32] But in practice, the maximisation of output seems to have been the primary objective: profit margins might be smaller, but total profits would remain, and the future could be assured through recapturing market shares. So there was little incentive for employers to assert some new form of direct control in the immediate post-war period. And although employers made some attempt to regain control by indirect ('responsible autonomy') means,[33] 1919 and 1920 were marked by an overall erosion of managerial control. It was at this time that the number of active AEU shop stewards in Edinburgh reached its peak.[34]

With the onset of the recession in 1920-21, the ground shifted. Engineering was hit early and hard.[35] The principle of 'efficiency' again found material support. Workers found themselves increasingly on the 'long side' of the labour market. This eased management's problems in one respect at least: the need to motivate workers diminished. To the extent that employers had tended to 'responsible autonomy' strategies and structures for this reason, they were now able to shift to tighter control over the workforce. But of course there were other reasons for employers' adoption of the 'responsible autonomy' approach, which were strengthened by the depression. Declining demand did not encourage the investment necessary to make direct control fully effective. Uncertainty of demand for central products put a premium on the ability to compete for orders over a relatively wide product range: this discouraged inflexible fixed investment, and positively encouraged reliance on workers' ability to adapt. Maintaining unwieldy management structures was increasingly risky, and its cost higher in relation to income.

In practice, Edinburgh's engineering employers seem to have steered a middle course. There was tightening-up, as employers attempted to reduce costs. According to a correspondent in the Labour Standard, 'the conditions in many shops [in 1925] are as bad as possible. Speeding up and time-checking even for the lavatory has been brought to a fine art.'[36] Although there is no reason to treat this as mere hyperbole, overall, Edinburgh's engineering employers seem to have sought less provocative methods of cutting costs. Working conditions were allowed to deteriorate; safety equipment and welfare facilities were inadequately installed:[37] the AEU noticed 'a steady increase in our sick members' during the years after 1921.[38] The conditions of apprentices (a minority group for which, in practice if not in rhetoric, few journeymen seem to have been prepared to fight) were undermined in two ways. First, they were taken on where adult labour was being laid off, leading to comments that engineering was 'overrun' by apprentices in the mid-1920s.[39] They seem to have been employed, in many cases, as semi-skilled labour: 'the[ir] time spent in the workshop has been very frequently upon repetition work of no educational value. Instead of apprentices they have developed into cheap labour for the bosses ...'[40] (Given the traditional attitude of journeyman to apprentice,[41] this may have had the additional effect of inducing the former to undertake informally, unpaid, even unconsciously, certain supervisory functions in relation to semi-skilled labour.) Second, apprentices seem to have been easily manipulated. 'During the last six years of trade depression,' wrote an 'engineer' in 1927,

> many apprentices have been stood off for weeks on end, and few boys have finished their four years' apprenticeship with more than three years actually in the workshop. The rest of the period they have been serving their time on the so-called dole.[42]

Often, they were dismissed when their indentures expired, and full wages became due; in other cases, they were 'threatened with the sack unless they continue to work at apprentice wages'.[43] In short, their ability to resist (or induce others to resist on their behalf) being small, apprentices were often treated as cheap, easily-manipulated labour.

Edinburgh's engineering employers then, generally continued their established managerial approach (which involved more than normal reliance on the craft responsibility of their skilled employees), but tempered it with cost-cutting measures of various kinds. Two qualifications should, however, be made. First, we must except those firms in which strides had been made toward standardisation, and where piecework was normal. This meant, above all, the gas-meter making industry. Although, taking the inter-war period as a whole, this was to be one of Edinburgh's successes (linked as it was to the market for 'consumer durables')[44] during the early 1920s it suffered.[45] The employers responded by cutting piecework rates.[46] In addition, foremen had a more important role in this sector, not merely supervising and coping with grievances, but directing jobs in detail, even undertaking initial negotiations with shop stewards on adjustments to piece rates.[47] It is likely that, after 1921, their role was enhanced.[48] Second, the bulk of the Edinburgh firms were federated within the East of Scotland Association of Engineers and Ironfounders[49] (and, through it, with the Engineering Employers' Federation). They showed no signs of reluctance in executing the policy of the Federation, notably in locking-out their employees in 1922, although there were signs that they were grateful for the opportunity it gave them to evade direct responsibility for policies. And, clearly, it was the 1922 lock-out which comprehensively set the tone for industrial relations in engineering during the remainder of the 1920s.

PRINT: TECHNOLOGICAL CHANGE AND INDUSTRIAL STRUCTURE

The printing industry during and after the war was emerging

from, and coming to terms with, a profound, technological revolution. The introduction into Britain of the Linotype and Monotype composing machines (in 1889 and 1899 respectively) rapidly undermined the skills of the hand compositor:[50] 'after four centuries of hand composing, in two brief decades the change, in larger offices, was complete.'[51] The Linotype came to dominate in newspaper printing, the Monotype in bookwork, which was central to Edinburgh's printing industry. They were both faster and more accurate than hand composing: 'a monotype machine sets 7,000 letters per hour as compared with 1,000 when they were set by hand, and sets them better'.[52] Making use of punched paper tape, which could be easily stored, the monotype enabled the setting of type for reprints to be done without a compositor: a considerable advantage in book printing. Less fundamental technological breakthroughs were also made, which either offered increases in productivity in areas where craft labour had not been used in any case (self-feeding printing machines, folding machines, and so on),[53] or represented advances in specialised sectors of the industry, as offset printing revolutionised lithography.[54]

Edinburgh had long been a centre for printing.[55] Although it had its quota of small, jobbing, firms, the core of the industry lay in a number of medium and large-scale companies, contracting and selling nationally, even internationally. Some specialised - as John Bartholomew, for instance, did in maps; others preferred to retain the ability to respond to demand across a wider spectrum. Whereas most firms produced to contracts from publishers, a few (notably Bartholomew, T. & A. Constable, and Thomas Nelson & Sons) were themselves publishers, thus achieving an important degree of vertical integration. The latter could specialise, rationalise, in pursuit of economies of scale internally. Thomas Nelson is the extreme case: employing nearly 1,000 workers, their Parkside works routinely produced 30,000 volumes daily, and could double this in an emergency.[56] All were published by the firm. Much of the plant was designed by a specialist engineering staff, retained by the company; some of it was apparently unique and secret.[57] Of course, all the firms specialised to some extent, and some of these which worked largely to contract had relatively stable relationships with publishers.[58] But on the whole Edinburgh's printers 'rationalised' and installed new machinery more slowly than some of their rivals, and notably in South East England; after the turn of the century Edinburgh's competitive advantage, largely gained through the employment of women compositors, was eroded for this reason.[59] Edinburgh's importance in <u>publishing</u> was diminishing, in London's favour, of course; and this did not help the city's printing industry: at least one firm, the Ballantyne Press, moved from Edinburgh to London.[60]

Nevertheless, by 1914 the new technology was quite widespread in the city: in comparison to engineering, it was easily introduced into printing. The reasons for this are important. The division of labour, particularly between compositors and machinemen (who operated the printing machines), and between them and bookbinders, warehouse-men, and so on, was long-established. It was built into the layout of virtually every printing shop (even those for which 'design' is too strong a word).[61] The monotype and linotype did not dismember the compositor's task: rather, each could carry it out entirely.[62] Thus gains in productivity could be achieved without the wholesale re-organisation of the division of labour - new workshop layouts, incentive payment systems, tighter supervision - which was necessary in engineering.[63] In addition, the pre-war printing market was a growing one, not least because the new machinery allowed for the production of cheap books for a new mass market.[64]

PRINT: CRAFT CONTROL IN WAR AND PEACE
The war did not have the profound effect on printing that it had on much of engineering: the trade was in part a 'luxury' one, and paper supplies were uncertain. Nevertheless, with recruitment into the armed forces and transfer of labour to munitions industries proceeding apace (often with employers' encouragement),[65] from 1916 there was a labour shortage. Dilution threatened.[66] The print unions did not resist this although they attempted to regulate it: mobility between jobs within firms, and between firms, were increased, and overtime restrictions and machine-manning quotas relaxed.[67] The effective condition for this was substantial wage increases. By the end of the war the 'stab' (or piece) rate in Edinburgh had risen to 66s (31s in 1914), and the rate for mechanical composition to 68s 6d (38s 6d in 1914).[68] Perhaps because women were already common in Edinburgh's printing offices, dilution seems to have had no major disruptive effect. Few women compositors, for instance, were taken on during the war: all were paid the full

male rate, and all were rapidly replaced after the war.[69]

During the post-war boom employers were willing to concede in the confidence that demand and prices would continue to strengthen. In 1919 and 1920 four increases were obtained, taking compositors' wages to the apex of the 'wage league'. Other wages in the industry followed them.[70] Although these were, since 1917, negotiated nationally, in Edinburgh the long-standing local grievance of the so-called 'mixed system' (by which earnings consisted of both piece- and time-work elements) was abolished by eliminating piece-work.[71] At the same time the major post-war problem began to emerge: a contraction in the (staple) book trade, which created some problems in the reabsorption of demobilised union workers.[72] And union attempts to organise the Edinburgh daily press - non-union since 1872 - were rebuffed.[73]

As the economy moved into recession, so too did printing. The years from 1920 to 1923 were marked by heavy unemployment and short-time working, although conditions began to improve from 1924 onward.[74] The decline of the book sector - particularly quality books - meant that Edinburgh continued to suffer more than the national average for the industry. Where employment in Scottish printing as a whole rose by 19 per cent between 1921 and 1931, the bulk of this was in newspapers and periodicals: in Edinburgh the total workforce fell by 5 per cent, although the number employed in newspapers and periodicals actually rose by some 50 per cent.[75] Yet the industry, even in Edinburgh, was less hard-hit than many. Throughout the inter-war period unemployment in printing, publishing and bookbinding was about a half the average for all industries nationally; and this seems also to have been true of Edinburgh.[76]

By the 1920s the typographical unions in Edinburgh as elsewhere had secured control over the new composing machines; printers were the best paid of manual workers; the employers recognised their right to restrict the number of apprentices.[77] This position had been achieved in Edinburgh chiefly by the strike of 1909-10 on the question of female labour (and, more centrally perhaps, control of entry into apprenticeships), and by the lock-out of 1913, after which employers accepted the principle of mutuality: that no working rules would be instituted without the agreement of the union.[78] Compositors secured control of composing machines, and although some ancillary workers were recruited, these were brought into the union - as, for example, monotype casters were admitted into the STA in 1918.[79] The role of the unions in the post-war period was largely the policing of these agreements: there was no major attempt by the employers to alter their terms.

This strong element of craft control, now but rarely based on skill, was associated with a peculiar management of work within the printing offices. Thus Carter Goodrich:

> The compositors do not choose their own foremen, but the 'father of the chapel', their shop steward, performs enough supervisory functions for the firm so that he is in effect an elected sub-foreman; and the 'clicker' chosen by a 'companionship' or team of compositors to do their bargaining with the firm and to allot piecework might also be thought of as an elected supervisor ... [80]

In the 1936 edition of Southward's Modern Printing, a standard handbook, the duties of the clicker are enumerated, and the supervisory element is clear:

1. To receive copy from the overseer, and with it full instructions as to the style of the work to be done ...
2. To give out copy in portions to the compositors working under him, and to provide them with directions as to style.
3. To keep an account of the copy given to each man.
4. To superintend the making up of the work.
5. To book each man's work, wages, etc., in a ledger.
6. To produce a general bill, showing to the firm the exact total cost at which the work is produced.[81]

Southward points out that this system saves the employer 'much time, ... [and] also tends to securing uniformity in the style of the work'.[82] As Goodrich recognised, it amounted 'in effect to a democratic form of sub-contract'; mistakenly, however, he saw it as an historical relic, not to be found in 'modernised industry'.[83] For it clearly was a rational form of managing workers given their strength, and the impossibility in practice of achieving sufficient unity among employers to break union regulation. It was also - albeit accidentally - a method of harnessing workers to the objectives of the enterprise through delegating substantial autonomy to officially-sanctioned work groups with strongly-imbued craft standards. In this way management might hope to minimise the development of dysfunctional group institutions, which tend to arise when management attempts highly individualised control methods.[84] It was, in short, a strategy of 'responsible autonomy' which in content rested heavily on the traditional structures of work organisation in the industry.

Certainly (save in the newspaper sector) employers do not seem to have been unhappy with the unions' role in the industry. Edinburgh's employers' concern about wages seems to have concerned relativities between towns within the industry, rather than their overall high level. But

> they seemed on the whole to consider that a high
> degree of union organisation made their task easier
> in some ways than if they had to deal with
> unorganised workers: the unions, for example, were
> co-operating to secure a good type of apprentice
> and to supervise his training; and, again, employers
> who needed men could get the kind of worker they
> wanted through the union, which knew its members
> and their suitability for particular jobs to a degree
> which an employment exchange could never do.[85]

The unions, then, gained substantial control over work organisation in the industry; but with this went the clear understanding that they would operate within bounds acceptable to employers. To this extent, Goodrich is clearly correct in categorising it as 'craft', rather than 'contagious', control.[86]

THE RUBBER INDUSTRY: TECHNOLOGY AND CONTROL

Edinburgh's rubber industry was quite different from engineering and printing. Having been established only since the 1850s, it lacked their long traditions. It was far more concentrated: one firm, the North British Rubber Company - the largest in any industry in the east of Scotland - employed three-quarters of the city's rubber workers at its Castle Mills.[87] This was by far the largest single factory in the city, and had, from its inception, operated a relatively complex internal division of labour; the essential methods established at the company's inception were still in use in the 1930s.[88]

In contrast to both engineering and printing, the rubber industry was highly vertically integrated. The North British carried out the manufacturing process from processing the raw material to wholesaling an array of finished articles:

roughly equivalent to a single firm not only making a variety of papers, but also books, stationery, and so forth. Consequently, it was necessary to co-ordinate a great variety of different production processes. On the one hand, the raw rubber had to be purified, and then mixed with sulphur and pigments to form a plastic 'dough':

> The dough is then passed through various machines for running it into sheet, tubing, or cord, from which are built up the articles it is desired to manufacture. A large portion of these articles have to be subsequently moulded. The manufactured article is then subject to heat for a length of time, which causes the sulphur to combine chemically with the rubber, producing a state of vulcanisation.[89]

During these years, however, many rubber products had to be strengthened with textile fabrics:[90] this was achieved by softening the dough with a solvent, generally naphtha, and then forcing it onto the fabric through rollers.[91] Much of the machinery was 'of an elaborate, heavy, and frequently dangerous type ..., and although some of the work consists mainly in machine-minding, much of it calls for a high degree of skill'.[92]

Whilst some materials, such as floor coverings, might be complete at this stage, many required assembly and finishing in separate departments. Here a variety of other skills was called for, some involving the operation of light machinery (as sewing the cloth uppers onto plimsolls, or piercing eyelets), but probably the majority being entirely hand-work. Of course, the skills required were rarely of a high level; no apprenticeship was involved, and although some workers completed, for instance, entire garments, many of the tasks were intensely sub-divided and simplified.[93] So management required substantial control over the production process, having to co-ordinate and organise, for instance, the production of various types of boots and shoes, waterproof coats, hot water bottles, golf balls, bicycle and motor car tyres, floats for fishing nets, and a whole variety of components for the car industry.[94]

Far more than in engineering or printing, management in the rubber industry retained control of the production process. There were a number of reasons for this. The process was very much the employers' creation: it was not constructed in dialogue with a body of craft knowledge. The company ensured that its superiority of knowledge about the design of the production processes was retained. Substantial managerial and technological staffs - nearly 100 of the company's clerks joined the union in 1919 - were responsible for a number of advances in product design.[95] It went to remarkable lengths to ensure control over recruitment. The company maintained its own employment exchange: mainly, recruitment was of boys and girls aged 14. All applicants were interviewed, and those successful subject to medical examination. Those with records of union activity might be refused employment.[96] Among women, at least, preference was given to those from areas of high unemployment around Edinburgh: New Craighall, Musselburgh, Leith and Broxburn. Indeed, special buses were operated for them. Women were expected to leave on marriage, but would then form part of a reserve labour force, to be taken on as seasonal workers (much of the work was seasonal: most obviously, golf balls and hot water bottles).[97] Finally, there seems to have been a careful planning of the internal labour market. There were clear distinctions between male and female jobs, with the men employed largely in the earlier stages of the process, and the women in assembly and finishing:[98] there is some evidence that management exploited potential and actual conflict between men and women in order to weaken (or, at least, control) union organisation. 'The women did not object to being sweated and used as a lever to keep down the wages of the men'.[99] Time rates and piecework were both used; despite a widespread dislike for the latter, union efforts to remove them were unsuccessful, perhaps because they offered the chance to earn up to 25 per cent more than time rates.[100] Of course, this does not imply that managerial control was in no way challenged; nor that the 'frontier of control' remained stationary throughout our period. On the contrary.

THE CASTLE MILLS IN WAR AND PEACE
The rubber industry was at the centre of the war effort; Whitaker's Almanack for 1920 recorded:

> The war absorbed an enormous quantity of rubber in the manufacture of aeroplanes (Palmer tyres of 1500 m/m x 300 m/m were fitted to Handley-Page Bombing machines), submarines, surgical appliances, anti-gas apparatus, field telephone cables, rubber boots, waterproof coats and sheets, and tyres for motor ambulances, motor cars, motor vans and lorries of every description.[101]

As one of the largest rubber works in the country, the Castle Mills fell under the aegis of the Munitions of War Acts, which brought the apparatus of state intervention: compulsory arbitration; regulations on hours of work, work discipline, attendance standards; liability to inspection by Ministry personnel, including the welfare inspectorate.[102] Strikes were outlawed; dilution encouraged, new products demanded (and the production of others intensified or discontinued). Nevertheless, the major impact was in the pressure of work and the involvement of statutory institutions; in production methods and work organisation the essential systems had been long set.

Rubber-making had always been a dangerous business. Apart from dangerous machinery, many of the chemicals were dangerous: some were also addictive.[103] The industry probably became more dangerous during the war; certainly many complaints arose from workers at the Castle Mills. Over one month, for instance, in the winter of 1917-18, three issues of health and safety were reported to consecutive union committee meetings. There was concern about 'replacing dressing for burns in solvent'[104] (not, interestingly, about the burns or the solvent themselves). 'The case of men suffering from lead poisoning was again raised'; the strategy selected was to ask 'the NB Co to insure these men specially'.[105] Finally, the problems of solvents recurred: two deaths were reported, 'and a discussion as to the cause of death and [what was seen as] the epidemic of disease in the solvent followed'.[106]

The involvement of statutory bodies and regulations in the organisation of production was a departure from pre-war practice. It is widely held that one intention of the Munitions of War Acts was to weaken union organisation; they were used to attack strong union organisation, as on Clydeside.[107] However, where union organisation was weak or non-existent, the Acts could lend recognition and legitimation, de facto, to trade unions; or hinder the development of a sharp employers' response to the early stages of union development. (The object, after all, was to maximise production: provoking a dispute on issues such as recognition or union existence can hardly have seemed justifiable to Ministry officials.) This view is consistent with union development at the Castle Mills.[108] The management had successfully prevented the formation of active or lasting union organisation for 60 years; nor did it suddenly become an advocate of union membership. In April and May

1917 a campaign by the Edinburgh organiser of the NAUL led to the establishment of a committee and a series of mass meetings: success was achieved so rapidly that on 21 May four branch officers had to spend two-and-a-half hours entering members and receiving cash.[109] Membership did not reach 100 per cent, save perhaps in certain departments, but the cases of members refusing to work alongside non-members suggest that the latter were in a minority.[110]

The Ministry of Munitions provided a mechanism for raising issues, a substitute in this sense for agreed procedures. Where previously the distance between organising in a union and achieving anything by this was considerable (in terms of dismissals, disputes, lost time, and so on) - now suddenly, it was reduced. An achievable end was in view; the role of the Ministry could be seen as a neutral one. Within weeks of its establishment, the union took up the case of three men who had been 'forced to sign an agreement accepting a lower rate than the minimum rate'.[111] The Ministry's representative confirmed that the company's action was wrong.[112] Later in the same year a strike occurred, which seems to have led to proceedings at a Munitions Tribunal, thus 'compelling Coy to negotiate'.[113]

The existence of a union at the Castle Mills meant that after the war, and more particularly after 1920, management could no longer rule in the old way. In early 1919 the union went on the offensive, demanding a 44 hour week, and the abolition of piecework and overtime. They won a 47 hour week, in place of the previous 55 (no mean achievement)[114] and substantial advances in pay, though piecework and overtime were not abolished.[115] By mid-1920, the union branch numbered about 3,900, and cannot have been far from 100 per cent membership in the industry in Edinburgh.[116] A Whitley Council was set up, with joint works committees in the various plants, a district structure to which disputes would be referred failing internal agreement, and a national industrial council: the union saw this as a major advance.[117] But, ultimately, employers' control was not in question.

Although the detail is obscure, after 1920 union strength was eroded, until by the 1930s, it was largely dependent upon managerial support.[118] During the war the company conceded the union presence reluctantly, defended - even aggressively - its right to employ non-union labour, used the latter against the union, and in no way discouraged inter-union competition for recruits.[119] After the war, redundancies soon began, with little union resistance.[120] Management's control of the internal labour market led to the transfer of nearly 100 clerks from the NAUL to the National Union of Clerks;[121] and attempts to establish a joint union committee including craft unions proved abortive.[122] Given an apparent tension between men and women, and a number of structural disincentives to union membership among the latter (high turnover, retirement on marriage, distinct socio-geographical origins), the increasing proportion of females in the industry's labour force must have been, at least incidentally, a strategy to weaken the union.[123] The decision to maintain a Welfare Department, particularly to deal with women, may also be seen in this light.[124] Certainly, the union began to suffer some set-backs. During 1922 or 1923 time and piece rates were reduced by between 21 and 32 per cent, and an hour was added to the working week.[125] Work was speeded up, and a number of disputes occurred: by 1925 union membership had fallen to 25 per cent, and no doubt suffered more after the General Strike.[126]

In short, the scale and technology of the rubber industry, especially in the Castle Mills, made direct control both possible and desirable. During the war, however, as union organisation developed, management appears to have edged toward an element of 'responsible autonomy': but in a form very different from that found in printing. Close supervision persisted in the work process itself, but some recognition was given to trade union organisation. Probably this openness to a union role was induced by government involvement, for after the war the company made a determined, and largely successful, attempt to weaken union organisation. As time passed, however, this itself seems to have brought costs: a number of sectional strikes occurred, which were difficult to settle, and so the company took steps to strengthen union membership.[127] For, as Milnes recorded after discussion with the company,

> In the absence of a recognised union when disputes arise, the firm is compelled to carry on negotiations with a specially elected workers' committee and discussions with such a committee are frequently futile since agreements made with them are generally impossible to enforce.[128]

THE RAILWAYS: STRUCTURE AND SERVICE

Although Edinburgh was far more than a railway town, over

4 per cent of the city's workforce was employed in the service of the North British and Caledonian Railway companies.[129] The railway companies were massive. The two which ran into Edinburgh were, by a very substantial margin, the largest industrial companies in Scotland.[130] They were vast employers of labour, not merely in operating trains - which had to be as nearly around-the-clock as possible - but in loading and unloading freight, building and repairing rolling-stock, and maintaining track, stations, and other fixed capital. In Edinburgh alone, in 1921, they employed over 8,000 men and women:[131] as drivers, firemen, guards, porters, clearly; but also as clerks, signalmen, permanent way men (maintaining track), and in the railway workshops in the entire spectrum of the engineering trades.

Some of these tasks were relatively capital-intensive: for instance, each engine crew operated in a machine of great complexity, as did signalmen. Their movements were prescribed in detail by timetables, although, of course, keeping safely to these timetables was a matter of great skill and responsibility. On the other hand, track maintenance was highly labour-intensive, requiring gangs of men to work, often with little more than hand-tools, and often many miles from their home towns. Railway engineering workshops had many of the characteristics of heavy engineering. Each company had developed a large central administrative organisation, which planned the operational aspects of railway work: timetabling in particular, but of repairs, maintenance, as well as of trains themselves. And each was marked by an internal division of labour of bewildering complexity.

A military model was fundamental to the organisation of work in the railway industry before and after the Great War. It was one of the few known methods of large-scale organisation when the railways were established.[132] In addition, the railways had to co-ordinate a network of employees (often, initially, from rural backgrounds) in widely varying jobs over vast areas. Basic work-disciplines had to be instilled, basic standards set: a process very similar to mobilising an army. It was necessary to instil not merely a sense of organisational goals, but also a common appreciation of their paramount importance. Not just the structural, but the moral, elements of the military model were taken over: company uniform and livery; the language of going on 'duty', 'absence without leave', being put on a 'charge', 'loss of rank'; unquestioning obedience to 'officers' and 'superior officers'.[133] During the nineteenth century these attitudes of 'the Service' were very largely internalised by railway servants and, in time, those joining knew what to expect. And if hours were long and pay was low, loyalty was rewarded by a security of employment almost unmatched in nineteenth century industry.[134]

Nevertheless, in time railway servants rebelled against 'all the petty tyranny'.[135] In doing so, however, they were hindered by another aspect of the military model: for in the railway service the division of labour became a fetish. There were (literally) hundreds of distinct job classifications and grades, and, in the army mode, workers were commonly addressed and referred to by job title as well as name. This was reinforced in everyday social interaction: drivers and firemen, for instance, working together in the same cab, would very likely drink in different bars and stay at different hostels.[136] The sense of 'the Service', the intensity and social meaning of the division of labour, the strictness of company discipline, made the development of united union organisation between grades difficult. Also, the companies were inclined to perceive union organisation (and, even more, strikes) as incipiently mutinous. It was, therefore, not until the decisive national strike of 1911 that the unions even achieved recognition from management;[137] and only in the wake of this was the National Union of Railwaymen formed, by amalgamation of several smaller unions.[138]

THE SERVICE IN WAR AND PEACE

When war broke out, the railway companies were placed under state control. A Railway Executive Committee was appointed, consisting of leading railway general managers, to operate the railways in the interest of the war effort. Railway company revenues were guaranteed at (record) 1913 levels. (There was no mention of workers' wages or living standards.)[139] At the same time, many railway workers left to join the forces; new sources of labour were found, particularly among women, but the main solution was to lengthen working hours and increase the railwaymen's workloads.[140] For the railways bore the brunt of internal transport demands - particularly great in Scotland with the Grand Fleet based at Scapa Flow, and using other anchorages at Invergordon, in the Forth, and on the west coast. So the war had a positive effect on the bargaining strength of the NUR. As the Edinburgh No. 1 branch recalled, 'with the international war, the wage war did not stop. The cost of living rose tremendously, and demands had to be made for increased wages.'[141] These were conceded in part (though only in the form of flat rate 'war bonuses'); but the important change from 1915 was that they were agreed nationally: company negotiations on wages were never revived.[142]

The 'truce' which the railway union leaders and managers agreed in October 1914 lasted through the war. The centralisation of negotiations was, of course, related to this, for the Railway Executive could be more confident of agreement with national leaders, such as J.H. Thomas, who were strongly associated with the national war effort. But this 'truce' did not end industrial conflict. The NUR's experience before 1914 had generated within it a militant element which drew inspiration and theory from syndicalists and socialists.[143] In Edinburgh during 1911 and 1912 the No. 1 branch became increasingly militant, and critical of its national leadership.[144] Whilst some aspects of the wartime experience weakened this movement (not least the blandishments of patriotism), the rising cost of living, especially when compared with the comfortable situation of shareholders, lent strength to demands for higher wages. Tensions (reflected in the increasing influence of district councils and vigilance committees) developed between the union's leading officials and many of its active members.[145]

Given their highly mechanistic organisation, dilution brought problems on the railways. The grade and classification structure was the foundation of an intricate system of status differences, and in peacetime an individual's progression through them was slow. During the war it accelerated: thus the social meanings attached to the various jobs, or work-roles, were severely dislocated. Very often the short-term response was a vigorous defence of existing standards. In Edinburgh in May 1918 the North British proposed to introduce women passenger guards. A special meeting of passenger guards appointed a deputation to 'state the[ir] objection' to the district superintendent: the union branch, covering all grades, shared the guards' view, rejecting an addendum to the effect

> That this meeting impresses upon the deputation of passenger guards the advisability of placing no obstacle in the way of women becoming passenger guards but will press for the best conditions being obtained for those who may be introduced.[146]

In the long run, however, the meaning-system was inevitably undermined. This did not imply the imminent collapse of the industry's division of labour (although there were several steps just after the war to simplify and standardise the classification and grading systems).[147] It did, however, still further weaken the effectiveness of 'railway values' in sustaining work disciplines; this was to create further problems for railway management after the war.

Three factors are crucial to understanding the post-war development of the railways: the enormous achievements of the unions in 1919 (and to a lesser extent, 1920); the deteriorating market environment; and the changing relationship between the industry and the state. Of 1919 much has been written. The eight-hour day was implemented in February, a landmark in the history of the industry (and particularly in the history of the ASLE&F).[148] The national rail strike in September was marked by great unity in action between trade unions ('The Associated [SLE&F], though having got a settlement, struck with us to a man');[149] by great membership support - although Edinburgh's claim 'All men and women out' should be qualified by the NUR No. 1 branch's interest in 'the question of Blacklegs';[150] by the use of the press on both sides;[151] by the government's capitulation. It was, above all, a massive achievement of organisation and morale: at the No. 1 branch's meeting on 9 November, a song written as a 'souvenir of the Railway Strike' by a branch member was sung; printed, it sold well.[152] Although doubts were subsequently voiced at the detailed national agreement,[153] 1919 seemed to have shifted the balance of power in the industry away from the employers.

Under the shadow of this defeat, the employers had to contend with a deteriorating market situation. After the war, especially after the onset of depression, the shipping surplus brought down coasting rates: Leith's coastal trade remained relatively stable after the war, and rose after 1923.[154] Except where speed was essential, or the destination inland, shipping was highly competitive.[155] In the 1919 rail strike, the lorry proved itself a dangerous competitor, especially over short distances.[156] At the same time, the recession reduced the total quantity of goods requiring transport, particularly on certain Scottish routes which had been heavily used in wartime.

Government control lasted longer on the railways than in other industries. Not until August 1921 was state control surrendered, although as this date approached the Railway Executive's members began to act in the interest of their companies, rather than of the state as such.[157] During the first two post-war years the government not only conceded on railway working conditions; it also prevaricated and vacillated on the question of control, first suggesting nationalisation but - having defused the issue until union strength had waned - finally returning the railways to the companies under the ineffectual aegis of a Ministry of Transport.[158] The Railways Act 1921 did intervene to 'regroup' the railways into seven large companies (with effect from 1924), but these were to be run commercially, for profit, rather than as a service.[159] The railway companies thus in 1921 regained authority over an industry which, for the previous seven years, had been operated with other (military and political) objectives to the fore. They attempted to increase their rate of return on labour and capital in two main ways during the early 1920s: by increasing the volume of traffic, and by reducing their expenditure on labour and capital. Advertising campaigns, cheap day return and weekly season tickets, and similar promotional devices were inevitably inadequate in the competitive environment after 1921.[160] So the companies' major efforts went into the direct cutting of costs. In the Edinburgh area, a number of small stations and branch lines were closed in the early 1920s;[161] the workshop at St Margarets was run down;[162] employment was reduced and greater efficiency demanded.[163]

Such moves required a reassertion of managerial control. But the effectiveness of pre-war work structures had been further weakened by the disputes over 'standardisation' which arose in the wake of the terms of settlement of the 1919 strike. The system of grades and classifications was simplified; but all kinds of inconsistencies arose, and dissatisfaction was rife. Speaker after speaker at the NUR branch meeting in March 1920 gave examples of the injustice of the new system. One will suffice: before the agreement, the grade 'Examiners' had been divided into four classes, 'Special', 'first', 'second', and 'third':

> now they were only one class, and all paid alike -
> 66/- falling to 56/-. Under him as examiner in
> Waverley [the speaker reported] he had tradesmen
> working - there were joiners, plumbers, who were
> simply refusing to accept the grading ... A man
> with two months service now, was as good as he

who had twenty years.[164]
This elision of grades stirred emotions which the grade system had so effectively fostered; but it also demonstrated that the structure was not immutable. What remained, therefore, was an hierarchic structure based upon a system of rules backed up by disciplinary sanctions; but less effective in mobilising opinion, in sustaining a common moral culture within the workforce.

Other aspects of the old notion of railway service were weakened by the financial policies of the railway companies after 1920. Cost-cutting policies brought an end to the 'job for life'.[165] Dismissals began in 1920: some were only temporary, but this only serves to emphasise the employer's new approach to labour.[166] At the same time, employment cuts were seen by the workers as an attack on the standard of the service. Threats to permanent way staff numbers, for instance, 'constitute[d] a grave menace to the travelling public';[167] whilst tightening up of working practices was held to have led to defective rolling stock, and thus accidents.[168]

The approach adopted by the railway companies in reasserting their control can be seen as a shift in the direction of a 'responsible autonomy' strategy: though a very qualified shift. Discipline tightened after 1919. Signalmen were suffering 'severe punishments for the technical offences';[169] a yard foreman exhibited 'Prussianism in its worst and [sic] malignant form'.[170] At the same time, piecework was introduced in certain jobs, particularly in the workshops.[171] The essence of the employers' strategy was to tighten control, intensify labour, in the everyday working of the railways; but to involve unions in the newly-instituted joint procedures and committees, thus reducing their ability to mobilise effectively. This had an effect both nationally and locally. The national leaders of the NUR regarded the recognition accorded to the unions by the 1921 Act as their major achievement, even opposing a 1924 ASLE&F strike because it was in breach of procedure, and instructing NUR members to work normally.[172] Locally, the attitude was similar:

> the National Wages Board and the Wages Board, with the Railway Boards, Sectional Councils, and Local Departmental Committtes, [are] all [bodies] ... which when our railwaymen are wise enough to organise sufficiently may provide them with the machinery that would give them complete control

of their industry.[173]

Union branches became involved in these bodies; representatives argued their members' cases, both individual and collective; some gained enviable reputations as advocates.[174]

In short, the railway employers' approach during the early 1920s attempted to integrate union organisation in a common conception, not so much of the aims of the railways, as of the values of recognition and procedure.[175] The companies were fortunate (in this respect) that unemployment lessened many of their problems of motivation, for while this integration of the unions could reduce the effectiveness of workers' resistance, it could not motivate as effectively as the old notions of the railway service. The employers were successful to the extent that the unions perceived the joint institutions gained in 1921 as their fundamental achievements, the basis of their ability to represent their members effectively. The railway unions had turned, perhaps perforce, from defending their members to defending the joint machinery they had won.

Edinburgh's employers, then, adopted a variety of strategies in attempting to achieve the control over labour necessary to enable them to attain their objectives. These strategies varied according to a number of factors; the structure of the firm and the industry, their market environment, the strength of labour. But some general trends are discernible. First, 'scientific management' in a strong sense was rare. During the years of greatest labour strength, change was too frequent to encourage investment in the control systems necessary to make such techniques effective; moreover, they required the goodwill and abilities of various groups of workers. With the depression, employers did 'tighten-up' in a number of ways, but this did not amount to 'scientific management' and it was often allied with attempts to win workers' commitment to enterprise objectives (either directly or through enlisting unions' interest in common aims, such as stability). Second, depression did not encourage attempts to achieve economies of scale: on the contrary, 'tightening-up' was an attempt to achieve greater efficiencies with existing plant. Third, although employers' control was never fundamentally in doubt, it was occasionally under severe pressure until about 1920. Thereafter, the balance of industrial power shifted decisively against the unions: nevertheless, there are grounds for supposing that, in the late 1920s, their position in Edinburgh remained stronger than it had been before the war.

Union development thus occurred on shifting and differing terrains. Although influenced by factors such as industrial structure and management strategy, other factors were also necessary to produce the major shifts in union strength which marked our period. It is to those factors which grounded the general union advance of 1917-20, and then the general retreat, that we now turn.

NOTES

1. A Gramsci, Selections from the Prison Notebooks (London, 1971), p.303.
2. R. Gray, The Labour Aristocracy in Victorian Edinburgh (Oxford, 1976), pp.38-9.
3. C. Oakley, Scottish Industry Today (Edinburgh, 1937), p.144; D. Keir (ed.), The Third Statistical Account of Scotland. The City of Edinburgh (Glasgow, 1966), p.616.
4. Keir, City of Edinburgh, p.616.
5. Ibid.; Oakley, Scottish Industry, pp.144-5.
6. W. Oliver, 'The Engineering Industries of Edinburgh', in Scottish Chamber of Commerce, Trade and Commerce between Scotland and the Empire (Glasgow, 1934), p.47.
7. Keir, City of Edinburgh, p.616.
8. G.T. Bloomfield, 'New Integrated Motor Works in Scotland 1899-1914', Industrial Archaeology Review, vol. 5 (1981), p.127.
9. Ibid., p.130.
10. Ibid., pp.126-8.
11. George Gray (ASE) in ESAE&I and ASE, 'Local Conference Proceedings: in re Engineers' Working Rules', 19 September 1919, p.29; see also ibid., p.6.
12. W. Wallace (Chairman, ESAE&I) in ESAE&I and AEU, 'Local Conference Proceedings: in re Outworking Allowances', 22 January 1923, p.11.
13. 'Workers normally employed in the shops who are sent outworking, normally to customers' works, to instal, maintain or repair plant manufactured by their employer': A. Marsh, Industrial Relations in Engineering (Oxford, 1965), p.177.
14. J. Hinton, The First Shop Stewards Movement (London, 1973), pp.93-6. Craft control should not be seen as any strong form of workers' control: cp J. Monds, 'Workers' Control and the Historians: a New Economism', New Left

Review, no. 97 (1976), pp.81-100, and Hinton's 'Rejoinder', ibid., pp.100-4.

15.   H.N. Blyth, 'An Apprentice Fitter, 1915', Industrial Archaeology Review, vol. 16 (1982), pp.223-32. Blyth (p.227) recounts one particularly revealing example of the treatment of his foreman. An Admiralty inspector visited to test a new engine. He passed it. 'The Managing Director was on the inspector's right and our foreman on his left. The inspector shook hands with the boss and our foreman hastily wiped a hand on the slack of his trousers in case it should be shaken too.' It was not: for foreman and workers alike, just 'a nod of approval'.

16.   ESAE&I and AEU, 'Conference Proceedings: Proposed Reduction of $12\frac{1}{2}$ per cent on Piecework Prices of Brass Finishers and Brass Moulders, in Gas Meter Making Works', 20 July 1922.

17.   Blyth, 'Apprentice Fitter', passim.

18.   Of course, this drew on deeper roots also, especially the notion of 'national efficiency' which had been central to Liberal Imperialism: see H.C.G. Matthew, The Liberal Imperialists (Oxford, 1973).

19.   A. Clutton Brock, Our Common Purpose, The Economics of Peace (London, n.d. [1919]), p.4. This pamphlet was issued by the National War Savings Committee, a statutory body set up to oversee and encourage saving following the first issue of National Savings Certificates in 1916. By 1920 it had dropped 'War' from its title.

20.   Labour Standard, 6 March 1926.

21.   On this, see Labour Standard, 17 October 1925, 2 January 1926 NUR Edin. No. 1 branch minutes, 10, 24 August, 7, 21 September 1924. The workshop was 'run down' over a period of years, and there are thus various figures on the numbers affected: from 469 (NUR Edin. No. 1 branch minutes, 7 September 1924) to 100 (Labour Standard, 17 October 1925). The closure was immediately a consequence of the reorganisation and rationalisation of the railway companies by the Railways Act 1921. But it was associated with the depression and especially the collapse of overseas markets: the North British Locomotive Company of Glasgow, the major Scottish engine-builder, had built 400 locomotives annually on average 1904-14, mainly for export; its 1921-31 average was 150. C. Harvie, No Gods and Precious Few Heroes, Scotland 1914-1980 (London, 1981), p.40.

22.   Cp ESAE&I, ASE and SBU, 'Conference Proceedings:

Brassmoulders' Rates - Levelling up to Ironmoulders', 4 April 1921, pp. 4, 6, 8, 12; ESAE&I and AEU, 'Conference Proceedings: in re Outworking Allowances', 22 January 1922, esp. pp.21, 23; E&AE(EofS)A and AEU, 'Conference Proceedings: in re Allowances for Repair Work on Diesel, Semi-Diesel and Oil Internal Combustion Engines', 23 October 1925, esp. pp.2, 4, 9, 31; E&AE(EofS)A and AEU, 'Conference Proceedings: in re Local Application for 20/-per week increase in wages', 22 April 1926, esp. pp.3, 7-8, 12-14, 16, 19-21, 23, 31-2.

23.   Blyth, 'Apprentice Fitter', p.225.

24.   ESAE&I and ASE, 'Conference Proceedings: Recognition of Shop Stewards as Officials of the Union', 18 January 1918, p.9. The vehemence with which the speaker (Wilson Coates, ASE) made this point may have been influenced by his several years as full-time national Organising Secretary of the National Union of Paper Mill Workers. On at least one occasion it appears he was upset by his members; his approach to trade unionism seems to have involved strong ties with employers, rather than organising workers directly. He was clearly upset also in 1916, when his union forced him to resign in unclear (but evidently unpleasant) circumstances. See C. Bundock, The Story of the National Union of Printing, Bookbinding and Paper Workers (Oxford, 1958), pp.186-7, 374. On the situation in Coventry, see Hinton, First Shop Stewards Movement, pp.223-5.

25.   ESAE&I and ASE, 'Conference Proceedings: Recognition of Shop Stewards', 18 January 1918, p.3.

26.   Ibid., p.4. The context of this conference needs some explanation. In December 1917, 13 unions reached agreement with the EEF on 'Regulations regarding the Appointment and Functions of Shop Stewards'. These did not include the ASE, which appears (from this local negotiation) to have felt that the national agreement gave overmuch autonomy to shop stewards. The Edinburgh District Committee was therefore attempting to negotiate a local agreement which would cover this point, but the employers were unwilling to depart from the national guidelines. Clearly there was little chance of the ASE's mobilising around an attempt to reduce shop stewards' autonomy, and the meeting broke up without agreement. (The national agreement is reprinted by Marsh, Engineering, pp.262-4.)

27.   G.D.H. Cole, Workshop Organisation (Oxford 1923), esp. pp.48-65; C.L. Goodrich, The Frontier of Control (New York, 1921) esp. pp.163-175; Hinton, First Shop Stewards

Movement, esp. pp.86-92; G. Brown, Sabotage (Nottingham, 1977), esp. pp.175-83.
28.   ESAE&I and ASE, 'Conference Proceedings: Recognition of Shop Stewards', 18 January 1918, pp.2-4.
29.   Ibid., p.4.
30.   Shop stewards had first officially been appointed by the ASE in 1892; the ASE's defeat in 1897-8 (following which its executive adopted a strategy of co-operation with the employers within the 1898 Terms of Settlement) left resistance de facto to stewards. See Hinton, First Shop Stewards Movement, pp.80-2; J. Zeitlin, 'Craft Control and the Division of Labour: Engineers and Compositors in Britain 1890-1930', Cambridge Journal of Economics, vol. 3 (1979), esp. 270-2.
31.   E.g., in the case quoted it was a recruiting officer's arrival at the factory which brought the shop steward to management's attention.
32.   On management theory, see, e.g., J.F. Whiteford, Factory Management Wastes (London, 1919). On public opinion, anti-waste, and the restriction of output, see Goodrich, Frontier of Control, pp.176-85; M. Cowling, The Impact of Labour 1920-1924 (Cambridge, 1971), esp. pp.45-59.
33.   Goodrich, Frontier of Control, passim.
34.   E. Lancaster, 'Shop Stewards in Scotland: the Amalgamated Engineering Union between the Wars', Scottish Labour History Society Journal, no. 21 (1986), pp.31-2.
35.   Harvie, No Gods, pp. 39-40; T. Dickson et al., Scottish Capitalism (London, 1980), p.247; W. Hannington, Unemployed Struggles 1919-1936 (London, 1936), pp.1-11.
36.   Labour Standard, 9 May 1925: 'Engineering Employers' Insult to Engineers'.
37.   See P. Collins, 'Work for Electricians in Edinburgh', Labour Standard, 1 August 1925.
38.   E&AEA(EofS) and AEU, 'Adjourned Local Conference Proceedings in re Local Application for 20/- per week Increase in Wages', 22 April 1926, p.6.
39.   Anon., 'How Capitalism has Ruined the Engineers', Labour Standard, 25 April 1925.
40.   'Engineer', 'The New Heriot-Watt Trust and Apprentices' in Labour Standard, 8 January 1927. The same point is made in Labour Standard, 25 April 1925. Cp the argument in ESAE&I and AEU, 'Local Conference Proceedings: Young Journeymen's Rates (Edinburgh District)', 4 April 1921, when employers 'wished to pay

young journeymen according to their ability', whilst the AEU pressed for regularisation.

41.   Cp Blyth, 'Apprentice Fitter', <u>passim</u>.
42.   <u>Labour Standard</u>, 8 January 1927.
43.   <u>Labour Standard</u>, 25 April 1925. A letter from 'Engineer' in response to this article alleged that 'One firm had the audacity to apply for more apprentices at the Labour Exchange to start their time when over twenty of their apprentices were drawing Unemployment Benefit': <u>Labour Standard</u>, 2 May 1925.
44.   Oakley, <u>Scottish Industry Today</u>, pp.145-6.
45.   Cp, e.g., ESE&IA and AEU, 'Conference Proceedings: Proposed Reduction of $12\frac{1}{2}$ per cent on Piecework Prices of Brass Finishers and Brass Moulders in Gas Meter Making Works', 20 July 1922, esp. p.9.
46.   Ibid., <u>passim</u>.
47.   ESAE&I and Brassfinishers' Society, 'Conference Proceedings; Brassfinishers' Piecework Prices - Application for Advance of 20 per cent', 29 October 1920, esp. pp.5-6, 8, 9, 18-19, 23.
48.   Cp <u>Labour Standard</u>, 9 May 1925.
49.   From 1925, the Engineering and Allied Employers' Association (East of Scotland).
50.   J. Child, <u>Industrial Relations in the British Printing Industry</u> (London, 1967), pp.155-8.
51.   Ibid., p.165.
52.   J. Gibson, 'Printing' in N. Milnes, <u>A Study of Industrial Edinburgh and the Surrounding Area 1923-1934</u>, vol. 1 (London, 1936), pp.204-5. A contemporary text-book (J. Southward, <u>Modern Printing. A Handbook</u>, vol. 1 (London, 1924), pp.160, 399) estimated that where an 'expert in fast [hand] type-setting' might reach 4,000 letters per hour, and the norm was nearer 1,000, a monotype operator could vary between 5,000 and 15,000.
53.   Gibson, 'Printing', pp.205-6.
54.   Child, <u>Printing Industry</u>, pp.158-9.
55.   On the development of printing in Edinburgh, see Gibson, 'Printing', pp.178-84; Keir, <u>City of Edinburgh</u>, pp.686-9.
56.   Child, <u>Printing Industry</u>, p.160.
57.   Oakley, <u>Scottish Industry Today</u>, p.138.
58.   J.S. Waterston, 'The Printing and Allied Trades of Edinburgh' in Scottish Chamber of Commerce, <u>Trade and Industry</u>, p.52.
59.   Child, <u>Printing Industry</u>, p.160; Gibson, 'Printing',

p.201.
60. In 1915: Gibson, 'Printing', p.183.
61. Southward, Modern Printing, vol. 1, pp.1-42.
62. Previous typesetting machines had been unable to cope with important elements of the job, e.g. 'distribution'. See Child, Printing Industry, pp.155-7.
63. Zeitlin, 'Craft Control', p.268.
64. Child, Printing Industry, p.159.
65. Ibid., p.220.
66. Ibid., pp. 220-6; S.C. Gillespie, A Hundred Years of Progress. The Record of the Scottish Typographical Association 1853 to 1952 (Glasgow, 1953), pp.141-2.
67. Child, Printing Industry, pp.221-2; Gillespie, Scottish Typographical Association, p.157.
68. Gillespie, Scottish Typographical Association, p.157; see also Chapter 3 above.
69. Gillespie, Scottish Typographical Association, pp.206-7. Women had first been introduced into skilled parts of the industry to break the 1872-3 Edinburgh printers' strike. At the 1911 census, 1,796 out of 5,259 'printers' were women. In 1910, however, apparently with the women's support, the STA negotiated (after a strike) an agreement with the employers that no women were to be apprenticed as compositors after 1916. This agreement seems to have held: dilution represented only a temporary reversal. See Gillespie, Scottish Typographical Association, pp.105, 203-7; Zeitlin, 'Craft Control', p.270.
70. Child, Printing Industry, pp.223-4; Gillespie, Scottish Typographical Association, p.158; Chapter 3 above.
71. Gillespie, Scottish Typographical Association, pp.72-6, 153, 163; this apparently simple achievement had eluded the union for 50 years.
72. Gillespie, Scottish Typographical Association, p.142.
73. One tactic successfully employed by the Scotman's management was to introduce a superannuation scheme for non-unionists only; it had the desired effect: TC EC minutes, 4 February 1919. Cp Gillespie, Scottish Typographical Association, p.222.
74. Gillespie, Scottish Typographical Association, p.142.
75. Gibson, 'Printing', pp.184-5; Census 1921; Gillespie Scottish Typographical Association, p.143. 'Printing' here includes publishing and bookbinding. Oakley, Scottish Industry Today, p.137 misquotes the 19 per cent figure, applying it to Edinburgh: he thus concludes that the situation in the city was 'satisfactory', despite other indications

to the contrary.
76. Child, Printing Industry, pp.234-5; Gibson, 'Printing', p.188.
77. Zeitlin, 'Craft Control', p.264.
78. Gillespie, Scottish Typographical Association, pp.217-8.
79. Ibid., p.202.
80. Goodrich, Frontier of Control, pp.118-9.
81. Southward, Modern Printing, vol. 2 (London, 1936), p.302.
82. Ibid.
83. Goodrich, Frontier of Control, p.120. The origins of companionships and clickers are discussed by Child, Printing Industry, pp.42-3.
84. Cp the classic work of D. Roy, 'Efficiency and "the Fix": Informal Intergroup Relations in a Piecework Machine Shop' in T. Burns (ed.), Industrial Man (Harmondsworth, 1969), pp.359-79; 'Quota Restriction and Goldbricking in a Machine Shop', American Journal of Sociology, vol. 57 (1952), pp.427-42.
85. Gibson, 'Printing', p.197.
86. Goodrich, Frontier of Control, pp.260-65.
87. Originally built as a silk-mill. For the story of the company's establishments, see Oakley, Scottish Industry Today, p.135; Milnes, Industrial Edinburgh, pp.242-4; Keir, City of Edinburgh, pp.637-8; G.A. Findlay, 'Rubber Manufacture in Edinburgh' in Scottish Chamber of Commerce, Trade and Commerce, p.60.
88. Oakley, Scottish Industry Today, p.135.
89. 'British Empire Industries: Rubber' in Whitaker's Almanack 1920, p.840.
90. E.g., the moulded hot-water bottle was only beginning to be introduced in the 1920s; the fabric bottle was still held to give 'a much longer life': Findlay, 'Rubber Manufacture', p.60.
91. Whitaker's Almanack 1920, p.840.
92. Milnes, Industrial Edinburgh, p.249.
93. Ibid., p.250; Findlay, 'Rubber Manufacture', p.60.
94. Milnes, Industrial Edinburgh, pp.249-50; Oakley, Scottish Industry Today, pp.136-7.
95. NUC Edin. branch minutes, 21 April, 5 May 1919; Oakley, Scottish Industry Today, pp.136-7.
96. Cp NAUL No. 292 branch minutes, 29 January, 5 February 1918, 25 March 1920.
97. Ibid., 29 January, 5 February 1918, 25 February, 17

June 1920; Milnes, Industrial Edinburgh, pp.250-2.
98.   Milnes, Industrial Edinburgh, pp.249-50.
99.   'North British Rubber Company Thrives on Sweated Workers', Labour Standard, 13 June 1925. The article also had some harsh comments on the male workers' allegedly docile attitudes. Cp Milnes, Industrial Edinburgh, pp.252-3.
100. T&LC ARs, esp. 1923 and 1924. A Rubber Workers branch quarterly meeting, at which pieceworkers formed the majority present, carried unanimously a demand for a 44-hour week, the abolition of piecework and overtime. They achieved only a 47-hour week. NAUL No. 292 branch minutes, 12 January, 23 February 1919.
101. Whitaker's Almanack 1920, p.840.
102. See N. Whiteside, 'Industrial Welfare and Labour Regulation in Britain at the Time of the First World War', International Review of Social History, vol. 25 (1980), pp.307-31; G.R. Rubin, 'The Origins of Industrial Tribunals', Industrial Law Journal, vol. 6 (1977), pp.149-64.
103. These dangers, including paralysis, hysteria and consumption (the incidence of which was specifically noted among Edinburgh's rubber workers), were well-established: see e.g., T. Oliver, 'Indiarubber: Dangers Incidental to the Use of Bisulphide of Carbon and Naphtha' in T. Oliver (ed.), Danger Trades (London, 1902), pp.470-4.
104. NAUL No. 292 branch minutes, 13 December 1917.
105. Ibid., 27 December 1917: emphasis added.
106. Ibid., 10 January 1918.
107. Cp Rubin, 'Industrial Tribunals', pp.152-3; A. Marwick, The Deluge (Harmondsworth, 1967), pp. 58-65; J. Hinton, 'The Clyde Workers Committee and the Dilution Struggle' in A. Briggs and J. Saville (eds.), Essays in Labour History 1886-1923, (London, 1971), esp. p.161.
108. For a modern discussion of the importance of recognition to union organisation, see E. Batstone, I. Boraston and S. Frenkel, Shop Stewards in Action (Oxford, 1977), esp. pp.154-77.
109. The formation of the NAUL No. 292 branch is described in its minutes for April and May 1917. The first membership figure relates to 14 August 1917, when 2,118 votes were cast in a ballot for Secretary (although by then members were also included from two small rubber works).
110. NAUL No. 292 branch minutes, 3, 5, 19 February, 8 August 1918, 16 January 1919.
111. Ibid., 28 June 1917.
112. But he added 'that the amount at issue being so small,

the matter was not worth proceeding with': ibid., 2 August 1917.

113. Ibid., 23 August 1917; see also 14 August 1917.

114. Ibid., 12 January, 23 February 1919.

115. See Chapter 3 above; TC AR 1920, p.42. By May 1919, pieceworkers were complaining at how their earnings had been cut with the shorter working week: NAUL No. 292 branch minutes, 8 May 1919.

116. This estimate is derived from the assertion (NAUL No. 292 branch minutes, 15 July 1920) that affiliation to the Trades Council on full membership 'would mean an affiliation fee of approximately £65'; affiliation fees were 4d. per member p.a. (TC AR 1920, p.55); the 1921 Census records 3,903 'workers in Rubber, Vulcanite, Ebonite', excluding employers, managers, foremen and overlookers.

117. NAUL No. 292 branch minutes, 8 August 1918, 10 January 1919.

118. Milnes, Industrial Edinburgh, pp.252-3.

119. See, e.g., NAUL No. 292 branch minutes, 3, 5 February 1918, 12 June, 17 August 1918, 21 August 1919.

120. Ibid., 3 July 1919.

121. Ibid., 21 August, 4 September 1919; NUC Edin. branch minutes, 6 January, 17 March, 21 April, 5 May 1919.

122. NAUL No. 292 branch minutes, 27 November 1919.

123. Cp ibid., 15 May 1917; Milnes, Industrial Edinburgh, pp.252-3. According to Milnes (p.244), the numbers effectively employed in Edinburgh's rubber industry were: 1923: 4,233 (50.2 per cent women); 1924: 4,584 (49.3); 1925: 4,682 (50.6); 1926: 4,827 (50.7); 1927: 4,356 (50); 1928: 4,480 (52.9).

124. Milnes, Industrial Edinburgh, p.251.

125. T&LC ARs 1922, 1923.

126. Labour Standard, 13 June 1925; F. Douglas, Zero Hour for the Forth (Edin., n.d. [1940]), p.12.

127. Milnes, Industrial Edinburgh, p.252; cp T&LC AR 1930, p.9; 1934, p.8.

128. Milnes, Industrial Edinburgh, p.252.

129. Census 1921. As a result of the Railways Act 1921, these became part of the London North Eastern and London, Midland and Scottish railways (LNER AND LMS) respectively.

130. J. Scott and M. Hughes, The Anatomy of Scottish Capital (London, 1980), pp.67-8, 109; the figures relate to 1920-1.

131. Census 1921.

132. Cp T. Burns and G.M. Stalker, The Management of Innovation (London, 1961), pp.104-5.
133. F. McKenna, 'Victorian Railway Workers', History Workshop Journal, no. 1 (1976), pp.27-8.
134. Ibid., pp.26-37.
135. The phrase is J.H. Thomas's, quoted in P.S. Bagwell, The Railwaymen. The History of the National Union of Railwaymen, vol. 1 (London, 1963), p.299.
136. Ibid., p.417; McKenna, 'Victorian Railway Workers', pp.42-8.
137. On the 1911 strike, see McKenna, 'Victorian Railway Workers', pp.54-65; Bagwell, The Railwaymen, pp.289-308; N. McKillop, The Lighted Flame. A History of the Associated Society of Locomotive Engineers and Firemen (London, 1950), pp.88-98.
138. Bagwell, The Railwaymen, pp.325-43.
139. Ibid., pp.346-7.
140. Ibid., p.345.
141. NUR Edin. No. 1 branch, Jubilee Souvenir 1876-1926 (Edin., 1926), p.26.
142. Ibid.; Bagwell, The Railwaymen, pp.348-9.
143. R. Holton, British Syndicalism 1900-1914 (London, 1970), esp. pp.97-9, 164-7.
144. Ibid., pp.108-9. Cp NUR Edin. No. 1 branch, Souvenir, p.23: 'About this time the socialist activity of certain members is worthy of notice as giving point to the discussion and interest to the meetings which had a good effect on the members'. In December 1913 James Larkin addressed 7,000 enthusiastic supporters in Edinburgh (Holton, British Syndicalism, p.196).
145. Bagwell, The Railwaymen, esp. pp.352-5.
146. NUR Edin. No. 1 branch minutes, 26 May 1918: the addendum was rejected by 11 votes to 2. G.D.H. Cole and R. Page Arnot, Trade Unionism on the Railways. Its History and Problems (London, 1917), pp.62-4, present a more optimistic view of dilution.
147. Bagwell, The Railwaymen, pp.417-18; McKillop, The Lighted Flame, pp.136-8: the immediate cause of these was the need to harmonise various companies' grading structures on grouping.
148. McKillop, The Lighted Flame, esp. pp.119-20.
149. NUR Edin. No. 1 branch, Souvenir, p.28.
150. The claim was made in a telegram to Unity House, London (Bagwell, The Railwaymen, p.387). On blacklegs, see NUR Edin. No. 1 branch minutes, 12, 26 October, 9

November 1919: the branch summoned them to a special meeting, and wished to see them expelled.
151. Bagwell, The Railwaymen, pp.392-5.
152. NUR Edin. No. 1 branch minutes, 9 November, 7 December 1919.
153. The NUR No. 1 branch (minutes, 18 January 1920; cp 28 March 1920) expressed 'its dissatisfaction with the Agreement and its inadequacy to meet our demands, while being forced to accept it'.
154. Milnes, Industrial Edinburgh, pp.148, 155.
155. There were, of course, extra hazards in coastal transport. Keyne's Economic Consequences of the Peace, printed in 1919 by R. & R. Clark of Edinburgh for Macmillan, first came to the public attention on the shores of Jutland, when a ship carrying 2,000 copies was wrecked. See R. Harrod, The Life of John Maynard Keynes (Harmondsworth, 1972), p.339.
156. Bagwell, The Railwaymen, p.390. But even in the mid-1920s the General Secretary of the carters' union 'was not convinced that the motor vehicle would dominate the future': A. Tuckett, The Scottish Carter (London, 1967), p.158.
157. Bagwell, The Railwaymen, pp.411, 419-21.
158. Ibid., esp. 404-14, for a full coverage of this; cp also K. Middlemas, Politics in Industrial Society (London, 1979), esp. pp.123-4, 149-51.
159. Bagwell, The Railwaymen, p.414.
160. All were tried in Edinburgh: D.L.G. Hunter, Edinburgh's Transport (Huddersfield, 1964), pp.162-3.
161. Ibid., 163-6.
162. NUR Edin. No. 1 branch minutes, 10, 24 August, 7, 21 September, 19 October 1924; Labour Standard, 17 October 1925, 2 January 1926.
163. Between 1921 and 1931 the number of railway workers in Edinburgh fell by 18.3 per cent, according to the Censuses, from 8,064 to 6,586. The number of insured railway workers fell 22 per cent, 1923-26 (Milnes, Industrial Edinburgh, p.154).
164. NUR Edin. No. 1 branch minutes, 28 March 1920.
165. McKenna, 'Victorian Railway Workers', pp.31-5.
166. For examples, see NUR Edin. No. 1 branch minutes, 4 July, 4, 15 August 1920, 27 February, 8 May, 31 July, 4, 18 December 1921, 11 March 1923, 29 June, 21 September 1924.
167. NUR Edin. No. 1 branch minutes, 29 June 1924.

168. Letter from 'Railway Worker', Labour Standard, 22 January 1927.
169. NUR Edin. No. 1 branch minutes, 23 April 1922.
170. Ibid., 22 October 1922; see also ibid., 1 February, 14 March, 9 May 1920, 2 July 1922, 15 July 1923, 18 April 1926; Bagwell, The Railwaymen, pp.440-1.
171. NUR Edin. No. 1 branch minutes, 13 July 1924.
172. Bagwell, The Railwaymen, pp.434-7.
173. NUR Edin. No. 1 branch, Souvenir, p.28.
174. An example: Nixon was requested by men from other departments, objected to by management, and offered promotion by the North British (NUR Edin. No. 1 branch minutes, 23 May 1920, 8 May 1921).
175. On procedure as an element of 'responsible autonomy' strategies, see A. Friedman, Industry and Labour (London, 1977), pp.96-8.

Chapter Six

TRADE UNION DEVELOPMENT:
MOTIVATION AND ORGANISATION

> New conceptions have an extremely unstable
> position among the popular masses; particularly
> when they are in contrast with orthodox
> convictions (which can themselves be new)
> conforming to the general interests of the ruling
> class.[1]

Trade unions develop in shop floor conflicts around the
'frontier of control', but they are not influenced by management strategy and industrial structure alone. They are
institutions consisting of, and created and sustained by,
working men and women. They are the authors, as well as
the victims, of social and political forces. As they reflect,
so they can help to shape, the outlooks and attitudes of their
members. They are political institutions in several respects:
they seek to achieve objectives through persuasion or
coercion; their power stems in large part from their ability
to mobilise people to certain forms of action; in attempting
to do this, they must deploy, employ, create, engage with,
principles which will make action seem legitimate to their
members (or others).[2]

The principles on which unions can develop action stem
from three main sources. First, they are generated by
groups of workers in their daily activity. Even where an
employer attempts to maintain a rigorous direct control,
there is ample evidence that workers develop social
institutions, and that these often support values of which
the employer would disapprove. They may, for instance, lead
to attempts to establish some collective control over
payments systems, or the pace or distribution of work, as in
notions of an 'effort bargain': a 'fair day's work for a fair
day's pay'.[3] Such principles derive from what Gramsci
described as workers' practical consciousness: they are
negotiations of fundamental economic values, but in relation
to a specific and limited context - rather than springing
from a general alternative ideology.

100

Second, however, dominant social values are brought into the workplace in at least two ways. They are reflected in workers' ordinary discourse, though often in a 'fragmentary, incoherent and inconsequential' form: Gramsci's 'commonsense'.[4] But they also underline and underpin management actions: employers' authority is buttressed by popular assumptions about the rights of property, the law of Master and Servant,[5] the necessity for profit,[6] and so forth. Third, unions can draw values from institutions of the wider working class movement: from other union institutions external to the workplace, from community organisations, the co-operative movement, from political parties, and so on.

So unions act in relation to principles, notions, which are shared by their members and - perhaps - others. Unless they are shared by significant numbers of union members, collective action will be difficult to achieve; if they are widely shared by others also, it will (very likely) be both easier to achieve, and more likely to succeed. (Of course, principles tending to support action may well exist alongside others which oppose it, even within the same person or group; this is part of the battle of ideas.)

The nature of the union institution is an important factor in whether (and how) collective action takes place. Thus a union workplace organisation may merely reflect and defend the principles developed by a work group. It may develop a network of shop stewards who can share information and provide mutual support. The shop-steward network may itself develop an elite group which can develop a relatively distinct vocabulary of motives, ponder strategy, even consider which principles should be deployed to achieve their end.[7] The organisational structure of the union, in the workplace and outside, will play a central role in determining what types of action are possible. At the same time, patterns of industrial relations play a part in shaping union structures. In this chapter, we explore the interplay of union organisation, industrial relations behaviour, and broader political and social movement.

MOBILISATION AND ADVANCE, 1917-18

The scale of union advance in Britain during and just after the Great War is a commonplace. The number of trades unionists more than doubled - to over eight millions - between 1913 and 1920. It was also reflected in other factors: increased state recognition, more widespread workplace organisation, the organisation of previously non-union groups of workers, the amalgamation and restructuring of a number of unions. But the growth in union membership during 1914 and 1915 was, if anything, slower than it had been during the preceding four years. It was not until 1916 that we can begin to speak of increases which were clearly war-related. A similar pattern appears in other labour statistics: for instance, the number of stoppages due to industrial disputes rose markedly in 1917 and 1918, as did the number of workers involved.[8]

In Edinburgh, as late as the spring of 1916, 'the difficulties in organising the large non-union element in the District' had, in the Trades Council's view, been 'greatly increased by the War'.[9] In contrast, 1917 was 'a record year so far as interest in and development of Trade Unionism is concerned',[10] whilst primary among 1918's 'marked features ... from the Trade Union point of view, apart from the general industrial unrest' was 'the strengthening and extension of the Trade Union movement'.[11] The NAUL's great success in organising the numerous rubber workers in Edinburgh won the Trades Council's 'Congratulations'.[12] Organisation began among chemical and hosiery workers,[13] among asylum and precious metal workers,[14] among dressmakers, milliners,[15] biscuit workers[16] and clerks.[17] This extension of the boundaries of trade unionism inspired the normally sober secretary of the Trades Council:

> Even in occupations which were usually regarded as
> outwith the influence of Trade Unionism has the
> gospel spread. The policemen have been arrested.
> The Insurance Clerks are thinking of a new policy;
> the Bank Clerks are combining to check economic
> pressure; the Teachers are growing class conscious;
> and the Domestic Servants are endeavouring to
> make a clean sweep of old and hard traditions.[18]

Where organisation already existed, the density of union membership increased. In some cases women, who had previously been excluded from membership, were recruited - as when the Bookbinders decided to admit women in 1918, and found their membership swelled by some 1,200.[19] In other cases there was a more general strengthening of organisation, as among the laundry[20] and road transport workers.[21]

Despite attempts to improve the structure of the movement,[22] the substantial evidence is that it was bedevilled by organisational failings. The constant theme of the Trades Council, for example, was just the 'lack of co-ordination, and consequent waste of effort'.[23] Competition between unions was rife, and associated with intense multi-unionism: laundry workers, for instance, were enrolled in 'five or six separate unions' even before J.H. Moore initiated the Laundry Workers' Union in 1917.[24] A conference called to 'arrange spheres of action for the unions which enrol[led] women workers' achieved little. The Paper Workers contested with the Bookbinders over the latter's new women members;[25] whilst the Bakers, the Shop Assistants, and the General Workers Unions, together with the NAUL competed for biscuit workers.[26] The problems were rooted too deeply to be solved on a local basis.

We cannot therefore successfully explain unions' ability to mobilise in organisational terms alone. Several factors were important. First, certain important principles giving legitimacy to the capitalist enterprise were eroded. Second, at the same time a number of - relatively general - legitimising principles, to which wartime developments lent support, began to be extended increasingly to trade unions. Third, the role of trade unions was recognised by the state, and while this did mean abandoning some union standards, it had positive effects too. Fourth, there was an undoubted, though intangible, strengthening of what we may term the self-image of the working class, generated by the sense of wartime sacrifice. Fifth, a number of issues were generated, within the workplace, which were clearly important in terms of both legitimising principles available at a societal level, and of those applicable to union organisation. Consequently, mobilisation became relatively easy. Let us look at these factors in turn.

The principal objective of the capitalist business enterprise is, inevitably, the making of profit. In general, this is lent support by the operation of a market economy; it is also supported, as a principle legitimising action, by its association with a number of other expressions. 'Efficiency', good 'organisation', opposition to 'waste', were all, however, during the war far more associated with the prosecution of the war effort: to oversimplify somewhat, their central meaning was derived from the military, rather than from the business, context, and associated with national rather than commercial interest.[27] State controls on profit, however ineffectual, further eroded the legitimacy of 'laissez faire'. Thus, certainly within the working class, 'profit' largely lost the support it had gained from these principles; conversely, it became associated with 'profiteering', a concept previously of little significance, but 'one of the emotional corrosives of the war period'.[28] Especially from 1916, 'profiteers' came under sustained attack from the popular press. This was reflected within the working class movement. In the Co-operative movement's advertisements, for example, by 1918 assumptions about 'profiteering' were uncontroversial enough to be central to the message:

THE OLD SYSTEM

must be scrapped and modern methods substituted. Other economies will, no doubt, suggest themselves, but the great break away from

PROFITEERING

will undoubtedly help to solve your difficulties. In your own interests, therefore, you should make arrangements to join[29]

and so forth. As the Commission of Enquiry into the Industrial Unrest in Scotland reported, in a sentence of inordinate complexity,

There is no doubt that the chief and fundamental cause of the existing unrest is the increased cost of living, which, in the mind of the workers, is the result of the Government having failed timeously, and effectively, to control the production, supply and distribution, of food, and thus opening the door to what the worker terms 'profiteering', by which he means the amassing by a few people, of abnormal wealth, out of the necessities of the country. The actual increase in the cost of living does not appear to be so important a factor in the worker's mind as the belief that 'profiteering' exists ...[30]

Our second factor is an associated one. As the legitimacy of 'profit' was eroded, in part by state action, in part by the assault on 'profiteering', but in part by its becoming distanced from related, normally supportive, legitimising principles; so some of the latter became increasingly open to employment in furthering trade union activities and objectives. It was not that unions necessarily started to use principles which they had previously shunned; rather that the latter now worked. For instance, the organising secretary of the NAUL had, very likely, been pointing out the importance of organisation for years before his 'stirring address' to the rubber workers: 'the employers having long since been organised it was up to the workers without delay to do the same'.[31] On this occasion, however, the notion - and benefits - of 'organisation' may have been more obvious to his audience, for, as we have seen, they joined in large numbers, and elected shop stewards. Again, much could be made of the 'discoveries' of the Welfare movement:

> The test of experience has proved to Government officials and to many others who, at the beginning of the War, desired to scrap every Trade Union regulation and restriction, that long hours are uneconomic and wasteful; that behind the rules put in force by trade unionists was a world of experience and industrial knowledge. Scientific study and enlightened and unprejudiced management are now reaching conclusions arrived at fifty years ago by thinking Trade Unionists.[32]

'Efficiency' then, was no longer the indisputable domain of the employer. Another example, though at one remove: the ideas of co-ordination, efficiency, elimination of wasteful competition, were important in giving legitimacy to plans to restructure the trade union movement. Amalgamation of unions would save 'expense and labour', and 'the petty, personal ambitions that spring out of the present competition would end'.[33]

The third factor which eased unions' problems of mobilisation was their recognition by the state. Clearly union leaders were consulted at a national level on many matters: to this extent they could no longer be entirely 'beyond the pale'. At the same time, the legal status of trade unions was enhanced,[34] and this had very immediate practical effects. In 1915 the NAUL started to organise workers at Musselburgh wire mills,

> who, although engaged on Government work, were being paid very low wages. Meetings ... were held to explain to the workers their position under the Munitions Act, and the advantages that would accrue from joining a trade union.[35]

Locally, the trade union movement was called to be represented on a variety of statutory, official, semi-official and voluntary bodies: exemption tribunals under the Derby Scheme, Relief of Distress Fund Committees, Local Pensions Committees, Food Control Committees, and so on.

Of course, the other side of trade union recognition was an attempt by the state to control labour by winning its leaders, together with a legal structure which severely circumscribed workers' freedoms. Naturally, this created problems for unions, such as the tendency for disputes to arise between union members and their own leaders, rather than with employers. But, certainly in Edinburgh, the trade unions seem to have taken a very sanguine approach: while broadly supportive of the war effort, and of the 'national interest', they retained a strong sense of class (as well as national) identity.[36] Thus the workers needed defence against 'the clutching hand of capitalism', even (perhaps especially) during wartime; the government showed, for instance, 'no capacity or desire to deal with the problem' of food price rises.[37] There were, at least by the end of the war, few illusions: 'no effective power was ever given' to the Food Control Committees, for instance, and

> What powers were given have been gradually diminished. The Food Control Committees are in reality mere rags to clothe the nakedness of bureaucracy. ... They have unlimited power to pass resolutions, but no power to put them into operation.[38]

Such an evaluation was complemented by a willingness to organise demonstrations and deputations on the issue in question, whilst being represented on the relevant committee.[39]

Our fourth coincident factor, the strengthening self-image of the working class, is more elusive. An historiographical commonplace,[40] we are suggesting a surge in confidence, rather than a legitimising principle as such: it is less easy to identify instances where this factor was important. The sense of war service having some kind of collective exchange value - homes 'fit for heroes', and the like - seems not to have been used publicly by Edinburgh's trade union movement until after the war (and until after it had entered the language of national politics).

It is on our final element that the others turn. The war generated a host of problems within the various workplaces. Industrial relations problems, however, are often beyond the ability of trade unions to influence, simply because they are unable to induce among their members (or potential members) a sense that the problem is a problem. Indeed the union organisation itself may see no problem. Our suggestion is that many of the industrial problems of wartime could be understood in terms of the legitimising principles which the war was making available. Thus, for the Clerks, whose union was small and lacked control over recruitment, dilution, for instance - the 'serious danger [to] which the Clerk is subjected by the influx of partially qualified people into offices' - could be understood in terms of the 'danger of inefficiency'.[41]

One major problem was present with ever-greater intensity during the later years of the war: the problem of rising prices. This provided a central focus for working class mobilisation, and for two main reasons. On the one hand, it provided a critical link between social distress and workplace organisation. As the Trades Council pointed out, it was 'in the trades and occupations which are not so well organised that the workers have been unable to maintain a proper standard of life'.[42] In well-organised establishments, achievement was frequent:

> Long period agreements have been suspended. The rapidity with which food prices have changed has necessitated the review of rates of wages at stated intervals. Wages in munition and some other trades are now open for reconsideration every four months.[43]

Of course, many of these rises were not achieved by 'dispute' but 'granted as the result of negotiation or arbitration'.[44] But the link between union organisation and adequate pay seems to have been clear.

On the other hand, however, rising prices - especially food price rises - was an issue which could draw on a range of legitimising principles, sustained not only within the working class, but actively propagated by national institutions. A major cause of the inflation was 'the rampant and rapacious profiteer';[45] the workers and their families were prepared to suffer hardship if the sacrifice was equal, but not 'to use glorified soup kitchens so as to keep the well-to-do from hardship and inconvenience', particularly when the government had only 'to completely control and regulate' food supplies[46] to overcome the problem: 'If all foodstuffs had been commandeered, and distribution regulated from the outbreak of war, and home production stimulated and encouraged, the present crisis could have been avoided.[47]

The achievement of the trade union movement - in recruitment and membership - during the later years of the war was, therefore, based primarily on the conjunction of favourable circumstances. There is little sign that, in Edinburgh, any major advances were made in the creation of institutions capable of generating legitimising principles or shaping issues – if we leave aside the one major achievement of large-scale recruitment and organisation at the workplace. In contrast to the engineering centres of the west of Scotland, Coventry and Sheffield, no strong shop stewards' movement emerged. In the rubber mills, and in many other sectors, the achievement was the simple formation of a union. Rather, the institutional structure of trade unionism remained relatively stable in form, even though far stronger in membership: it seems to have been capable of deploying, often quite effectively, legitimising principles which were already available, and of translating them into the working environment. It could 'negotiate' the meanings of principles originating elsewhere. But in essence, its victories were achieved using weapons forged by others.

By way of concluding this section, we may look briefly at two disputes which occurred late in the war. The first, in the spring of 1917, concerned the dressmakers, 'whose low wages and miserable earnings were proverbial'. Whilst previous efforts had failed, the Shop Assistants Union attempted to recruit, and 'Once a start was made, the women flocked into the union, and a spirit of revolt was born'. The tactics of the union seem to have been canny. A 'modest and fair' wage claim was put to the employers, and had the effect of splitting them. Some firms conceded; but the larger ones did not. 'A strike ensued. The spirit, the loyalty and the courage of the girls won the fight after a six weeks' struggle.' The Trades Council held that 'The fine fight by the Dressmakers against a strong combination of employers was one of the factors that led to the successful organising efforts of other unions ...' Another important factor was that 'a section of the press - The Evening News - several prominent citizens, and the general public, were all on the side of the women'. This was almost unprecedented in a strike in wartime (indeed, in any strike); although to be sure a strike in dressmaking could not be presented as unpatriotic so easily as a strike in, say, munitions. Of course, the unions mobilised labour and working class opinion effectively too: demonstrations were held, union organisations of various kinds contributed £84 13s 11d to a strike appeal. Labour councillors were brought into action.[48] Probably this played a part in swinging 'public opinion', but such methods had previously failed too often for us to believe they can alone account for the breadth of support. They were able to employ a vocabulary of motives which was, temporarily, biased in favour of the workers.

The second dispute occurred at Middlemas & Son's biscuit factory in the city, in September and October 1918. The workers, again largely women, sought union membership in order to 'level up their rates of pay' in line with other factories in the industry. Management raised no objection to union membership in principle. But then, according to one account, some of the women joined the union, and were 'straightway dismissed': 'Some of their fellow-workers struck in sympathy.'[49] In another version, management refused negotiations, and the women thereupon struck.[50] In either event the firmness of management's approach is clear. With some workers out (apparently about 60), but many others still working, the employer reduced the hours and raised the wages of those still at work, while refusing to reinstate those on strike 'in a body'.[51] Conversely, the unions seem to have been in disarray. It seems that the workers joined the Shop Assistants Union (or perhaps only approached it for financial assistance and advice) only after they had struck (or been dismissed).[52] The Shop Assistants were at this precise time in the midst of a demarcation dispute over recruitment of biscuit factory workers.[53] The women were under pressure from their families to return to work:[54] we should not forget that the cost of living in 1918 was extremely high, and compensated for only by rising pay levels. 'In the end,' the Trades Council recorded, 'the contest had to be temporarily given up. The arbitrary power of the management, and the fear of dismissal, held in check the natural instincts of the bulk of the employees of the firm.'[55]

So although both disputes occurred in previously non-union workplaces, one was successful, while in the other the employer prevailed. These cases illustrate several points. Even during this period, unions were not guaranteed success: organisational failings, combined with astute tactics on the employers' part, could make matters at least very difficult for the unions. Particularly in those sectors only recently organised, success depended largely on the ability to mobilise people into forms of 'industrial action'. But this in itself was dependent on the ability to mobilise opinion more widely: union organisation did not seem able to sustain of itself legitimising principles strong enough to 'justify' large-scale or long-term industrial action. Finally, even in war-time, the fear of dismissal was not negligible.

'A STATE OF FLUX',[56] 1919-20

The Armistice was a momentous event; yet few trade unionists seem to have regarded it as fundamentally altering their purpose. Alexander Caldwell, the Trades Council's vice-president, an eloquent painter, opening the first post-war meeting, referred from the chair to

> the fact that the week just closed had seen the cessation of hostilities in the devastating war of the last four years; and while expressing hope that the resulting peace would be a just and lasting one, he trusted that no political or other changes would distract our attention from the task of overcoming the enemy on the home front.[57]

The attitude elsewhere was equally matter-of-fact: the Rubber Workers dispatched a congratulatory telegram to Sir Douglas Haig 'on the Great Victory achieved by Greater Britain and her Allies in the War, now happily over', and then got down to business;[58] the Railwaymen considered a motion 'that the EC be called together on the cessation of hostilities for the purpose of declaring a General Strike to establish a dictatorship of the proletariat in this country', rejected it, and did likewise.[59] Looking back six months later, the advent of peace did not seem to the Trades Council one of the 'marked features of the year from the trade union point of view'.[60]

In the world of 1919 and early 1920, mobilisation of trade union members remained quite straightforward. Again, in seeking to explain this, the coincidence of a number of factors is important. First, there was a significant, though temporary and partial, loss of self-confidence by important elements of capital and the state. This was associated with increased problems of co-ordination between employers, and between employers and government. Middlemas has written of 'the government's near-panic early in 1919' as it confronted a national coal strike with the loyalty of army and police in doubt.[61] State control of industry could no longer be justified, yet the employers lacked representative organisations which could engage in negotiations with the government.[62] Mistrust, already sown by the state's wartime 'interference' in management, was intensified when government appeared to be conceding demands to unions without consulting employers.[63] In addition, an important section of opinion within government - especially, it seems, within the Ministry of Labour - and increasingly too among employers, accepted that there could be no return to pre-war labour relations. The problem was not how to re-establish the old forms of labour control, but how to re-establish control, given the increased power of the shop floor: thus Whitley Councils, thus the National Industrial Conference of 1919-21.[64]

Our second factor: after the war issues remained which were legitimate in terms of principles generally available, and which were also relevant to union action at workplace level. Two are outstanding: inflation, and the shorter working week. 'During the past year,' recorded the Trades Council in 1920, 'the mad race between wages and prices has continued.'[65] There seems to have been little initial need for industrial action: there were few, if any, organised trades which did not obtain some increase during these years. However, union success was at best mixed.[66] Despite the wage increases, the city's unions found it difficult to maintain their standard of living in these years.[67] The problems they encountered in fully regaining ground lost to inflation, and the frustrations engendered, are reflected by the Trades Council's decision to hold a demonstration on the High Cost of Living in July 1920, and in the terms of the motion proposed: 'That this meeting - holding that high prices are due to causes under human control, calls upon the Government to take the necessary steps to reduce prices or to give place to those who will.'[68]

The other linking issue was the shorter working week. The 40-hours movement gained some support in Edinburgh; but, perhaps more important, hours were reduced in virtually every organised trade, as Table 6.1 shows. Again the bulk of these reductions were achieved by negotiation. The Rubber Workers, for instance, demanded a 44-hour week in January 1919; six weeks later they settled for a nationally-agreed 47 hours.[69] In sum, then, issues were available which were both amenable to action within the workplace and trade union context, and clearly achievable by such means.

The third coincident factor was the redefining of national (and community) interest. The threat to the nation was no longer so conspicuous; the national interest therefore became more controversial, and class and sectional interests were strengthened. We have seen that, during the war, the trade union movement was quite capable of proposing, at least, a somewhat negotiated version of the national interest: 'support was given to the war in the hope that the country would win and be able to formulate such conditions of settlement as should make for permanent peace.'[70] Still

Table 6.1: The Basic Working Week in Certain Edinburgh Trades 1914-27

	1914	1918	1919	1920	1921-2	1923-4	1925-7
Brewery Workers	56	n.a.	50	50	50	n.a.	n.a.
Electricians	50-4	n.a.	47	47	47	47	47
Engineers	54	54	47	47	47	47	47
Sheet Metal Workers	51	51	47	47	47	48	48
Bricklayers	51	50	44	44	44	44	44
Masons	51	50	44	44	44	48	48
Painters and Slaters	50	50	44	44	44	44	44
Compositors and Bookbinders	50	50	48	48	48	48	48
Railway Drivers and Firemen	60	n.a.	48	48	48	48	48
Rubber Workers	55	55	47	47	47	48	48
Bakers	48-55	48-52½	48-51	48-51	44	45-7	45
Shop Assistants	over 60	60	48	48	48	48	48
Laundry Workers	n.a.	54	48-52	48	48	48	48
'Labourers'	50	50	44	44	44	44	n.a.

Source: TC and T&LC ARs 1918-27.

more, after the war, were questions asked about the objectives of the national struggle. The fact that 'brutal' employers still received 'public and civic honours' showed 'that the old regime has not passed, that sweaters and hypocrites need not yet fear social ostracism.'[71] The government could not be trusted: it had made use of the workers in a national emergency, but was not thereafter prepared properly to acknowledge their aspirations. This sense grew as 1919 became 1920:

> if one tithe of the energy and Statesmanship displayed in the production of munitions had been transferred to work of real national importance, unemployment would have been wiped out of existence. But the path of the present Government has been one long trail strewn with broken pledges.[72]

Nonetheless, the sense of renewal, of national reconstruction and a common purpose, was one to which the establishment paid at least lip service - a fact which trade unionists were prepared to exploit. Thus, in negotiation with the employers' federation, an ASE negotiator accepted

> that during the war that was not a suitable time to discuss alterations of byelaws, but now that we are come to the period of reconstruction when we are trying to make the land fit for heroes to live in, we propose to put these [draft working rules] as our part in trying to reconstruct things in this district, and in this particular industry ... [73]

In short, the nation now included the working class, whose aspirations were valid. And the employers in September 1919 could make no response to this argument (although defending their position on other grounds).

We are, then, arguing that the trade unions' advance was due to their being offered a set of legitimising principles, supported by the dominant institutional order, which was relatively open to action in their interests - rather than to their having themselves generated quite independent principles. But the unions knew they were engaged in an ideological struggle, especially in relation to the national interest, and to the war. Like the government, the Trades Council, in the months after the Armistice, put much effort into strengthening its links with ex-servicemen. According to one study, the 'spectre of red and white armies haunted capital and Labour respectively'.[74] Yet more prosaic fears were also important in Edinburgh. Former soldiers and sailors sought their old jobs back, often vainly. A large pool of unemployment quickly formed, and the authorities attempted to divert responsibility onto trade union practices.

> The return of the ex-Servicemen has been made the occasion for fresh attacks on the Unions. Time and again on public platforms the slander is reiterated by responsible ministers of the Government that organised Labour is placing obstacles in the way of the ex-Serviceman's return to industrial life.[75]

The local unions, through the Trades Council, considered the problems of demobilisation and resettlement in two special conferences as early as February 1919: in May and June a joint committee was established between the Trades Council and the Discharged and Demobilised Sailors' and Soldiers' Federation (it seems first to have been referred to in the Trades Council minutes as a 'Workers' and Soldiers' Council').[76] But such initiatives were to be frustrated. Although some 'useful work' was done, and an 'interesting campaign against certain "ultra-patriotic" employers' planned,[77] the joint committee seems to have broken up 'owing to the influence of interested politicians and a party Press'[78] - although the immediate cause was the Trade Council's amalgamation with the Labour Party.[79] Thereafter 'a continuous crusade of slander' was 'conducted in the Press and on many platforms for the purpose of alienating the ex-Serviceman from the Trade Unions'.[80]

The fourth factor requires less discussion. We have discussed the role during the war of those legitimising principles associated with the language of organisation, planning and efficiency; they remained influential thereafter. The reorganisation of the TUC after the war drew on both parallels with the bureaucratic organisation of the Civil Service and 'the terminology of war'.[81] The reorganisation of the Edinburgh Trades Council sprang in part from similar motives.[82] Of course, such language was often not associated directly with wartime experiences: we have seen, for instance, how organisation, efficiency, planning were given meaning by their use in industry. During 1919, too, the notion of 'profiteering' was still a powerful source of legitimisation; we shall look at this in more detail below.

Fifth, the status and prestige achieved by - or granted to - the trade unions during the war could not be immediately withdrawn. In particular, the government's anxiety to isolate the 'revolutionary' or 'political' element by strengthening national union leaderships was also an acceptance of an important role for the movement.[83] Edinburgh's trade unions were deeply involved by 1919 in aspects of what we may term the state apparatus; to this extent their status was enhanced. Inevitably they were involved in the administration of pensions and unemployment insurance.[84] Virtually every trade had representation on the Education Authority's Advisory Council.[85] Several of the city's leading trade unionists were JPs: it seems, for instance, to have been almost automatic for those who held senior office in the Trades Council, at least for more than one year, to have been honoured in this way.[86] Certainly the Trades Council imagined that 'Our influence is distinctly felt in our local governing bodies, and Government departments consult us more freely than in the past.'[87] No doubt there was an element of 'incorporation' here, but (for instance) in rhetoric at least, some of the trade union justices were militant, anti-government and conscious of class interest. Nor should we imagine that this enhanced 'status' had no implication for the business of union workplace organisation. Two instances may be given here. Firstly, the Whitley Councils, whatever their real, or long-term effects, were undoubtedly perceived by some unions as likely to strengthen their organisation.[88] In addition, union JPs were - at least during the heady days of 1919-20 - acceptable arbitrators in industrial disputes.[89]

We now turn to our final coincident factor: the rising level of union morale. The ability to mobilise can itself constitute a most effective argument for union negotiators. Thus in September 1919 the ASE took a grievance to the employers' association. After prolonged argument, the patience of the union men broke:

We both talk from the strength of the case which we have, and this is probably the strongest position which we are in, namely, that the men have absolutely got their backs up in the matter, and it will not be very difficult for us to stop them from going, and that is the biggest argument in the matter.[90]

In addition, confidence that others will join in common action is an important justification for taking action. Thus the Edinburgh Railwaymen's telegram claim, 'All men and women out', during the 1919 strike, though technically incorrect,[91] nonetheless played a role in legitimising the action.

UNION ORGANISATION 1917-20

Whilst union mobilisation remained quite easy during 1919 and 1920 - and union victory was the rule - the achievements were based on factors which were not the conscious creation of the movement itself. Substantial concessions had been made to the trade union movement and the working class during the war, and action against them was consequently more difficult to co-ordinate and justify. Broadly, the trade union movement in Edinburgh did not generate mobilising institutions of any real strength during the period from 1917 to 1920. It knew that the gains might be transient: 'If our gains in 1919 are not to be ephemeral, there must be more unity of purpose and more co-operative action than the past has shown.'[92] Yet, for several reasons, lessons were not - or could not be - learnt.

The first reason also reflects the nature of the gains of 1917-20. In almost all unions, existing organisational structures were placed under severe strain. The clearest cases are in those unions, largely of unskilled, semi-skilled, and white-collar workers, which grew beyond recognition. In some cases entirely new structures had to be created, as the NAUL in the rubber works. Here, the union had to assimilate over 2,100 new members within three months of its formation:[93] even simply to administer such numbers was a major task.[94] Thus within two months of its formation, the branch committee had to be enlarged as 'so many sections of the works' were unrepresented.[95] Inevitably, all this had to be achieved by men and women who were inexpert at managing a union's affairs, and in their spare time.[96] The growth of the National Union of Clerks was less spectacular, but still created major problems. In September 1917 the Edinburgh branch had 25 members: by the end of the year this figure had doubled to 57; by September 1919 it stood at 378.[97] Here, an existing structure was altered markedly:[98] from being a somewhat exclusive group, composed largely of trade union and political activists,[99] the branch became one with a mass membership, and with large sections of its members in various firms.[100]

In short, effective organisation (even just efficient administration) was by far the most immediate concern of union organisation during this period: its absence could easily be a major failing. In January 1919, for example, the

Clerks were approached by a disaffected member of the NAUL at the Castle Rubber Mills: 'he thought there was a possibility of the clerical staff, of 100 members, ... transferring to the NUC'.[101] He and his colleagues 'had been rather badly treated by their present union.'[102] After some effort by the NUC, they 'transferred':[103] such was the Clerks' euphemism. To the NAUL this was 'encroachment', even 'poaching': and indeed, prima facie, such it was. But in protesting to the Trades Council,[104] the NAUL encountered problems. They had been affiliated to the Trades Council only for a short period, had appointed only four delegates, of whom only one attended regularly, and he was hardly a prominent member.[105] They had, in short, made little effort to consolidate their relationship with the trade union movement outside their own place of work. The Clerks had done so assiduously: one of their delegates, a member of the Executive Committee of the Trades Council since at least 1916, was articulate and able enough to be elected to the General Council of the STUC - just the third woman to be so.[106] For the Rubber Workers this was a matter of principle. They demanded the Clerks be reprimanded. The Trades Council would clearly do this only after much persuasion, if at all; it therefore invited both parties' executives to a conference. This was a final insult to the Rubber Workers:

> after considerable discussion [at their branch meeting] it was ... unanimously agreed to decline to meet the Nat[ional Union of] Clerks Executive, as we were the injured party and we as a Union cease to be affiliated to the Trades Council owing to their failure to protect our interests.[107]

The greater ability of the Clerks to create institutional links allowed them to emerge unscathed from a situation in which they had acted without scruple. The Rubber Workers' appointment of shop stewards and accident stewards was an institutional development of comparable significance within the Castle Mills.[108]

If the organisational development of the trade union movement was hindered, in part, by the sheer scale of the administrative tasks imposed by its very success in recruitment, there was also a second reason: the concept of 'organisation' available, at least within the mainstream of the trade union movement. We argued in Chapter 4 that the metaphors of work organisation used by management were, in the main, mechanical and military; and that this limited

117

the extent to which managerial strategies relying on some workers' responsibility could be developed. For the unions' activists, the position was not dissimilar. Their illustrations of organisation also drew on mechanical and military analogies: the union should be an 'effective weapon';[109] the great claim of those who created the Trades and Labour Council was to 'have succeeded in producing a machine ... capable of giving adequate expression to the aims, the hopes and the aspirations of the working class of this city'.[110] The problem with this 'nuts and bolts' understanding was that it treated organisation as an instrument, rather than as a relationship.[111] In reality, of course, organisation itself required constant legitimisation, and yet was a vital element in shaping an issue, and thus in mobilising union members. In short, the concept of organisation as a machine left activists as 'mechanics', in some sense external to the machine - its operators: the generals in an army whose will to fight could be taken for granted.

This mechanistic image of organisation was also constrained by the tendency to see administration as the fundamental aspect of organisation. Within a year of its formation, for example, the Trades and Labour Council felt in need 'of fully equipping our machinery with cash and staff';[112] a year later it believed that it 'would never be able to give the maximum assistance to the Working-Class Movement locally until the present system of spare-time officials is superseded by a more progressive method.'[113] This 'more progressive method' was nothing more grand than the appointment of a full-time Secretary.[114] We have seen above how important quite basic administrative tasks were to a union organisation based on voluntary, spare-time labour; such efficiency, of course, had a bearing on the legitimacy of union organisation itself. When a shop steward at the Victoria rubber works lost 52s. of union money (nearly a week's wage for one of his members) it was important to raise a subscription not merely to recover the money, but because 'it would strengthen the bona fide nature of the case'.[115] But to see union organisation primarily in terms of administrative (or mechanical) analogies hindered the development of thought about the role of organisation in, and its relation to, the mobilisation of union members and institutions. In the years before 1921 the effect of these weaknesses could pass unnoticed. Solidarity could be assumed. Failings could be explained in terms of failing in organisation - organisation as it was then understood - or in terms of betrayal. Or both.

'FIGHTING ON THE DEFENSIVE'
The good times did not last long after the war: as early as the spring of 1920 the Trades Council was sounding a note of warning.

> During the war period the average worker has become lulled to a sense of security by the comparative ease with which increases of wages and improvement of conditions have been obtained, but signs are not wanting that the employing classes have been strengthening their position, and are marshalling their forces for the great struggle which is undoubtedly imminent.[116]

A year later, this 'prophecy [had] ... indeed, come true': 'A struggle has begun, the rules of which are the laws of the jungle'.[117] During subsequent years the struggle ebbed and flowed, but real union achievement was rare. So successive Trades Council annual reports moved from recognising the 'extraordinary difficulty'[118] the movement was facing (and the defeats suffered) in 1921-2; to stressing the heroism of the struggles, the loyalty and example in defeat. Our explanation for this deterioration in the trade union position concentrates on, first, the changes which occurred in the principles by which actions could be legitimised and, in the next section, the effect of developments within the trade union movement at the level of organisation. Of course, the economic terrain on which these struggles were fought out had changed to the disadvantage of workers in relation to their employers.

Let us turn to the legitimising principles by which trade union action in the working class interest could be justified. We have argued that these were unusually wide during 1917-20, and found resonance within the workplace. Clearly, our assumption is that the balance of legitimation shifted significantly away from the working class after 1920: several aspects deserve exploration.

First, the institutional support for certain aspects of trade union activities or objectives, especially in important sections of the press, rapidly evaporated during the early post-war years. The press had never, of course, been supportive of trade unions; but for just a few years they shared certain assumptions. Whilst in 1919 and early 1920 trade unions had been able to enlist newspapers' support, and to 'rouse' public opinion in some disputes, this seems rapidly to have dissipated. 'The Press that pled with such sweet reason for Whitley Councils and Conciliation when the sword was in the hand of the Trade Unions, today urges the mine-owners to be relentless', complained the Trades Council in 1921;[119] while a year later rather than supporting the just demands of labour, 'The millionaire-owned press has now changed its headlines and leaders to read that Britain is a poor country with limited economic resources'.[120] This refrain continued through the 1920s.

Second, the government's recognition of trade unionism implicit in joint consultation, 'Whitleyism', and the National Industrial Conference altered profoundly. In 1919 and 1920 the government's intent was to divide responsible leaders from those (shop stewards, industrial unionists, and the like) who represented an illegitimate and unacceptable form of trade unionism. From 1920 the definition of illegitimacy expanded as the strength of all forms of union action waned. All strikes - indeed, any form of union action likely to prove effective - were no longer to be countenanced:

> the employers have been, either openly or secretly, assisted by a Government which, while proclaiming its impartiality and its 'inability to take sides' has placed the full weight of the machinery of the State against the comparatively mild demands of organised Labour.[121]

At another level, trade union justices of the peace found their role narrowed. With the employers' offensive, arbitration was no longer so desirable (or necessary) from their point of view: arbitrators who were trade unionists must have seemed particularly inappropriate. Trade union JPs were, therefore, confined to the bench. At the same time, it seems no longer to have been so important to appoint trade unionists.[122] In short, 'recognition' was conferred not on trade unions as such, but on ever-narrower definitions of trade union activity.

At the same time, thirdly, the memory of certain legitimising principles (particularly those deriving from the war) became more distant. Many were re-interpreted in the light of new conditions and events, particularly those associated with the economy. During the war certain legitimising principles (such as efficiency), which had previously been closely associated in meaning with notions of profit, became more closely associated with notions of organisation and planning. This was particularly true in industrial contexts. Now, after the war, state control over the economy was rapidly abandoned; companies, broadly speaking, returned to traditional objectives in a market context.[123] This put the meanings of efficiency and its associated principles under pressure. This was increased as press campaigns against 'waste' developed.[124] Employers and managers had in any case been less wholehearted about the organisational benefits of war, often interpreting it more in terms of interference and inefficiency.

An illustration is to be found in the notion of 'profiteering'. Common currency in wartime, this became more rare and played but a small part in explanations of industrial and other developments. In 1919 the Co-operative movement, for example, reminded trade unionists that it was still 'the sworn enemy of profiteering in any shape or form, and for that reason <u>alone</u> deserves their warmest support'.[125] By 1920 awareness of separate class interest remained in the claim that

> The financial and other benefits which are inseparable from CO-OPERATIVE TRADING make an irresistible appeal to all who find it necessary to economise. Only people who have plenty of the world's goods can afford to be outside this helpful movement.[126]

but 'profiteering' no longer seemed important. And indeed, the word hardly appears in trade union minutes, reports or publications after 1919.[127] A commonsense explanation of economic development, with strong emotive content and supported by powerful established institutions, was no longer commonly available.

The effect is illustrated in the changing language used by negotiators in the engineering industry. Where in 1919 and early 1920 the unions' negotiators could argue in terms of their members' feelings (and win their case, very often), from 1920 this became more difficult. The employers now held the trump card: the state of the economy. The argument was not, of course, new: it was the stock-in-trade of employers in negotiations. It was used in 1919 and 1920: but in those months it was both weakened by the war, and outweighed by the unions' confidence.[128] Thus we find a reversal in methods of negotiation. In 1919 the union negotiators tend to deploy a simple case, based on their ability to mobilise their members; the employers generally introduce other principles in an attempt to confuse the issue - or, at least, to provide the trappings of relevant and reasoned judgement. Rules should not be altered in 1919 because it would be 'panic legislation' in 'abnormal conditions'; apprentices' pay should not be too high because 'there are evil influences at work' on such boys; some issues are too 'big' to be dealt with locally; 'political argument' should be kept out of industrial negotiation; 'order and ruling' are desirable; 'constant confusion and trouble' (allegedly the result of workplace negotiations) are to be shunned.[129]

From 1920 the employers could deploy a simple case: that they were all, employers and employees, subject to the exigencies of a market over which there was no control. Work was not 'plentiful', trade was 'slack': the consequences, though regrettable, were inescapable. The argument came in several forms: from mild reminders ('the trade ... has fallen upon bad times'),[130] through strong reminders ('we do not think we are pressing hard at all, but only fighting to get back to a level [of pay] where we can make our jobs attractive to the buyers'),[131] to outright threats:

> I think most men who have a job, and a steady job,
> are very happy just now, and any of them who have
> contracts are very pleased and there is no change
> ... that is going to better the conditions[132]

thus one employer in 1923; while another, in 1925, averred: 'It is that time and quarter that is just driving work across the other side of the water. It makes things impossible.'[133] The union representatives, in contrast, drew on a wider range of legitimising principles: parity ('in all districts where brass moulders and iron moulders are working the principle is generally admitted - that the rates should be paid practically the same'); precedent ('the principle was recognised in July of last year'); the 'effort bargain' ('it is far more unhealthy work than that of an iron moulder, and the brass moulders' work is just as exhaustive').[134] These could be effective in securing marginal or sectional improvements, but rarely when an employer resisted resolutely, for they were of relatively narrow application.

The unions continued to use, on occasion, the broader principles on which they had earlier mobilised so effectively (such as wartime promises), but to little effect: they no longer mobilised union members. In a revealing exchange in January 1923, the employers show a quiet confidence in the workers' quiescence:

> The CHAIRMAN: You will ... perhaps adjourn and
> ... discuss what are your real proposals in
> connection with Clause 6 on the country allowance,

because we certainly cannot go to the length of [raising it from 4/- to] 5/- per day. Mr. STUART [AEU]: Then, I do not think there is much use in our coming back. That is the last word we had on it with the men.

The CHAIRMAN: But the last word is that the men are working at 4/- ...

To Stuart's assertion that 'We are not here to bluff you on this matter', the Chairman responded, 'Well, I do not know what word you put upon it, but ...'[135] He would not move beyond 4s.; he knew he did not have to.

For the employers, moreover, 'the market' could undercut almost any argument the unions could produce, and justify almost any move by management. It could even explain why unions could not be informed about the state of trade: 'we never see these cuts [in the price of gas-meters sold] and never get any proof of them,' complained an AEU man in 1922. The employers' chairman retorted: 'I assure you it is done, but we cannot go on revealing all our business to Tom, Dick and Harry because it gets abroad and spoils trade.'[136] In 1926 the union even attempted to argue for increased wages by using the employers' own argument in reverse: because there had been a 'definite improvement in trade'. This was forlorn, for having accepted the premise of the employers' case, the union could not escape the logic of their riposte: 'we should be perfectly justified ... to ask you to help us to get work by reducing further the [wage] costs.'[137]

The fourth aspect of the shift in the balance of legitimation is crucial. The economic downturn changed the nature of the issues confronting trade union organisations. Where the problems of 1917-20, notably inflation, had been very amenable to solution by union activity at the workplace, the problems of depression were not. When the markets began to disappear, when the relative cost of employing workers rose, when profit margins contracted, workplace organisation could win few concessions. The distance between hope and realistic expectation grew; and, in due time, hopes were either dashed or adjusted downward. Whilst unions were conscious of unemployment (members were out of work, memberships in decline),[138] they could do little about it. Their members were increasingly hard to mobilise; it was still harder to mobilise them successfully, since success now generally required action at an industrial - rather than sectional or workplace - level. The scale of action required had escalated greatly; the possible benefits from action had become smaller, or at least more distant.

Many employers, of course, used the depression to tighten their control over labour. This generated issues relevant to union organisation, but did not mean that union action could achieve improvements. The gas meter making firms, for instance, in 1922 determined to reduce their piecework rates. As an AEU representative pointed out, the men's view was unambiguous:

> we had a very representative meeting of the whole
> of the gas meter making shops in the city ..., and
> the men instructed me to point out that the $12\frac{1}{2}$
> per cent reduction that you propose is totally
> unwarranted.[139]

But after the unions' recent defeat in the national lock-out, the employers had an answer to every argument - 'to get prices down to increase business and induce managers to order more meters'.[140] During the 1920s, in contrast to 1917-20, 'commonsense' seemed to support the employers' interpretations of economic necessity. On no occasion, before 1926, did an engineers' negotiator attempt to criticise the economic assumptions of the employers' case for limiting or reducing wage costs.

TRADE UNIONISM AND ORGANISATION IN THE 1920s

Broadly, then, the political 'space' which had been created in the brief period around the Armistice closed quite rapidly as the post-war boom passed. Labour organisations proved unable to sustain this space, to create or sustain the necessary principles, of themselves. During 1919 and 1920 union organisation had developed with an administrative, rather than mobilising, orientation. Union organisational thought was marked by military and mechanistic images, and by the immediate imperatives of efficient internal administration. The movement failed to address the relationship of union organisations to their members: union organisation was apparently working, as increasing membership made plain; whilst the ready availability of issues at the workplace made it unnecessary to think deeply about how to mobilise members. This administrative orientation influenced strongly the subsequent development of union behaviour.

As the depression set in, the context in which union organisational structures functioned changed. Membership of TUC-affiliated unions fell by 32.6 per cent over the

Figure 6.2: NUR Edinburgh No.1 Branch: Membership Statistics 1918–27

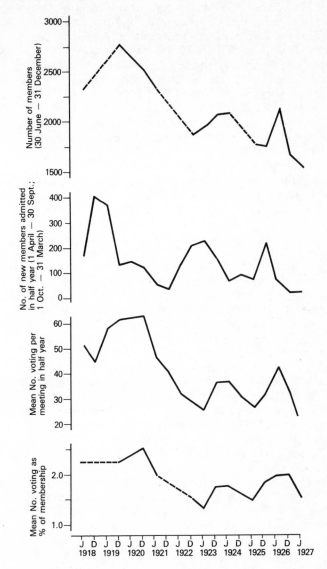

Source: NUR No.1 branch minutes, <u>passim.</u>

three-year period beginning in December 1919.[141] The decline in membership of the Railwaymen's No. 1 branch - the only Edinburgh union organisation for which we have figures - was almost identical, at 32.3 per cent (see Figure 6.2). The number of union branches affiliated to the Trades Council fell from 95 to 70 in just one year, 1920-1 (see Figure 6.3); financial pressure caused by loss of membership and unemployment was an important reason. The Painters reported between 180 and 200 of its 1,200 members idle in November 1920;[142] the following year the orchestras cut back, causing 'large unemployment' among the Musicians' members;[143] the Penicuik branch of the Printing and Paper Workers withdrew from the Council because trade depression was affecting branch income.[144]

But the depression's impact on union organisation was uneven. There were problems in integrating newly unionised workers into union institutions, and new union institutions into the existing organisational structures of the trade union movement. Three aspects deserve discussion. Firstly, involvement in union activity by union members did not change significantly during the year after the war. Among the Railwaymen the mean number voting at meetings (the only available indicator) only rose as a proportion of membership as the latter began to fall in 1920 (see Figure 6.2). So the (quantitative) increase in union membership was not accompanied by a (qualitative) change in the meaning of union membership. Participation in union meetings declined by 47 per cent as a proportion of membership between the winter of 1920-1 and the summer of 1923, despite the fact that the falls in the number of new members, and in total branch membership, had been stemmed between six and 18 months earlier. Although participation rose again, it never rivalled the proportions of 1918-20.

Turning, secondly, to the Trades Council, we can see in Figure 6.3 that when the number of organisations affiliated to the Council, and their size, were greatest, each delegate attended the fewest meetings, and the average attendance at each meeting was lowest. In short, the infusion of new members into the movement in 1919 and 1920 could not be consolidated in organisation, attitudes or behaviour. After 1921, the number of Trades Council affiliates began to rise, but the membership of affiliated organisations (reflected, if approximately, in the number of delegates) never reached the 1920 level. The level of activity of the average delegate, as represented by the number of meetings

Figure 6.3: Edinburgh Trades Council: Membership Statistics
1915-27

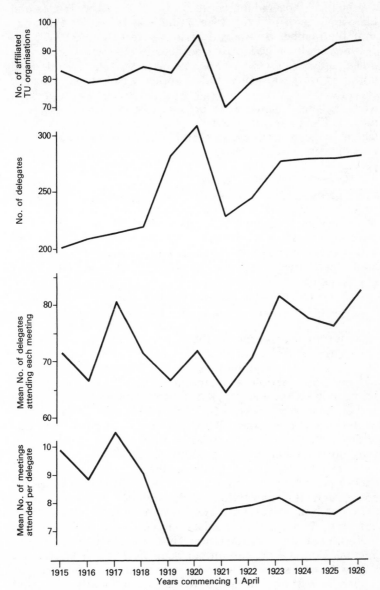

Source: TC and T&LC ARs, 1916-27.

attended, never again approached its levels of 1915-18.

Thirdly, union branches new to the movement formed the bulk of those which ceased affiliation to the Trades and Labour Council in 1921. (See Table 6.4; it was in this year that the number of Council affiliates fell the most.) Of the 16 unions which had affiliated since 1915, a majority was made up of unions in the 'growth sectors': semi- and unskilled workers, white-collar workers, and so on. Overall, therefore, it was among the more recently organised workers, and unions, that organisation was weakest, and most liable to erosion; but the trade union movement as a whole found it difficult to sustain the level of membership participation in its affairs that had characterised the war years.

After 1920, then, the unions' inability to consolidate their gains of 1917-20 began to be exposed; at the same time, the context in which they operated altered. There consequently developed (alongside a debate about strategy), intense discussion of certain organisational questions. The major problem was identified as the inability of unions to hold their own against an alliance of employers and government:

> When it has come to meeting the attacks of those whose interests lie in the maintenance of the status quo, or in reaction, the Trade Union Movement, fighting on the defensive, has been out-generalled and out-manoeuvred, and the combined weight of the employers' attack has been felt by separate sections at different times.[145]

This analysis seems to have been shared widely. The proposed solution was reflected in the title of a special conference on 'Hours, Wages, Unemployment, and Co-ordination'.[146] If the problem had been disunity in action, the solution, clearly, was to co-ordinate.

Yet whilst the perceived problem had changed from the earlier period, the solution was found in the same essential conception of organisation. With diminishing memberships, efficient branch administration was no longer a key issue, but the image of organisation remained mechanistic: hierarchical and militaristic. Thus the language of the Special Conference resolution: 'Complete co-ordination of policy is necessary within the trade union movement,' it declared, setting out steps to be taken locally 'to assist National Unions and the Trade[s] Union Congress to this end.'[147] In the debate, all drew on mechanistic images of

128

Table 6.4: Trade Union Branches which Ceased their Affiliation to Edinburgh Trades and Labour Council 1920/1

Branches not affiliated to Edinburgh Trades Council in 1915:

       Asylum workers (Morningside)
       National Union of Clerks (Engineering)
       Electrical Trades Union (North)
       Electrical Trades Union (Cinema Operators)
       General Workers (Meter)
       General Workers (Tobacco)
       General Workers (Drug)
       Gold, Silver and Allied Trades
       Pottery Workers (Portobello)
       Prudential Staff Federation
       Railwaymen (Edin. No. 3)
       Scale, Beam and Weighing Machine Makers
       Woodworkers (Amalgamated No. 4)
       Woollen Workers
       Workers' Union (No. 2)
16   Workers' Union (Musselburgh)

Branches not affiliated to Edinburgh Trades Council in 1915; possibly then affiliated to Leith Trades Council:

       National Amalgamated Union of Labour (Leith)
       Corporation Employees (Leith)
       Machinemen (Leith)
       Painters (Leith)
       Shipwrights
       Tailors and Tailoresses (Leith)
7   Woodworkers (Leith No. 2)

Branches affiliated to Edinburgh Trades Council in 1915:

       Electrical Trades Union (West)
       Farm Servants (Dairyworkers)
       Furnishing Trades
4   Tramway and Vehicle Workers

Source: TC and T&LC ARs, 1916, 1921, 1922.

organisation. There are two main problems with this approach. One we know: its tendency to divorce organisational questions from those of legitimising mobilisation. Sectionalism, for instance, was an organisational problem which co-ordination could solve. The second problem is related: such a model of organisation can be effective in some circumstances only. To employ the military metaphor, it may be appropriate to using a well-motivated army in a 'war of manoeuvre', when the objectives are clearly specified and attainable. (Thus it provided the basis for local strike committee organisation in 1926, which has so impressed many historians.)[148] But the 'army' after 1920 was not well-motivated: its morale was low; its willingness to take action could not be assumed. In short, the concept of organisation available tended to conceal the relationship between organisation and the legitimisation of action. Instead, it laid stress on the direction of action: it emphasised tactics at the expense of strategy.

Of course, as the depression became more entrenched, an awareness of other problems developed. A 'Trade Union Organising Committee' established by the Trades and Labour Council at the end of 1922, for instance, 'acted on the principle not only that it was necessary to get Non-Unionists into Unions, but that a working class consciousness should be created'.[149] This was no small task, and similar statements echoed plaintively through the succeeding years: 'If Trade Unionism is expected to kill poverty and assist in uplifting mankind, there must be solidarity'.[150] Yet the tendency was to distinguish organisation from propaganda, but to view the latter simply as one task to be executed by the former. An example of this is the 'Back to the Unions' campaign of 1923: initiated by the TUC with a self-explanatory purpose, it was pursued in Edinburgh by a series of public and works-gate meetings, demonstrations and marches, with handbills, posters, and rejoining forms. Yet the campaign made no recommendations about union behaviour, let alone union structure, although it was necessary to set up ad hoc committees (of district union officials, and on organising women) to run it - perhaps implicit recognition of the inadequacy of existing institutions for the tasks now necessary.[151]

Some debate on the relationship between organisational structure and the attitudes and actions of union members did arise in the mid-1920s. But it did not move beyond existing notions of organisation. Whilst there began to be an awareness that 'For the successful work of the Trade Unions, understanding and performing their work is not enough; special knowledge, tact, and ability are the essentials', this was to be 'combined with a disciplined sense of confidence in the authoritative decisions of a local or national General Council. The tendency towards amalgamation in the Trade Union world is in the right direction'.[152] In short, notions of hierarchy and discipline continued to rule supreme. The two main sources of criticism illustrate this. The first drew on the tradition of industrial unionism:

> A policy of scientific amalgamation is needed. Not the haphazard amalgamation which consists in knocking two or three unions into one, regardless of whether the financial product is a homogeneous whole, but amalgamation on industrial lines, so that there may be one union for each industry, in which will be organised all the workers of that industry - manual, clerical, technical and adminis-trative. When we see the necessity for sinking sectional differences and interests, and organising on these lines, we will have taken a tremendous step in the direction of workers' control of industry.[153]

Thus even the industrial unionists, so closely allied in basic thinking to syndicalism, attempted to change union organisation only to another mechanistic structure. The second source of criticism likewise came from the left. It did stress the importance of decentralising decision-making to local trades councils and the like. Yet there was no attempt to explore the relationship between organisation and the legitimation of action and - if anything - the authority of the localised committee was to be even more absolute. The view is perhaps most clearly put in a conference motion:

> That this conference agrees to endeavour to co-ordinate all sections of the working classes locally. No one section of workers to act independently of any others, but submit all questions to a Central Committee appointed by this Conference, which shall act in conjunction with the Trades Council for the purpose of defending all the interests of the Working Class.[154]

Trade Union Development

Three inter-related factors suggest why such images of organisation continued to be important in the 1920s. Managerial images of organisation were strongly influenced by analogies with machines, weapons and armies; the managerial mood of the 1920s shifted toward tighter control of work, closer discipline, and more centralised, hierarchical, decision-making. Taylorism began to acquire institutional backing in Britain as consultants applying versions of Taylor's methods were set up.[155] There was, in short, little basis in management thinking for the type of critique of trade union organisation and methods we have discussed.

Second, within the labour movement contributions to thinking about organisation came largely from the political side. The formation of the Communist Party during 1920 and 1921 highlights the process by which the syndicalist tradition was integrated into a 'political' organisation, losing much of its contribution to trade union debate. The Communist Party also soon adopted a view of Bolshevik organisation which led to a concentration on the importance of hierarchical centralist organisation in trade unions also. The Labour Party was in the process of re-organisation into a national, membership organisation in which formal control was centralised. After 1918 (indeed, also before) there was no critique of organisation to threaten the direction being taken.

The major factor in sustaining mechanistic union structures, however, is to be found in the development of industrial relations. During the 1920s, there was a movement toward national bargaining both in engineering and on the railways. Such industries as these set the pace and tone of industrial relations in the 1920s; they were strongly represented in the general institutions of the Edinburgh labour movement. Of course, national bargaining meant something slightly different in each case. But, above all, it regulated: it reduced uncertainty, introducing an element of stability into the framework of decision-making and planning. It reduced differences in labour relations practice between firms, areas, or divisions to a minimum. It meant that where disputes did occur, the employer had advance warning, and thus time to prepare. It reduced the danger of disputes that occurred in one firm disrupting the work of others which bought from or sold to it. Agreed national bargaining structures also enabled employers to enlist union leaders' support in certain tasks: immediately, they became committed to the method and timings for settling disputes; subsequently, they might become committed to the terms of substantive agreements. In short, national bargaining brought order.

National bargaining had certain advantages for unions in common with employers: it reduced the unit costs, particularly in terms of time, of negotiation; it allowed for the development of expertise (though whether this opportunity was exploited is less clear); it increased the stability, and reduced the uncertainty, of the bargaining situation. But there were apparent advantages to the union rather than the employer. The NUR leaders, for instance, seem to have seen their negotiating machinery agreed in 1921 as a means of preserving some of the gains made during 1919 and 1920, in the face of threatening 'decontrol'.[156] In engineering, it could ensure a basic standard in nearly all firms: 'if that is so then so much the better' was the response of an ASE negotiator when assured that his belief that 'the worse [sic] offenders' in the disputed matter 'do not come under the Federation at all' was incorrect.[157]

One of the advantages of a national negotiating machinery to unions' leaders was the prospect of stabilising external conditions so that their internal affairs could be sorted out. Administrative effectiveness was an urgent priority for national as for local union organisations in the years of rapid membership growth. According to one NUR member, for instance, where 38 clerks had been employed at Unity House in 1914, there were 51 in 1920;[158] visiting the Headquarters,

> he had found the clerks on the point of revolt, because their claim of a 50 per cent [sic] had been thrown back on them by the EC: who had been told they had refused to work overtime when the truth was they were working excessive hours.[159]

There were clearly administrative problems. And, as memberships began to fall after 1920, union leaders faced the problems of managing decline: the need to cut costs, even to reduce their establishment of officials and staff, whilst having to cope with the problems generated by the onset of depression.

We now turn to the implication of national negotiations and procedures for union organisation, and images of organisation. If agreements were reached above plant level, then the leaders who negotiated them had in some way to ensure their members' compliance (or to find some acceptable reason for not doing so).[160] One method, clearly, was only to make agreements which were assured of members' enthusiastic acceptance: whilst this was difficult even during 1917-20, it became far more so thereafter. Another was to persuade members that an agreement was the best possible in the circumstances: it may be that this was easier in depression. A third option was to ensure compliance rather than endorsement. This might mean the persuasion of members not by reference to an agreement's merits, but rather by reference to other principles: unity, loyalty to the union, discipline, and the like. It might, however, mean the coercion of members into compliance, through sanctions of various kinds.

This implied an important shift in the functional focus of union structure: whereas in 1917-20 the main function of union structures was to assimilate new members, during the 1920s it became the control of members. Before 1920 union achievements were likely to commend them to their members; during the later period successes were few. Military commanders are wont to equate morale with discipline. Where motivation failed, discipline could replace it. In the aftermath of the General Strike and the humiliating terms of settlement on the railways, an NUR branch member 'in no uncertain manner condemned our Leaders for their signing such a settlement and then fining our members for taking part in the strike'.[161] In general, measures were taken to strengthen leadership control at an earlier stage, as the NUR introduced extra tests for prospective organisers in 1924.[162]

Unions are, of course, inherently difficult to discipline. They contain important elements of legitimate authority at both 'top' and 'bottom', and institutions able to articulate opposition to centralised leaderships. Among the Railwaymen, where branches could be large and strong, there was a strong tradition of 'unofficial' organisation. Thus the NUR No. 1 branch conducted a war of words with their National Executive Committee throughout the early 1920s. (Even so, the principle of loyalty to the union could be a strong one, especially where its own members were not involved: the branch could approve even of the Executive Committee and J.H. Thomas in their action against an 'unconstitutional' strike - it was necessary 'to take every step to safeguard the constitution of our Society'.)[163] It was, therefore, impossible for this process totally to transform union structures.

But the influence of nationally agreed procedures was felt not only nationally: indeed their essence was just the involvement of union officials (permanent and lay) at all levels. So the Engineers participated in district conferences, the Railwaymen in departmental committees, even though they might doubt their power and effectiveness:[164] in so doing, local activists too came to rely - in part - on the disciplining functions of union structure. Although they might object to the authority of national officers, local activists themselves came partially to rely on union organisation to ensure their agreements were adhered to: there was, in short, no constituency with power to mobilise resources within the unions which did not also have some stake in the way they were organised.

INDUSTRY, MANAGEMENT AND LABOUR

The Great War and the years that followed it was a period of rapid and contradictory change for industry, work organisation and trade unions. Our examination of four diverse sectors of Edinburgh's economy has shown a spectrum of responses. There was no ineluctable trend toward larger-scale production and tighter, direct, control of labour. Indeed, during and just after the war, employers adopted strategies which (in various ways) reflected an accommodation to labour strength, and a reliance on the technical abilities of at least some workers. Neither was strong direct control the immediate resort of employers when depression came. Probably such methods were technically feasible only in the larger enterprises (such as the Castle Mills, and the railway companies); even there, strong and well-established unions could temper it (as on the railways), while the North British Rubber Company learnt that eliminating union strength could also bring problems. The structure of Edinburgh's engineering industry generally hindered the development of large-scale enterprises, and its products relied heavily on workers' skills. So even when labour was economically weak, employers could not ignore the unions. Union strength in printing was well-established, and little eroded.

In these conditions unions were able to make substantial advances until about 1920 or 1921. These were based on wider influences: in particular, the war generated problems which were amenable to union action, and shifted the language of industrial motivation in directions which furthered union interests. At the same time, trade union organisations developed along lines which discouraged them from taking vigorous, mobilising, roles. Their organisational structures became more centralised, at every level. This meant that after 1920 (when circumstances turned against them) the trade union movement could resist less effectively. It also meant that, as it became more difficult to find principles which would persuade members to take effective action, unions tended to rely on notions of institutional loyalty (to the union) - even, in the last resort, on disciplinary action.

NOTES

1.   A. Gramsci, Selections from the Prison Notebooks (London, 1971), pp.339-400.
2.   For a helpful discussion of these processes, see P.J. Armstrong, J.F.B. Goodman and J.D. Hyman, Ideology and Shop-floor Industrial Relations (London, 1981), esp. pp.35-56.
3.   The industrial sociological literature on this area is now large. See e.g., D. Roy, 'Banana Time: Job Satisfaction and Informal Interaction', Human Organisation, vol. 18 (1960), pp.158-68; H. Beynon, Working for Ford (Harmondsworth, 1973), esp. pp. 129-50; H. Behrend, 'The Effort Bargain', Industrial and Labor Relations Review, vol. 10 (1957), pp.503-15.
4.   Gramsci, Prison Notebooks, p. 419.
5.   K. Wedderburn, The Worker and the Law (Harmondsworth, 1971), esp. pp. 52-3, 264.
6.   Armstrong et al., Ideology, esp. pp.68-70.
7.   E. Batstone, I. Boraston, S. Frenkel, Shop Stewards in Action (Oxford, 1977), esp. pp.23-76.
8.   G.S. Bain, R. Bacon, J. Pimlott, 'The Labour Force', in A.H. Halsey, Trends in British Society since 1900 (London, 1972), p.127.
9.   TC AR 1916, p.2.
10. Ibid., 1918, p.4.
11. Ibid., 1919, p.2.
12. Ibid., 1918, p.4.
13. Ibid.
14. Ibid., 1919, p.2.
15. Ibid., 1918, pp.7-8.
16. TC minutes, 10 September 1918.
17. NUC Edin. branch minutes, 4 March 1918.

18. TC AR 1919, p.2.
19. Ibid., 1918, p.7.
20. Ibid., 1918, pp.4-7.
21. Ibid., 1919, p.5; A. Tuckett, The Scottish Carter (London, 1967), pp.134-5, 144-5.
22. E.g., TC AR 1916, p.2; ESAE&I and ASE, 'Local Conference Proceedings: Recognition of Shop Stewards', 18 January 1918, passim.
23. TC AR 1918, p.7; cp ibid., 1917, p.16.
24. Ibid., 1918, pp.4-7. On J.H. Moore, see Labour Standard, 9 October 1926.
25. TC AR 1918, p.7.
26. TC minutes, 17 September 1918; see also 30 July, 13, 20, 27 August, 10 September, for a dispute between Wiredrawers and Workers unions.
27. Cp A. Marwick, The Deluge (Harmondsworth, 1967), esp. pp.162-78. On wider uses of 'efficiency' before the war, see H.C.G. Matthew, The Liberal Imperialists (Oxford, 1973), esp. pp. 225-64, 291-5.
28. Marwick, Deluge, p.131.
29. TC AR 1918, p.6. These were placed by the Scottish Co-operative Wholesale Society; St Cuthberts, the main Edinburgh store, placed separate (and more commercially-oriented) advertisements. Cp also Marwick, Deluge, pp.132-3.
30. Cd. 8669, p.3.
31. NAUL No. 292 branch minutes, 1 May 1917.
32. TC AR 1918, p.8.
33. Ibid., p.7; cp ibid., 1916, p.2.
34. Notably by the Munitions of War Acts. E.g., the 1917 Act (s.9) reads: 'No worker employed on or in connection with munitions work shall be discharged on the ground that he has joined or is a member of a trade union, or that he has taken part in any trade dispute and if any employer discharges a workman on any such ground he shall be guilty of an offence ...'
35. TC AR 1916, p.2; a branch was formed, and wage increases won.
36. Cp B. Waites, 'The Effect of the First World War on Class and Status in England, 1910-1920', Journal of Contemporary History, vol. 11 (1976), esp. p.42.
37. TC AR 1916, pp.5-6.
38. Ibid., 1919, p.13.
39. See, e.g., ibid., 1918, p.12.
40. E.g., Waites, 'Effect of First World War'; Marwick,

Deluge, esp. pp.218-26, 316-7.
41. NUC Edin. branch minutes, 5 August 1918.
42. TC AR 1919, p.5.
43. Ibid., 1918, p.8.
44. Ibid.
45. Ibid., 1919, p.5.
46. Ibid., 1918, p.12.
47. Ibid., 1917, p.8.
48. The account of this dispute is drawn from ibid., 1918, pp.7-8, 20.
49. TC AR 1919, p.6.
50. Ibid.
51. TC minutes, 10 September 1918.
52. Both TC AR 1919, p.6, and TC minutes, 10 September 1918, give this impression.
53. TC minutes, 17 September 1918 (cp also 12 February 1918). Arbitration was a normal part of trades councils' activities at this time: see A. Clinton, The Trade Union Rank and File (Manchester, 1977) esp. pp.20-1. The dispute was eventually resolved in the Shop Assistants' favour: see TC minutes, 5 October 1918.
54. TC minutes, 17 September, 15 October 1918.
55. TC AR 1919, p.6 (see also p.22).
56. W. Wallace (employers' chairman) in ESAE&I and ASE, 'Local Conference Proceedings: in re Engineers Working Rules', 19 September 1919, p.7.
57. TC minutes, 19 November 1918. For personal information on Alexander Caldwell, I am grateful to Mr F. Lawson.
58. NAUL No. 292 branch minutes, 14 November 1918.
59. NUR Edin. No. 1 branch minutes, 10, 24 November 1918.
60. TC AR 1919, p.2.
61. K. Middlemas, Politics in Industrial Society (London, 1979), p.145.
62. Ibid., pp.128, 146-7, 160-1.
63. P. Maguire, 'Employers Attitudes to Industrial Relations and Government Policies 1915-20', paper read to Society for the Study of Labour History conference, 27 November 1982 (abstract); cp Middlemas, Politics, p.127.
64. R. Lowe, 'The Failure of Consensus in Britain: the National Industrial Conference 1919-1921', Historical Journal, vol. 21 (1978), pp.649-75; V. Allen, The Sociology of Industrial Relations (London, 1971), pp.83-90; H. Ramsay, 'Cycles of Control: Worker Participation in Sociological and Historical Perspective', Sociology, vol. 11 (1977), esp. 485-8;

Middlemas, Politics, pp.137-41.
65. TC AR 1920, p.2.
66. Ibid.
67. See above, Chapter 3; TC AR 1920, p.2; TC minutes, 21 September 1919.
68. TC minutes, 18 July 1920.
69. NAUL No. 292 branch minutes, 23 February 1919.
70. TC AR 1919, p.17.
71. Ibid., p.6.
72. Ibid., 1920, p.5.
73. ESAE&I and ASE, 'in re Engineers Working Rules', 19 September 1919, p.3.
74. D. Englander and J. Osborne, 'Jack, Tommy and Henry Dubb: the Armed Forces and the Working Class', Historical Journal, vol. 21 (1978), p.620.
75. TC AR 1920, p.5.
76. TC minutes, 20 May 1919.
77. TC AR 1920, p.10.
78. Ibid.
79. TC minutes, 11 November 1919. The TC was divided on - at least - how to tackle the problem of ex-servicemen. An attempt (ibid., 18 November 1919) to try to maintain the connection with the ex-servicemen's federation was agreed by just 34 votes to 27.
80. TC AR 1920, p.10.
81. Allen, Sociology of Industrial Relations, esp. pp.169-81; cp A. Bullock, The Life and Times of Ernest Bevin, vol. 1 (London 1960), pp.107-11, 147-9.
82. See TC AR 1920, pp.10-13; Chapter 8 below.
83. See Middlemas, Politics, pp.146-51; J. Foster, 'British Imperialism and the Labour Aristocracy' in J. Skelley (ed.), The General Strike 1926 (London, 1976) pp.31-6.
84. E.g., TC AR 1919, p.37; cp Whiteside, 'Welfare Legislation and the Unions', pp.857-74.
85. TC AR 1919, p.35.
86. The following TC officials were JPs (with dates of appointment as justices): Alexander Smith, Secretary 1911-25 (by 1915); Andrew Eunson, President 1916-19 (1917); Alexander Caldwell, Vice President 1918/19, President 1919/20 (1919); George Hogg, Secretary, Leith United TC and LP 1920-1 (by 1921). Other trade union JPs (1916-20) included J.R. Bell (NUR) and J. Campbell (Bookbinders: by 1919 local organiser of the Shop Assistants).
87. TC AR 1920, p.2.
88. See NAUL No. 292 branch minutes, 8 August 1918, 16

January 1919.

89. See. e.g., 'Award by the Referee [A. Eunson, JP] in the Dispute between the Amalgamated Engineering Union and the Scottish Motor Traction Company Limited', 23 August 1920. In this case the union JP found in the union's favour.

90. J.F. Wallace (ASE) in ESAE&I and ASE, 'in re Engineers Working Rules', 19 September 1919, p.31.

91. See above, Chapter 5.

92. TC AR 1919, pp.9-13.

93. NAUL No. 292 branch minutes, 14 August 1917.

94. Ibid., April, 11, 15, 21 May 1917.

95. Ibid., 28 June 1917.

96. Although an 'all-day man' was appointed as Secretary in August 1917 (ibid., 15 July, 14 August 1917), and the works seems to have been a major object of the local (full-time) NAUL organiser's attention.

97. NUC Edin. branch minutes, 7 January 1918, 13 October 1919.

98. Ibid., 12, 19 May 1919.

99. For its size, the Edinburgh NUC contained a remarkable number of men and women active in the local labour movement. The following can be identified as NUC members between 1911 and 1916 (when branch membership was about 25) and as active in the local movement during the following decade:

T.A. Cairns (first referred to in NUC minutes: 3 June 1912): T&LC Treasurer 1922-5, President 1925/6, EC 1926-30; SDF Edin. branch EC 1921/2, delegate to T&LC 1922/3.

William Elger (1 July 1912): T&LC EC 1920/1, President 1921/2; SDF Edin. branch EC 1921/2; NUC Edin. branch President 1913-15; STUC General Secretary 1922-46.

Grace Mewhort (1 July 1912): T&LC EC 1916-20, Vice-President 1920/1; STUC General Council 1921/2; LP Town Council candidate 1919.

Frank Smithies (7 October 1912): T&LC Librarian 1922/3, Political Officer 1923-35; SDF Edin. branch EC 1921/2.

George Williamson (1 September 1913): T&LC Treasurer 1920-3; ILP Edin. West branch delegate to T&LC.

J.P.M. Millar (6 September 1915): ILP Central branch member; NCLC Organising Tutor for Edin. c.1921-3, General Secretary 1923-63.

100. E.g., about 100 at the North British Rubber Co., about 60 in the Ministry of Labour: NUC Edin. branch minutes, 17 March, 5 May 1919.

101. Ibid., 16 January 1919.

102. Ibid., 17 March 1919.
103. Ibid., 21 April, 5 May 1919.
104. TC minutes, 13 May 1919.
105. TC ARs 1918, p.26, 1919, p.26; TC minutes 1918-19, passim.
106. TC ARs 1916-21; S. Lewenhak, 'Women in the Leadership of the Scottish Trades Union Congress 1897-1970', Scottish Labour History Society Journal, no. 7 (1973), p.14.
107. NAUL No. 292 branch minutes, 4 September 1919; cp TC minutes, 9 September 1919.
108. NAUL No. 292 branch minutes, 15 May 1917, 14 May 1918, 29 January 1920: their activity was probably confined to collecting dues and dispensing benefit.
109. TC AR 1919, p.5.
110. Ibid., 1920, p.13.
111. Cp S. Macintyre, A Proletarian Science. Marxism in Britain 1917-1933 (Cambridge, 1980), pp.177-80, for the very similar social democratic ('Labour Socialist') view of the state.
112. T&LC AR 1921, p.9.
113. Ibid., 1922, p.8: the T&LC sent a circular to this effect to its affiliates on 7 December 1921.
114. Ibid., p.11.
115. NAUL No. 292 branch minutes, 29 January 1920.
116. TC AR 1920, p.5.
117. T&LC AR 1921, pp.5-6.
118. Ibid., 1922, p.4.
119. Ibid., 1921, p.6.
120. Ibid., 1922, p.4. On the popular press, see M. Cowling, The Impact of Labour 1920-1924 (Cambridge, 1971), esp. pp. 45-59; on the state and the press, see Foster, 'British Imperialism', pp.32-7; Middlemas, Politics, pp.153-4.
121. T&LC AR 1922, p.4; cp Middlemas, Politics, pp.158-61.
122. Only one T&LC official became a JP 1920-7: Peter Herd (AEU East branch; T&LC Assistant Secretary and Secretary), in 1922 or 1923. The names of 'Working-Class Justices of the Peace' were recorded in T&LC ARs from 1922. In 1922 there were 12 such JPs (of whom 5 were current or former councillors or parish councillors, and 5 can be identified as trade union officials). In 1923 and 1924 these figures had become respectively 18, 6 and 7; in 1925-7 they were 20, 6 and 8.
123. See R.H. Tawney, 'The Abolition of Economic Controls 1918-21', Economic History Review, vol. 13 (1943), pp.1-30;

P. Abrams, 'The Failure of Social Reform 1918-20', Past and Present, no. 24 (1963), pp.42-64; R. Lowe, 'The Erosion of State Intervention in Britain', Economic History Review, vol. 31 (1978), pp.270-86.

124. See Cowling, Impact of Labour, pp.51-2, 55-8.

125. TC AR 1919, p.4: emphasis in original.

126. Ibid., 1920, p.12: capitals in original.

127. Perhaps the sole exception is in a somewhat theoretical discussion of the origins of unemployment in T&LC AR 1921, p.5: 'Capital interest is being paid from a camel's hump, begot of artificial prosperity and profiteering, while unemployment stands sobre and foreboding over every worker's home.'

128. Cp ESAE&I and ASE, 'Local Conference Proceedings: Marine Repairs (Shore and Marine Engineers)', 30 April 1920, when the union accepted that 'if we were to take up a stiff-necked attitude ... the [ship] owner will naturally say, "we are not going to Leith, we will send them [their ships] to where we will get them repaired without trouble" '. But other principles outweighed this: the quality of work done, precedent, the respective expertise of the ship and shore engineers, the need to share work equitably - above all, the union's claim, evidently believed, that its members were incensed, and would take action.

129. ESAE&I and ASE, 'In re Engineers Working Rules', 19 September 1919, pp.9, 11, 15, 31, 37.

130. ESAE&I, AEU and SBU, 'Local Conference Proceedings: Brass Moulders' Rates - Levelling up to Ironmoulders', 4 April 1921, p.8.

131. ESAE&I and AEU, 'Local Conference Proceedings: in re Outworking Allowances', 22 January 1923, p.3.

132. Ibid., p.23.

133. E&AE(EofS) and AEU, 'Local Conference Proceedings: in re Allowances for Repair Work on Diesel, Semi-Diesel and Oil Internal Combustion Engines', 23 October 1925, p.29.

134. ESAE&I, AEU and SBU, 'Brass Moulders' Rates', 4 April 1921, p.3.

135. ESAE&I and AEU, 'In re Outworking Allowances', 22 January 1923, p.16.

136. ESAE&I and AEU, 'Conference Proceedings: Proposed Reduction of $12\frac{1}{2}$ per cent on Piecework Prices of Brass Finishers and Brass Moulders in Gas Meter Making Works', 20 July 1923, p.9.

137. E&AE(EofS) and AEU, 'Adjourned Local Conference Proceedings: in re Local Application for 20/- per week

Increase in Wages', 22 April 1926, pp.12-14.

138. See, e.g., NUR Edin. No. 1 branch minutes, 29 January 1922: the continuing fall in membership 'was accounted [for] by the number of dismissals, &c'.

139. ESAE&I and AEU, 'Piecework Prices of Brass Finishers and Brass Moulders', 20 July 1922, p.3.

140. Ibid., p.11.

141. Bain et al., 'Labour Force', pp.123-6.

142. T&LC minutes, 16 November 1920.

143. Ibid., 28 June 1921.

144. Ibid., 1 November 1921.

145. T&LC AR 1922, p.4.

146. T&LC Minutes, 4 March 1923: about 150 delegates attended.

147. Ibid., 18 March 1923: the conference had been adjourned from a fortnight earlier to debate this, its last motion.

148. Cp the Methil Council of Action organisation chart in E. Burns, General Strike 1926. Trades Councils in Action (London, 1926); I. MacDougall, 'Edinburgh' in J. Skelley (ed.), The General Strike 1926 (London, 1976), esp. 148-9.

149. T&LC minutes, 16 December 1922.

150. T&LC AR 1925, p.15.

151. T&LC minutes, 8, 15 May 1923.

152. T&LC AR 1924, p.13.

153. Labour Standard, 10 October 1925.

154. T&LC minutes, 18 March 1922. Trades councils' role may have been stressed as a likely source of alternative (left-wing) policies, rather than from a commitment to decentralisation as such.

155. G. Brown, Sabotage (Nottingham, 1977), esp. 231-51.

156. P. Bagwell, The Railwaymen, vol. 1 (London, 1963), pp.408-11.

157. ESAE&I and ASE, 'Marine Repairs', 30 April 1920, p.5.

158. NUR Edin. No. 1 branch minutes, 28 March 1920. According to another member (a member of the NUR's NEC), there were 100 clerks at Head Office in 1920. NUR membership grew from 273,362 to 481,081 during 1914-19; in 1920 it fell back to 457,836 (Bagwell, Railwaymen, pp.699-700).

159. NUR Edin. No. 1 branch minutes, 14 March 1920.

160. The legitimacy of procedure and agreement might be outweighed by other principles - e.g., absurdity - as when an AEU negotiator pointed out that 'our members are very discontent on this question ... [I]t would be very absurd for

our men to say, "Oh, wait till a national agreement comes along and we will start the job when it is completed". Yet that is an analogous position'. See E&AE(EofS) and AEU, 'Allowances for Repair Work', 23 October 1925, p.43.
161. NUR Edin. No. 1 branch minutes, 11 July 1926.
162. Ibid., 23 March 1924.
163. Ibid., 29 June 1924.
164. Cp an NUR member's comment (Edin. No. 1 branch minutes, 22 October 1922) 'on the power of these [departmental] comittees [sic] which he had doubts about'.

Chapter Seven

LABOUR POLITICS AND THE IMPACT OF WAR

What was previously secondary or subordinate, or
even incidental, is now taken to be primary -
becomes the nucleus of a new ideological and
theoretical complex.[1]

We have drawn little distinction between trade unions and
political parties, concentrating on what is common to both:
persuasion, mobilisation, collective action, and so forth.
There are, of course, differences: trade unions typically
have a narrower constituency (the members of a certain
factory or industry); parties tend to deploy more general
principles in seeking support for action; parties and unions
normally concentrate on different institutions (parliament
and local councils on the one hand, for instance, disputes
procedures and joint conferences with employers'
federations on the other). Commonly much is made of these
differences: thus, for instance, sustained attempts to define
trade unionism narrowly in terms of workplace activity, or
to define legitimate political action in terms of certain
formal political institutions. But stressing the shared
characteristics of trade unions and political parties reminds
us that there can be many definitions of the political 'party'.
Indeed, labour politics during and after the Great War can
be seen in terms of an internal struggle for mastery between
adherents of divergent concepts of political action.

In late Victorian and Edwardian Britain, and through the
war, just as there were varying conceptions of socialism, so
there were varying conceptions within the labour movement
of the institutions which could bring an advance to
socialism. This has been little-investigated by historians.[2]
For instance, Ross McKibbin's invaluable study of the
Labour Party's organisation shows how important trades
councils were even after 1918, yet does not consider
whether this reflected quite different views of the party's
role (rather than mere administrative convenience).[3] And
Robert McKenzie, while contrasting the self-images of

Labour and Conservative parties, does not suggest the latter changed with the passage of time, certainly after 1918.[4] The general assumption has been that we know from contemporary observation the characteristics of a mature political party; the historian's role is to show how a particular party developed into its mature form.

Organisational forms, however, are not neutral. They are related to political practices: the adoption of an organisational structure will affect a party's political activities, and even outlook, while organisational structures are themselves in part the products of political processes. That a certain type of organisation was adopted by the Labour Party in the 1920s is, therefore, a fact of great significance to the subsequent shape of labour politics. We explore this aspect of the development of political organisation from two points of view.

On the one hand, we use categories from the sociology of organisations (bureaucracy, organic and mechanistic structures, and so forth) which we have found helpful in our discussion of industrial and trade union development. On the other, we suggest a distinction between direct and indirect mobilisation. A trade union or political party (or other group) mobilises people directly when it generates the principles which will persuade them to take action, and makes contact with them, alone. To mobilise indirectly involves the union or party deploying principles generated by others, and persuading other institutions to undertake (or join in) the process of persuading people to act. Thus a party may contact the people directly, through propaganda meetings, canvassing, posters, broadsheets, and the like; or it may try to influence or mobilise them indirectly, by winning publicity in the press, by activity on local authorities, by working through trade unions, and so forth.

Of course, in reality trade unions and political parties tend to operate both directly and indirectly; but the balance between the two is important for two reasons. First, indirect mobilisation involves, in effect, constructing alliances with mediating institutions: these will rarely be on precisely the basis which motivates the initiating institution, and thus the meaning of the action will be (as it were) negotiated. Since most political action involves indirect mobilisation, political institutions are (consciously or otherwise) engaged in continual negotiations with other social institutions, so that the meaning of political actions is constantly under review. Second, enlisting the support of another institution involves an engagement between the values and social patterns of the two institutions; and both may change in the process. This may lead to tensions within (say) a party between those deeply committed to its long-standing outlook or methods, and those who value the potential gains from alliances: tensions which may, in extremis, render the party ineffectual, or lead to its disintegration.

LABOUR AND SOCIALIST POLITICS BEFORE 1914

When socialist organisation began to emerge in Edinburgh in the 1880s there was already 'a relatively autonomous working-class industrial and political movement, conditioned by the position and outlook of the labour aristocracy, and effectively contained within the forms of social hegemony characteristic of the period':[5] in effect, this meant containment within a Liberal coalition, and an orientation toward achieving representation on those bodies where political power apparently resided. By the later 1880s the socialists had found some measure of support, at least on certain issues, although their support was unstable.[6]

Socialism in the 1880s was marked by great faith in the powers of propaganda, of direct, almost missionary, methods to win men and women to the 'cause'.[7] With the surge of unionisation from the late 1880s, other strategies became possible. By 1892 a branch of the Independent Labour Party had been formed, and in that year fielded a parliamentary candidate in the Central division.[8] The socialists' electoral impact during the early 1890s, together with their offering a programme relevant to industrial issues, led to a 'definite shift' by the Trades Council 'towards co-operation with the socialists, on an "independent labour" basis'.[9] A new organisation was created to further this end. The Workers' Municipal Committee (from 1899) provided for the affiliation of union branches, co-operative societies and political bodies, paralleling - indeed, anticipating - the formation of the national Labour Representation Committee. Within a year a 'substantial number of trade union branches, a well as the ILP and the SDF', had affiliated; and at the election of 1900 the election of the first 'Labour' councillor was secured.[10]

So it was characteristic of the socialist movement - from the 1890s at least until the end of the Great War, and at least in Edinburgh - that when it wished to pursue a new strategy, rather than adapting an existing institution, it

147

formed an entirely new one for the purpose. This meant there was a considerable overlap in the membership of socialist and labour organisations. It also tended to emphasise the range of objectives and methods within the movement, and to differentiate them from one another, so that by the later 1890s ideological differences were becoming more important. The SDF, for instance, was riven during 1901-3 by a dispute over how far socialist principles should be compromised in a pursuit of political power.[11]

In as much as politics can be reduced to political institutions, the politics of labour in Edinburgh after 1900 can be sketched thus. For electoral activity, there was the Workers' Municipal Committee: or, from 1905, a branch of the Scottish Workers' Representation Committee, which in April 1907 changed its name to 'The Labour Party, Scottish Section, Edinburgh Branch'.[12] The unions' organisational and political break with Liberalism was not yet reflected in co-operation with socialists on an explicitly socialist basis. Even the Labour Party's object after 1907 was just 'The Independent Representation of Labour on all Governing and Administrative Bodies'.[13] To the Labour Party the Trades Council was affiliated, and through the Labour Party it pursued its electoral ambitions: many of its other activities were, however, political in other senses and were pursued independently - as its support for a 'Right to Work Committee' ('We believe the claim ... to be one of simple justice');[14] or its attempts to improve technical education facilities in the city. [15] Trade union branches could pursue 'non-industrial' issues by affiliation to the Trades Council (as 51 branches did in 1908);[16] a few also affiliated to the Labour Party, but most were involved in this electoral activity only at one remove, through the Trades Council.

These trade union bodies were joined, in the local branch of the Labour Party, by the ILP. Although explicitly a socialist organisation, the ILP's strength 'was not the possession of a coherent political philosophy, but the religious fervour with which it attacked the immediate tasks it saw before it'.[17] Central control was weak; it was an organisational home for many who wished to associate themselves with socialism, but with no particular version of it. The ILP became the Labour Party's public face. Its members carried out the propaganda and fought the elections; trade unionists who actively supported Labour joined it. Its importance was well-recognised: let us look at the only Parliamentary division fought by Labour before the war (Leith, which was contested in January 1910 and at a by-election in February 1914). An experienced Labour campaigner, who had already fought North Belfast twice, wrote to Ramsay MacDonald on receiving a 'unanimous invitation to ... address a meeting with the view of selection as Candidate'. MacDonald, then Secretary of the national Labour Party, asked his 'present view of the candidate's chances there',[18] thought it 'a good constituency', but would not commit himself to 'very strong advice', just because 'I was never altogether satisfied with the character of the men, taken as a whole, who composed the ILP there. If I have any hesitation about it, it is owing to this latter fact.'[19] In short, other affiliates to a Labour Party could not compensate for weaknesses in the ILP.

By 1914 the Labour Party had made substantial advances: a councillor was returned in 1909, joined by two others in 1911, and three more in 1913.[20] Three Labour members were returned to the School Board in 1911; a Labour Parish Councillor was elected in 1908.

Apart from the ILP, the most vital socialist party in Edinburgh during the early years of the century was the Socialist Labour Party. This broke with the SDF in 1903, led by a number of the Scottish branches and heavily influenced by the American Marxist, Daniel De Leon: Edinburgh and Leith were at the head of this movement, and indeed the party's national headquarters, and its publishing house, were in Edinburgh until the war. In Edinburgh, the SLP was the main representative of Marxist socialism. Whereas the ILP was an essentially open organisation, with little dogma (but, by the same token, little theory), and tolerant of a wide range of views within its membership, the SLP was based on a highly specific theory of social change. It would have no truck with parliament; 'pure and simple' trade unions blocked the way to socialism, and should be replaced by socialist trade unions. Members were expected to adhere rigidly to the party's principles. Indeed Neil Maclean, its most prominent member, was expelled when in 1908 he joined the Edinburgh 'Right to Work' Committee and took part in its delegation to the Town Council.[21]

From about 1908 the SLP began to suffer a number of problems. Its theoretical clarity was eroded, as De Leon gave his support to the Industrial Workers of the World's amalgam of socialism, syndicalism, and industrial unionism: the way ahead now called for industrial, rather than social- ist, unions.[22] The labour unrest provided contemporary examples of trade unionism which, if not socialist, were neither pure nor simple.[23] Thus internal debates on strategy developed, which led to disputes about party organisation. Members were permitted to address outside bodies and hold trade union office.[24] The Edinburgh branch claimed that the SLP

> had allowed itself to be dominated by an official
> gang. A large number of members had only a dim
> conception of what the Party stood for. Suffice it
> to say that fully three-fourths of the Party consis-
> ted of members who were connected with shop
> stewardism.[25]

In 1911 the branch was expelled. (Its members in June 1912 established the British Section of the International Socialist Labour Party,[26] an organisation whose subsequent record lends credence to the view that the nominal grandeur of socialist organisations is inversely related to their significance.)

Nonetheless, the mainstream of the SLP gained in influence as its members began to involve themselves in the trade union movement. Its influence was particularly strong in the NUR at the height of the union's flirtation with syndicalism and industrial unionism; and in the infant Labour College movement. Thus John S. Clarke, one of the SLP's most accomplished propagandists, gave a series of lectures to the Edinburgh No. 1 branch of the NUR, under Central Labour College auspices, from 1912 or 1913;[27] and, from the branch's post-war attitudes, there is every reason to believe he made some impact - no doubt on fertile ground. Yet the party's major activities during the pre-war period were public propaganda: its methods were similar to those of ILP, SDF, and others. Meetings were held, on street corners in large part, but predominantly in two places: on the Mound, just off Princes Street, close to railway station, bus terminus and the centres of working-class residence in the Old Town; and in the East Meadows. Here John S. Clarke (and other good speakers) could gather 'as many as 2,000 people at a time';[28] Hyman Levy, who grew up in the city, described its impact on him thus:

> On Sunday nights the Mound ... became a hotbed of
> political discussion and social analysis. Here a vast
> crowd, sober, washed and clean-collared, fore-
> gathered to listen to speakers, of all political
> complexions ... How was one to disentangle the
> respective differences, if any, of the British

Socialist Party, the Socialist Labour Party, or the
Social Democratic Federation? Time and again
with a copper I could ill afford, I bought a penny
pamphlet with a picture on the outer cover of a
heavily-bearded gentleman called Karl Marx.[29]

So when war came, labour politics in Edinburgh were
not set upon an unchangeable course. Trade unions had allied
with the ILP for electoral purposes; this alliance was
beginning to mark up some successes, but was not on a
socialist basis. The Labour Party was little more than the
name of this electoral coalition. The main activity of the
ILP and of other socialist parties was propaganda; a
relatively unmediated presentation of socialist theories and
analyses to the public. The major exceptions to this were
the ILP's involvement in electoral politics, and the SLP's
attention (from about 1909) to trade unions. The ILP
recognised the importance of working through the Labour
Party, and with trade unions, if socialists were to achieve
practical power; the SLP began to develop an analysis which
allowed it to apply its Marxism to problems of trade union
strategy and organisation. Involvement with bodies of
different political outlook could have caused problems for
both organisations. The ILP escaped serious harm by virtue
of its ideological flexibility: little was demanded of
members save a general belief in socialism; hard labour in
the cause was welcomed, but enforced only by moral
sanctions. In the SLP theory was all; changes in strategy led
to dispute. The solution was a discipline which showed no
favour even to its most noted members.

WAR: NEW ISSUES AND INSTITUTIONS

Though there was a significant anti-war minority within
Edinburgh's labour movement, the necessity of the conflict
was generally accepted. This reflected a patriotism common
to all classes. Returning to Edinburgh from Portobello, the
pacifist Clifford Allen found on his tram a 'state of slight
drunkenness and great hilarity and much hatred of
Germans'.[30] Among the bourgeoisie, vigorous opposition
developed to the establishment of a German chair in
Edinburgh University; even major intellectuals denounced
the language and its literature as unworthy of study.[31] In
the Trades Council, 'many discussions' took place 'on issues
arising out of the European conflict. In the main a general
support has been given to the war and the policy of the
Government'.[32] When, for instance, in 1915 the Council's

executive opposed the Derby Scheme, it argued that the government should instead 'compulsorily organise the nation for the purpose of more effectually prosecuting the War'.[33] Although it was mainly socialists who opposed the war outright, many socialists did not. Of the three wartime Labour councillors of whom we have information, for example, one at least was strongly pro-war, and the other two volunteered for war service, though all three were ILPers.[34] Those opposed to the war seem to have been isolated in the main. The limits of acceptable action were defined by the national interest. But this was often understood in ways which government and employers would have rejected: 'No military necessity, no national peril, can justify punishment without trial - the annul[l]ing of the elementary rights of citizenship'.[35] On specific issues, therefore - trade union questions, say, or civil liberties - the war's opponents could sometimes win allies.

There were four main levels on which the war altered the character of labour and socialist politics. First, just as it generated a host of new issues which were amenable to solution through union mobilisation on a sectional or workplace basis, so it also generated problems which such action was unlikely to solve. The main issues mentioned in the wartime Trades Council and Labour Party annual reports, for instance, were prices and the cost of living, conscription and recruitment, housing, food control, pensions, the plight of disabled ex-servicemen. Of these, prices and the cost of living, together with some aspects of military recruitment, workplace mobilisation could tackle. The remaining problems, however, demanded other forms of action; as they were perceived within the Labour movement as issues on which it was legitimate to take action, so mobilisation of various kinds was attempted - though often unsuccessfully.

The war, secondly, widened labour's institutional horizon. Fundamental to this was the importance of the working class to the war effort: the government needed channels through which to maintain the commitment of the working class, and perhaps the most important lay through the established organisations and leaders of labour. Many labour leaders became deeply involved in affairs - major and minor - of state, thus acquiring 'a stake, if not in the country, at least in the country's official business'.[36] If there were risks, so there were opportunities; it was an awareness of the latter which underlay a discussion of 'The War and the Future' in the 1916 Annual Report of the Trades

152

Council:

> Since hostilities began, the Trade Unions and the
> Labour Party have been specially consulted, and
> their advice sought on matters directly affecting
> their interest. The Prime Minister and Secretaries
> of State have met with them in secret, and private
> information has been given them. Special
> Congresses have been called to be addressed by the
> Government and their military chiefs. Recruiting
> schemes have been hatched with their aid. Labour,
> too, now sits in the Cabinet. On the many
> Committees set up to deal with the industrial and
> other problems arising out of the war, Labour has
> been provided with statutory representation.[37]

In short, there was a plausible view that access to government, and quasi-governmental, institutions, from which it
had previously been excluded, gave labour a greater ability
to defend its interests. The institutions open to labour
representation multiplied locally. There were some, of
course, even before the war; by early 1916 the Trades
Council had assisted with the Derby Scheme, and was
represented on exemption tribunals under the Military
Service Acts;[38] as the war continued, not only was there
increasing labour representation on war-related committees
(such as War Pensions and Food Control),[39] there was also a
new tendency for labour representation to be invited onto
other bodies (such as the Royal Infirmary's Board of
Management).[40]

There were good reasons for imagining that these
processes were concessions, to be exploited to the full while
the opportunity lasted; rather than cunning strategies perpe-
trated by those bent on subduing the working class anew.
Certainly the Trades Council debated the matter:

> The Council had either to face this responsibility
> and the expense it entailed and take that part in
> public administration which opportunity gave, or
> recede to a position of critical aloofness. It wisely
> chose the first alternative ... practically unani-
> mously ...[41]

This form of involvement of labour representatives followed
immediately the rapid expansion of Labour representation
on Town and Parish councils during 1910-13; and coincided
with the period when the new councillors were beginning to
participate in council committees. Perhaps, with just six
councillors, winning representation on the various council

committees was itself an achievement. Thus in 1911/12 the
Edinburgh Labour Party Annual Report contains a Town
Council report which is perfunctory and general, and a plea
from the first Labour councillor that there was 'a good deal
to be learned about City affairs, and the effectiveness of a
representative is not greatest until he has mastered a lot'.[42]
Just six years later Labour councillors were reporting in
detail on a wide range of social issues: housing, transport,
pensions, child welfare, education, food control, and so
forth.[43] This must have been a learning process; the terms
of the representation, and their implications, may not
always have been clear. For leaving aside those areas where
it was achieved through election, labour representation was
granted on restrictive terms. On the Local Food Committee
there were only six labour members out of 15 (and this after
'agitation', and including representatives of the Co-
operative movement);[44] when the Royal Infirmary Board
agreed to workers' representation, it did so by adding five
such representatives to its existing 21.[45] When the Town
Council appointed a Tribunal under the Military Service Act,
it elected two Trades Council nominees (in a Tribunal of 25);
it also elected two Labour councillors 'to sit as Labour
representatives' in an apparent attempt to impose not only
the quantity, but also the character of Labour
representation:

> The Trades Council, while having every confidence
> in the judgement of these two councillors, objected
> to their being regarded as Labour representatives
> in the sense of the provisions of the regulations.
> The Trades Council held, as they were appointed by
> the Town Council to complete the number of Town
> Councillors who were entitled to sit on the
> Tribunals, to call them Labour representatives was
> to give them a dual qualification, and to allow
> more representatives of other interests to take
> office.[46]

It seems that the point was conceded; but the attempt is
clear. So whilst the involvement of labour representatives in
the machinery of government increased substantially, and
thus increased the institutional compass of labour politics,
the representation was limited both in number and in terms
of its involvement.

WAR: THE POLITICAL INSTITUTIONS OF LABOUR
The third way in which the war altered the character of

labour politics was in expanding the movement's institutional resources. For the trade unions, growth had of course
involved organisational problems: successes were achieved
largely on a sectional basis, supported by favourable
economic and ideological circumstances, but with little
support from the movement's institutional structures. In
Edinburgh's labour politics, the restricted role of the Labour
Party continued (and probably became even more limited);
the role of the Trades Council was enhanced; the Trades
Council became somewhat distanced from the Labour Party.
The vitality of an organisation which was, in essence, a
coalition for electoral purposes, inevitably declined during a
period of electoral truce:[47] its rationale had evaporated.
The Edinburgh branch met, on average, every two or three
months during 1917 and 1918. Its discussions appear to have
been desultory: the occasional protest;[48] sporadic attempts
to form ward committees;[49] a letter from Arthur Henderson
suggesting a General Election was imminent: perhaps an
attempt to invigorate the organisation.[50] Labour
representatives on public bodies do not seem to have
reported to the meetings; nor even to have attended.[51] So
the Edinburgh Labour Party was neither electorally
effective (perforce), nor did it effectively supervise its
councillors. It had, in short, little to do.

This contrasts with the position of the Trades Council,
involved as it was in attempts to develop and co-ordinate
union action, and in the apparatus of wartime civil
administration. With certain qualifications (such as the
Town Council's attempt to minimise its representation on
Military Service Tribunals), it was widely perceived as the
representative body of labour in the city - which enhanced
its role within the movement. Clearly the character of the
Trades Council was changed somewhat by this engagement
with government. In 1917 the Annual Report recorded that

> the extra work thrown on the [Trades] Council in
> connection with new administrative bodies formed
> to deal with matters arising out of the war, and the
> lost time of representatives that had to be paid,
> have added materially to the expense of the
> Council's work.[52]

But although the Trades Council was extremely busy, and
although its status was enhanced, it made no real attempt to
strengthen or extend the political institutions of the labour
movement itself. We shall look at two aspects of this.

On the one hand, the Trades Council still found issues

155

on which the joint administrative machinery was manifestly inadequate. This might mean despatching a deputation to the authority which could mend the wrong: arguing 'reasonably', within the vocabulary of motives acceptable to the authority. Or it might mean generating additional or alternative legitimising principles: this might imply creating institutions which could sustain such principles. Housing was the main issue on which labour was excluded from the processes of government and administration. Although the Trades Council's approach was not unsophisticated (and at various times popular discontent ran deep), it was unable to capitalise on this in the form of deep-rooted or lasting organisation.

In 1915 the Clydeside rent strike and the Rent Restriction Act (apparently cause and effect) led directly to the formation of the Scottish Labour Housing Association.[53] But apart from the rent strike's tradition of working class 'direct action', the SLHA also drew on more mainstream patterns of protest. Where the rent strike had involved the development of community-based organisation, the SLHA concentrated on co-ordinating the existing institutions of labour in relation to housing. Over several years, this had some effect on the terms of debate, and played a part in eliciting the government's concessions after the war. But the SLHA's approach was an implicit acceptance that the movement's structure was adequate to deal with housing - in its pattern, if not in extent. Yet there is little sign that this was so.

The Edinburgh Trades Council's involvement with the SLHA reflected this approach. During 1916, for instance, having participated in the Association's founding conference in January, it took up the major grievance of housing for workers at Rosyth Naval Base (many were of course living in the capital).[54] A deputation was sent 'to gain particulars concerning the type of houses provided for workers at the Naval base'; it reported to a Conference of 'Trade Union Branches, Labour and Socialist Bodies, and Women's Guilds',[55] which sent a protest resolution and deputation to the Town Council. 'The deputation protested strongly against the suggested renovation of closed slum property and stated that if new houses could not be provided, that large houses now standing empty, should be commandeered for the workers' use.'[56] Such proposals did not commend themselves to a Town Council replete with property-owners. A subsequent deputation to the Admiralty in London fared little better.[57] The Trades Council's dilemma was that its assertive tone contradicted its suppliant style of approach; yet the latter was inevitable given its unwillingness (or inability) to attempt any restructuring of the movement, and its fundamental commitment to a national interest in the war effort.

The second aspect of the Trades Council's inattention to the institutional base of labour politics is shown in its wartime attitude to the Labour Party. Previously, it had maintained a relatively firm control: the party's Secretary had also been Secretary to the council;[58] as late as 30 July 1914 the council had endeavoured to send its own delegates to a conference to appoint a Scottish Advisory Committee of the Labour Party.[59] During the war, the Trades Council's interest was reduced: the Labour Party served no electoral purpose, and there was no need to deal with Labour councillors through an intermediary. The delegates to the local party elected by the council between 1916 and 1920 (see Table 7.1) were trusted and probably conscientious delegates, well-known to the Trades Council in most (but not all) cases, but not active at its highest levels. (Its Executive Committee was 15 strong during these years.) This is not detailed intervention. Even the records of those who were EC members tell the same story: two were EC members for just one year each; a third who was a member for two years apparently elected against being a delegate to the party in the second. Only one, Wallace, was a man of obvious substance in the council, becoming President in 1920. Yet by 1919, with amalgamation of the two organisations on the immediate agenda, the surprise is that the council was content to have only one EC member as a delegate.

Nor was this institutional lack of concern counteracted by the individual delegates. No Trades Council delegate served on the Labour Party branch executive for 1917/18.[60] In 1918 the council agreed that the attendance of its delegates 'could not be considered satisfactory'[61] (though it made no move to remedy the position: indeed, three of the delegates whose performance was thus criticised were returned again the following year). Neither was there any substantial overlap between leading Trades Council and Labour Party members. No-one who was a member of the Labour Party's executive committee in 1917/18 was also a member of the Trades Council's EC in that or the previous year: there was one common member with the council's

Table 7.1: Edinburgh Trades Council: Delegates to the Labour Party, Edinburgh Branch 1916-20

		Attendance at Trades Council meetings (preceding year)		Trades Council Status
		Actual	Possible	
1916-17				
H. Earl	Nat. League of Blind	24	26	-
John Williamson	Typefounders	22	26	-
J. Murphy	Corporation Employees	24	26	E1916
R. Simpson	Shale Miners	8	8	E1916 & 1917
1917-18				
Jas. Kelly	NU Railwaymen No. 1	15	27	-
J. Rutherford	Shop Assistants (Hairdressers)	13	27	-
J. Coates	Coachmakers	9	13	-
J. Hogg	Rail Clerks	18	27	- (A)
1918-19				
Jas. Kelly	NU Railwaymen No. 1	23	26	E1918
J. Rutherford	Shop Assistants (Hairdressers)	21	26	-
J. Hogg	Rail Clerks	19	26	- (A)
J. Elliott	NU Railwaymen No. 3	12	26	-
1919-20				
Miss Moffat	Postal & Telegraphic Clerks	4	4	-
A. Bain	Furnishing Trades	17	19	-
J. Rutherford	Shop Assistants (Hairdressers)	22	25	-
J.F. Wallace	Engineers (West branch)	22	25	E1919; P1920

Notes: E. On executive committee in year beginning March.
P. President in year beginning March.
A. Whilst not on the executive committee, Hogg was the TC's auditor during the years 1917-18, 1918-19 and 1919-20.

Source: TC ARs, 1916-19.

executive of 1918/19 (but this was the Labour Party's chairman in the period immediately before amalgamation).[62] The Trades Council, then, whilst busy, did not intervene actively to change the institutional structure of labour politics markedly during the war. Yet its involvement in so much quasi-governmental politics inevitably shifted the orientation of labour politics.

We may suppose that the shifting roles of Labour Party and Trades Councils also affected socialist politics in the city: unfortunately, the surviving influence is limited. Probably the ILP suffered a loss of momentum with the suspension of elections; its value to the trade unions - as an electoral ally - was reduced. At the same time, it was riven by the dispute about commitment to the war. Yet what is most striking is the extent to which the ILP absorbed these problems. There is no record of a discussion about the war in the surviving wartime minutes of Edinburgh Central branch.[63] The common attitude seems to have been to concentrate on areas where agreement within the party could be found: issues such as 'Land Socialisation' and opposition to wartime encroachments on civil liberties.[64] Thus it escaped the splits which affected the BSP over the war question. The ILP seems to have been growing at least in 1917 and 1918, and was almost certainly the largest socialist organisation in the city. In 1917 its three branches had a combined membership probably exceeding 300, and the (key) Central branch alone was able to pay its affiliation fee to the Labour Party in February 1919 'on 200 members'.[65] The meetings of the Central branch were held fortnightly, and the average attendance seems to have been about 30: in May 1918 40 members attended a meeting, and this was considered 'good';[66] a few weeks previously about 80 had been 'a good turnout of members' for the branch's annual general meeting.[67]

By the later years of the war the ILP had close informal connections with the trade unions. Of the twelve officials and executive committee members of the Central branch in 1917/18, for instance, certainly four, probably five, and quite possibly more were active trades unionists; so too were many others of the branch's leading members.[68] At the same time, however, there is no sign of any attempt to intervene in union affairs, or to mobilise unions in pursuit of some party objective. The ILP's priorities are well-defined by the committees which the Central branch appointed: two on 'propaganda' (one for the summer's outdoor work, one for the winter); one each on 'Halls', 'Social', 'Labour Party (Edinburgh branch)' (presumably the ILP's delegates), and 'Parliamentary campaign'.[69] In short, 'politics' for the ILP continued to mean, primarily, propaganda in which there was direct contact between the Party and the people; trade unionists who were also socialists might join the ILP, and their socialism would be reflected in their union work. But it was an individual rather than a collective intervention in union affairs.

Among the other socialist bodies, the schism in the BSP led to the formation, by the pro-war group in Edinburgh, of a Scottish Socialist Federation. Though small, this contained several who were influential in the city's labour movement.[70] Branches of the BSP, SLP and BSISLP continued to function.[71] We may assume that all continued their propagandistic work; and it seems that the last-mentioned was largely restricted to this. Certainly its theoretical position excluded most other activities and its contact with the remainder of the labour movement may have been restricted to the occasional debate.[72] In contrast to its national policy, the BSP branch in Edinburgh was not affiliated to the Labour Party; which may signify either its dissent from the policy, or its insignificant size. The limited Edinburgh evidence is consistent with the pattern of such organisations' development found elsewhere. This suggests that wartime militancy, and particularly the unofficial shop-stewards movement, provided the mechanism through which BSP and - above all - SLP militants began to turn from politics qua propaganda and education to a consciousness of the political dimension of industrial organisation and mobilisation.[73]

WAR: POLITICAL MOTIVATION

We look now at the fourth level at which the war affected labour and socialist politics. We have argued that the war changed the motivational context of industrial politics. Similar changes occurred in politics more generally. 'Profiteering' was a social, not merely an industrial, vice; 'efficiency', and 'organisation' were not seen as entirely, or even primarily, industrial principles - but as relevant to society as a whole; sacrifice in France was in no way closely associated with industry as such. In the workplace, these notions found an institutional context which made them relevant as principles legitimising action: we must consider how far labour and socialist politics offered a context which turned a sense of grievance into motives for action. In part, the war can be seen as a period when the labour movement was in internal dispute over the definition of political action. There were two poles in this dispute, and each provided a framework which enabled general principles to become principles legitimising specific courses of action. The labour movement did not split clearly between these two definitions: not least because many individuals subscribed to elements of both.

The first pole can be characterised as an enhanced view of the powers of the state, coupled sometimes with an optimistic view of the possibility of labour's gaining control of it, or at least influencing it. As early as 1916 an awareness was growing that 'there are great latent possibilities in the powers now in force whereby the State can commandeer supplies, take over businesses, assume control of factories, and run the transport services'.[74] As the intricacy of state control increased with the length of the war, so this awareness grew deeper roots. To be conscious of the state's power for good did not imply a belief that it could never be misused. 'The powers contained under the Defence of the Realm Act, and under the Munitions Act, may be a starting-point for a reactionary and repressive policy.'[75] Nor was it believed that state control always operated effectively: it was, indeed, often an article of faith that it did not, either because the state wished it so, or because of the influence of entrenched vested interests. The Trades Council accused the Town Council, for instance, of attempting 'to frustrate or delay direct municipal action [on housing], and to provide a new field of operations for the discredited speculator', rather than accept the full recommendations of the Royal Commission.[76] But commonly the belief seems to have been that the possibilities of state control, planning and organisation had been amply demonstrated: inadequacies could be blamed on failures of will. Thus in 1917 food scarcities led the Government to urge local authorities

> to start Communal Kitchens, but the suspicion was raised that there was an attempt to get the workers and their families to use glorified soup kitchens so as to keep the well-to-do immune from hardship and inconvenience.[77]

There was no question about the appropriate solution. A demonstration in the Meadows demanded 'that profiteering be ended, that steps be taken to completely control and regulate the food supplies, and that the Government disclose their plans for rationing'.[78] We have already seen how 'the status Labour has secured, and its call to the counsels of the nation',[79] provided a framework through which labour could hope to gain control - or at least some influence - over the apparatus of the state. The experience of state power during the war offered a ready example of its importance.

The second pole in the debate about the meaning of political action drew not so much on the power of existing government structures as on that of the existing trade union movement. Political strength lay in the trade union movement. Such a view was not unreasonable (if perhaps over-optimistic). Apart from the growth of union strength during the war, it owed much to pre-war syndicalism and industrial unionism. Pre-war British syndicalism was a movement encompassing a variety of understandings about politics and trades unionism, rather than a coherent, unified, body of theory; but it was an important element in the political reasoning of a large number of labour militants. When James Larkin spoke in Edinburgh in December 1913, 7,000 supporters turned out to hear him. 'The platform was stormed by sympathisers eager to shake Mr. Larkin by the hand.'[80] Such men and women experienced the war with dispositions which comprehended 'direct action'; which believed labour unionism (of some kind) could form the basis of a new society; which saw in the state more dangers than possibilities.[81] This general outlook, stressing solution through industrial organisation and action, was strengthened by the importance of the SLP in Edinburgh, and by the success of shop stewards and other trade union movements during the war.

Such understandings underlay widespread labour fears about the trend of government policy:

> there is another view of War precedents ... The munition trades are disarmed; the strike is an illegal weapon, and those that suggests its resumption find that penal servitude is their portion. All this may be explained on the ground of military necessity, but it seems an ominous invasion of industrial liberty.[82]

Such was the view of the Trades Council, so heavily involved in the apparatus of government, not simply of a few extremists. Within the mainstream of the movement there was an ambivalence, very often: developments and possibilities were perceived simultaneously in terms of both understandings of 'politics'.

Safety from the dangers that lie ahead will only be
found in stronger industrial and political organisation, by the workers assuming the power to control
their own destinies, and not remaining content with
a share as a polite and gracious concession.[83]

Thus the Trades Council again. It was, therefore, by no
means inevitable (if we were to abstract Edinburgh alone)
that wartime developments would lead to the dominance of
the post-1918 Labour Party.

NOTES

1.   A. Gramsci, Selections from the Prison Notebooks
(London, 1971), p.195.
2.   The main exception is J.M. Winter, Socialism and the
Challenge of War (London, 1974), esp. pp.52-9, 215-23, 259-
63, but Winter concentrates on the views of a few leading
socialists.
3.   R. McKibbin, The Evolution of the Labour Party 1910-
1924 (Oxford, 1974), esp. pp.137-44.
4.   R.T. McKenzie, British Political Parties (London,
1963), esp. pp.9-15.
5.   R.Q. Gray, The Labour Aristocracy in Victorian
Edinburgh (Oxford, 1976), p.163.
6.   On this period, see ibid., esp. pp.144-64, 177; I.
MacDougall (ed), The Minutes of Edinburgh Trades Council
1859-1873 (Edin., 1968), esp. pp. xxx, 303, 437; E.P.
Thompson, William Morris. Romantic to Revolutionary
(London, 1977), pp.350-1, 414.
7.   A term preferred by Edinburgh members of the
Socialist League to 'religion' in referring to socialism in the
1885 Socialist League manifesto. See S. Yeo, 'A New Life:
the Religion of Socialism in Britain, 1883-1896', History
Workshop Journal, no. 4 (1977), p.49; cp Thompson, Morris,
pp.732-40.
8.   Gray, Labour Aristocracy, p.177. The ILP branch was,
strictly, a branch of the Scottish Labour Party. The election
result: SLP 434, Liberal 3,733, Liberal-Unionist 1,758.
9.   Ibid., p.181.
10.   Ibid., p.182: similar developments were occurring
throughout the country.
11.   Particularly vehement in Scotland, where in 1901 the
SDF withdrew from the Scottish Workers Representation
Committee; in Edinburgh and Leith a majority of SDF
members broke away to form the Socialist Labour Party.

See W. Kendall, The Revolutionary Movement in Britain 1900-21 (London, 1969), pp.8-22; R. Challinor, The Origins of British Bolshevism (London, 1977), pp.9-26.
12.   LP Edin. Branch AR 1920, in TC AR 1920, p.21.
13.   LP Edin. Branch, official letterhead: see, e.g., letter R.T. Parker to A. Henderson, 25 July 1914, in LP Library, LP/PA/14/1/155.
14.   TC AR 1908.
15.   H. Mackinven, 'Edinburgh and District Trades Council Centenary 1859-1959' in TC AR 1959, p.53.
16.   TC AR 1908.
17.   A. Marwick, 'The Independent Labour Party (1918-32)', unpublished B. Litt. thesis, Oxford University, 1960, pp.16-17.
18.   Letter, W. Walker to J.R. MacDonald, 20 February 1909, in LP Library, LP/CAN/06/2/244.
19.   Letter, MacDonald to Walker, 22 February 1909, in LP Library: LP/CAN/06/2/245.
20.   R.A. Fox, 'Members of the Labour Party Elected to Edinburgh Town Council', unpublished typescript, 1971, at Edin. TC offices, pp.1-2.
21.   Challinor, British Bolshevism, p.109; Kendall, Revolutionary Movement, p.68.
22.   Kendall, Revolutionary Movement, pp.66-7.
23.   See R. Holton, British Syndicalism 1900-1914 (London, 1970); Challinor, British Bolshevism, pp.56-106.
24.   Challinor, British Bolshevism, p.118.
25.   R. McCaig, Report on the Decline and Fall of the SLP (Airdrie, n.d.), p.5, quoted ibid., p.119.
26.   Challinor, British Bolshevism, p.119.
27.   J.P.M. Millar, The Labour College Movement (London, n.d. [1979]), p.20, gives the date as 1912; J. Atkins, Neither Crumbs nor Condescension. The Central Labour College 1909-1915 (Aberdeen, 1981), p.70, gives it as 1913/14; R. Challinor, John S. Clarke (London, 1977), p.25, records the class as a marxist interpretation of prehistoric archaeology', attended by 35 railwaymen, which ran for at least two years.
28.   Challinor, J.S. Clarke, p.33.
29.   H. Levy, Social Thinking (London, 1945), p.8. The BSP and SDF would not have been debating with each other: the SDF became the Social Democratic Party in 1909 and the BSP in 1911.
30.   Quoted in A. Marwick, Clifford Allen. The Open Conspirator (Edin., 1964), p.51.

31. E.g., Sir James Crichton-Browne, FRS, wrote: 'The German language forsooth, is not a language, but a hideous guttural throatage. As for German literature, that part of it which is not poisonous is of the most stodgy and indigestible description. We have Schiller, Goethe, Lessing and Kant of the ante-depravity period in Germany adequately represented in translations, and we don't want any more German literature.' See A.W. Ewing, The Man of Room 40. The Life of Sir Alfred Ewing (London, n.d.), p.211; on Crichton-Browne, apparently an otherwise enlightened man, see The Compact Edition of the Dictionary of National Biography (Oxford, 1975), p.2536.

32. TC AR 1916, p.12.

33. Ibid., p.2; the full TC overturned this by 'a small majority' in favour of the Derby scheme.

34. John A. Young (Councillor 1909-20, parliamentary candidate, Edin. west 1918) was a member of the SSF, and allegedly had a 'relation with the British Workers' League through A.B. Stewart' (ILP Central branch minutes, 20 September 1918). William Graham (Councillor 1913-19, MP, Edin. central 1918-31) though a 'pacifist', volunteered, but was rejected on medical grounds (T.N. Graham, Willie Graham (London, n.d. [c. 1948]), pp.60-1). Gerald Crawford (Councillor 1912-20, 1926-42) volunteered in 1914; he was discharged in October 1917 as 'no longer physically fit for War Service' (letter, G.W. Crawford to J. McCorquodale, Secretary, ILP Edin. Central branch, 21 October 1917).

35. TC AR 1916, p.9.

36. R. Miliband, Parliamentary Socialism (London, 1973), p.47; K. Middlemas, Politics in Industrial Society (London, 1979), esp. pp.71-81, 88-90, 98-119, argues a similar case.

37. TC AR 1916, pp.6-9.

38. Ibid., p.5. The main pre-war non-elective labour representation was in Education Advisory and Pension committees.

39. TC AR 1918, pp.12-15.

40. Ibid., 1917, p.8.

41. Ibid., p.4.

42. LP Edin. branch AR 1911/12.

43. Ibid., 1917/18, pp.4-7.

44. TC AR 1918, p.12.

45. Ibid., 1917, pp.8-11.

46. Ibid., 1916, p.5.

47. By agreement, no seats were contested during the war (except in November 1914, when three retiring Labour

members were opposed, but returned with large majorities): see Fox, 'Labour Members of Edin. Town Council', p.2.
48. E.g., at the disenfranchisement of conscientious objectors: LP Edin. branch minutes, 13 December 1917.
49. Ibid., 22 November 1917, 14 February, 13 June 1918.
50. Ibid., 22 November 1917.
51. At one branch meeting, two members had to be appointed to meet Labour councillors anent housing policy (Ibid., undated fragment (c. 11 October 1917 but marked '1918', probably by NLS staff)). Town and parish councillors submitted written reports to the branch annual report, and probably attended annual general meetings. School Board representatives reported more often.
52. TC AR 1917, p.4.
53. J. Melling, 'Clydeside Housing and the Evolution of State Rent Control, 1900-1939' in Melling (ed.), Housing, Social Policy and the State (London, 1980), esp. pp.147-51.
54. TC AR 1916, p.10.
55. Ibid., 1917, p.11.
56. Ibid., pp.11-12.
57. Ibid.
58. Fred Hamilton: see ibid., 1908.
59. Letter, Alexander Smith to A. Henderson, 30 July 1914, LP Library LP/SAC/14/13: representation was refused, despite the Glasgow precedent. Cp letter, J.S. Middleton to Smith, 1 August 1914, LP/SAC/14/14.
60. LP Edin. branch AR 1917/18.
61. TC minutes, 7 May 1918.
62. LP Edin. branch minutes, 3 December 1917.
63. ILP Edin. Central branch minutes, from 11 January 1918.
64. Ibid., 21 June, 27 September 1918; letter, Ernest A. Bartlett, to Secretary, ILP Edin. Central branch, 20 September 1918.
65. LP Edin. branch AR 1917/18, p.8; ILP Central branch minutes, 28 February 1919.
66. ILP Edin. Central branch minutes, 3 May 1918.
67. Ibid., 29 March 1918.
68. ILP Edin. Central branch, 'List of Officials and Standing Committees for the year to 28 February 1918'.
69. Listed in this order. Ibid. The list also names those responsible for 'Dues', 'Literature', 'District Federation ILP', 'Workers Educational Association'.
70. Not to be confused with the SSF which linked SDF and Socialist League in the late 1880s, nor with that formed by

Edin. ILP branches which preferred to secede from ILP rather than LP in 1931.

71. ILP Edin. Central branch minutes, 16 May 1919.

72. E.g., letter, T. Tait, Organiser, BSISLP Edin. branch to Secretary, ILP Central branch, 20 January 1918, challenging ILP to debate 'The ILP is unworthy of working class support'.

73. J. Hinton, The First Shop Stewards Movement (London, 1973) is probably the best study of this, but see also Kendall, Revolutionary Movement, esp. 103-69; Challinor, British Bolshevism, esp. pp.150-70.

74. TC AR 1916, p.9. Cp A. Oldfield, 'The Growth of the Concept of Economic Planning in the Doctrine of the British Labour Party, 1914-1935', unpublished Ph.D. thesis, Sheffield University, esp. pp. 99-121, on the impact of wartime planning.

75. TC AR 1916, p.9.

76. Ibid., 1918, p.17; cp Report on the Royal Commission on the Housing of the Industrial Population of Scotland, Cd. 8731, 1917.

77. TC AR 1918, p.12.

78. Ibid., cp A. Marwick, The Deluge. British Society and the First World War (Harmondsworth, 1967), pp.206-8.

79. TC AR 1916, pp.9-10.

80. Liverpool Daily Post and Mercury, 12 December 1913, quoted Holton, British Syndicalism, p.196.

81. The most comprehensive study is Holton, British Syndicalism, but see also R. Holton, 'Syndicalist Theories of the State', Sociological Review, vol. 28 (1980), pp.5-21; Brown, Sabotage, esp. 23-40.

82. TC AR 1916, p.9.

83. Ibid., p.10.

Chapter Eight

THE REORGANISATION OF LABOUR 1917-1921

> The new Trades and Labour Council is not a
> debating society, an economic class, or a school of
> sociological philosophy. It is a machine! We are not
> schoolmasters; we are mechanics![1]

At the end of the war labour politicians entered a new
world. Two important changes occurred which generated an
uncertainty about their movement's aims and methods.
First, the institutional framework was altered. From 1918
the parliamentary franchise included all working class men;
though not all voted Labour, the Edinburgh party was
encouraged by the election of its first MP - William Graham
in the Central division.[2] The local government franchise
remained restricted, and Labour showed poorly when Town
Council elections resumed in 1919.[3] After the Armistice,
demobilisation proceeded apace. Ex-servicemen, largely
unemployed, became - briefly - an important political
constituency, wooed and feared by both labour and
government. They were a target for the press (itself
increasingly a target of government news management):
certainly the Trades Council believed an 'active anti Trades
Union campaign [was] being conducted by a certain section
of the Scottish Press' in early 1919,[4] and a year later was
complaining of 'a continuous crusade of slander ... in the
Press and on many platforms for the purpose of alienating
the ex-Service man from the Trade Unions'.[5] At the same
time the government was sponsoring the creation of various
'non-political' and 'independent' bodies to 'combat
Bolshevism' among the working class.[6]

Second, the stock of principles which could justify
political action was shifted by the end of the war itself, and
by the Russian revolutions of 1917. The ending of war
weakened, and reoriented, the language of 'nation' and
patriotism. Labour's political activities were no longer self-
regulated by an over-riding sense of national interest. Many
of the arguments by which members of the labour movement

had justified their support for the war now assumed greater weight just because they had become important elements in labour's (negotiated) 'war aims'. Popular definitions of the 'nation' now often saw labour as an important estate: 'national' concepts could be used to legitimise actions which might have been supported by principles of fairness, but with less force. Thus the Trades Council could argue, in relation to government policies on housing, that

> If the money is there to lend it is there to tax, and no national purpose is served by making the housing scheme a pretext for fixing on the backs of the workers an idle money-lending class and maintaining them in perpetuity.[7]

But in part, too, patriotism had been justified by the ascription to the enemy of unacceptable political character-istics. So the war was fought, it was claimed, not against Germans so much as 'Kaiserism', a form of 'despotism'.[8] Where such supportive beliefs could buttress the national effort in time of war, they might redefine it when the threat had passed.

'A Revolution has taken place in Russia. Despotism has been overthrown and former war aims revoked.'[9] Undoubtedly the revolutions of 1917 added to labour's self-confidence in Britain, but their impact was complicated. The October revolution raised questions of socialist method which were related to debates within the British movement. The nature of Bolshevism was itself a matter of dispute: inevitably associated with the question of war aims, it was highly susceptible to interested interpretation. In due course it was complicated by allied intervention in the Civil War. Within the movement in Edinburgh, there is evidence of an attempt to use the spectre of Bolshevism to perpetuate, in peacetime, the alignments which had been supported by patriotism in war. This effort focused on the Edinburgh branch of the National Socialist Party (which had its origins in the pro-war faction of the BSP). In January 1919 its secretary attended a 'Committee appointed to consolidate Pro Ally Socialist activities in Scotland':[10] probably as a result of this came its decision to become a branch of the NSP. A battle ensued: the national leadership, together with a group within the Edinburgh branch, appears to have seen Bolshevism as the issue which could replace the war as a political rationale for the Party. 'A circular and 3 collecting Cards were received from the Ex[ecutive] Committe[e] of the N.S.P.[:] the Funds were required to kill Bolshevism.'[11]

The branch agreed to accept the cards by eight votes to six: but Bolshevism was not to be so easily vanquished. When a member wrote a week later 'intimating his resignation from the Branch owing to his disagreeing with the effort to collect money to fight Bolshevism', the mood had changed. It was unanimously agreed to 'write asking him to reconsider and intimating the Branch was in sympathy with him',[12] and by the early summer of 1919 the branch was responding positively to a BSP request 'to take joint action to protest against the Government action in Russia. Conscription and espionage'.[13] Yet the attempt was made, and may have been part of a wider, government sponsored, strategy.[14]

Within the ILP we can see another aspect of the impact of the October revolution: initial fascination and curiosity, tempered by an apprehension about method; but in the course of time providing support for a re-assessment of political method. Just four months after the Bolshevik revolution, the Central branch endorsed a resolution protesting against attacks on the Bolsheviks made by Labour leaders:

> It is up to the rank and file of the ILP to make
> ourselves felt and to insist that the ILP shall rally
> to the cause of the Bolsheviks, which is the cause
> of International Socialism. Their methods may not
> be our methods, but their cause is ours.[15]

At much the same time the branch ordered twelve copies of a BSP book 'The Bolshevik, etc.'; by July it was ordering 156 copies of Lenin's pamphlet, 'Lessons of the Russian Revolution', also from the BSP.[16] Towards the end of the war sympathetic curiosity began to be associated with concern at allied intervention in Russia;[17] when the war ended intervention was no longer clouded by patriotism. In January 1919 a 'Hands Off Russia' conference was called, to which the Central branch sent a delegate:[18] in the following months the Edinburgh 'Hands Off Russia' Committee began to make an impact on both trade unions and political organisations. Although, according to one of its members, the Edinburgh Committee was 'a hole-and-corner organisation ... run by a little group of engineers who worked in Rosyth dockyard, mostly Englishmen transferred from Portsmouth',[19] it ensured that the issues of intervention were constantly raised.[20] The outbreak of the Russo-Polish war in April 1920 gave the Committee further impetus, and showed that sympathy for the revolution was widespread. 'It held crowded meetings on Sunday night in the old Pringles Picture House',[21] and further trade union support was won.[22] And when, in July, the tide turned against the Poles and British involvement against Russia seemed a real possibility, the Labour Party was able to mobilise and threaten 'direct action': a telegram from Arthur Henderson claimed the risk of war was 'extremely menacing' and urged that 'local parties immediately organise citizen demonstrations against interventions and supply of men, munitions. Demand peace negotiations, immediate raising blockade, resumption trade relations. Send resolutions Premier and Press, deputise local MPs.'[23] Labour's action in early August was widely held to have prevented British intervention: it shows how widespread was sympathy with revolutionary Russia, yet this was linked with popular revulsion at the prosect of further war. 'Primarily it was war weariness that sustained the "Hands Off Russia" agitation,' Fred Douglas recalled:[24] but war weariness alone could not have 'packed' the Usher Hall on 22 August to hear William Gallacher's report of his visit to the Second Congress of the Communist International in Moscow.[25] By the second half of 1920, Russia was the object of fascination and solidarity from virtually all sections of the labour movement: the Trades and Labour Council's Executive, encompassing a wide spectrum of political attitudes, accepted an invitation to appear on the platform of the Gallacher meeting.[26]

If the war had upset labour politics, it had also provided the basis and context for the development of new perspectives and allegiances which - though subjected to great strain, especially as union strength grew - survived until the Armistice. Peace, together with Russia's revolutions, again altered the political context: wartime outlooks and alliances were no longer relevant - or, at least, required justification in other terms. Two trends of thought co-existed within the wartime labour movement. One focussed on the wartime role of the state, drawing credence from its evident strength, and from labour's involvement with it. The second, focussing on the political potential of industrial organisation, was the stronger for the trade unions' advances. Individuals drew on both trends, which cut across the entire movement from left to right: during the immediate post-war years, briefly, strategic debate occurred as much within each as between the two.

With the labour movement's political alignments thus in the melting-pot, the possibility of common action across its political spectrum was unusually great. Notions related to 'efficiency' and 'organisation' had been raised in status during the war, and could legitimise action - particularly institutional change - across a wide range of opinion. This was the background to three developments: the Labour Party's new constitution in 1918, the amalgamation of Trades Council and Labour Party in 1920, and the restructuring of Marxist organisation between 1918 and 1921 (which is often seen as culminating in the formation of the Communist Party).

EDINBURGH LABOUR AND THE 1918 CONSTITUTION
Historians of the Labour Party have made much of 1918. For G.D.H. Cole, the 1918 Constitution (together with the new programme Labour and the New Social Order) 'unequivocally' committed the party to 'Socialist objectives'.[27] Ralph Miliband argued that the party was 'transformed ... from a loose federation of affiliated organisations into a centralized, nationally cohesive Party with its own individual members, organized in local constituency parties and subject to central party discipline'.[28] More recent research has qualified these assertions. The commitment to socialism - Clause 4 - was grafted into a constitution that 'confirmed the triumph of the unions and the defeat of the socialists' (and the unions cared little about socialism):[29] on this view, Clause 4 was merely 'a rallying point' around which the adherents of different ideologies and interests could assemble, without committing themselves to anything very significant.[30]

In the Edinburgh of 1918, however, there is no evidence that Clause 4 acted as a rallying point for labour; nor did trade unions show much desire to control the Labour Party. Indeed, the new constitution evoked little enthusiasm outside the party itself, although it was widely taken to be a good thing simply for reasons of organisational efficiency.

In view of its subsequent significance, the apparent unimportance of Clause 4 in discussion of the new constitution is remarkable. There is no record of its having even been mentioned, let alone discussed, in Labour's Edinburgh branch meetings in late 1917 and early 1918. The ILP did not consider it;[31] neither did the Trades Council.[32] Reporting on the party's special national conference, Edinburgh's delegate concentrated on 'the big question of the Conference - The New Constitution': but he did not mark Clause 4 as worthy of mention.[33] This resounding silence suggests that the socialist objective, at least in the language of Clause 4, was uncontroversial; but, by the same token, that it was not judged to be an effective 'rallying point' at the time.[34] The constitution was seen as important for other reasons.

Table 8.1: Trade Union and Political Affiliations of Officers and Executive Committee Members of the Labour Party, Edinburgh Branch 1917/18

Office:	Name:	Affiliations identified:
Chairman	T. Hamilton	Workers' Union Rosyth No. 3 National Guilds League, Edin. group President
Treasurer	P. Gray	Postmen's Federation
Secretary	A.S. Wylie	ILP Central branch; Workers' Union District Secretary
Executive Committee:	A. Cameron	Painters, Central Branch
	J. Grassick	National League of the Blind, ILP Central branch.
	F. Halliday	NAUL No. 292 branch
	W. Hodgson	Corporation Workers
	A. Pollock	(None identified)
	J. Rollo	NUR No. 1 branch

Sources: Labour Party, Edin. branch AR 1917/18; ILP minutes and correspondence; NUR Edin. No.1 branch minutes; NAUL No. 292 branch minutes.

Although, again, the 1918 constitution may have increased unions' control over the Labour Party nationally, there is little sign that this was a motive for union support for the change in Edinburgh. The Trades Council, as we have seen, preferred loose supervision to close control over the Labour Party. Before 1918 this was complemented by a somewhat deeper involvement of other trade unionists. Table 8.1 shows that, even before the 1918 constitution was brought into force in Edinburgh, union members had effective control within it. To be sure, some - perhaps a majority - had political links, with the ILP and so on; but they were trade union delegates in the main. So trade unionists did not need to wrest control of the Labour Party: they already held it.

If there was a struggle for control of the Labour Party in Edinburgh, it was between those who had already identified themselves with avowedly 'political' groupings: even this, however, seems not to have surfaced until after the new constitution was agreed. It would 'vitally affect ... the position of the Local Labour Parties':[35] in particular, the proposed individual membership was an implicit threat to the ILP. This was not an issue within the Edinburgh ILP in late 1917, but during 1918 the implications became clearer. Early that year the Edinburgh Labour Party appointed a new Secretary: James J. Pottinger was a member of the SSF, and seems to have pursued its interests as Secretary.[36] This meant the ILP's influence was weakened during a crucial year. The new Secretary was assiduous in upholding the constitution of the Labour Party to counter the interests of the ILP, which was, of course, distrusted by labour 'patriots'. The ILP, apparently attempting to increase its hold over the Labour Party, began to press for the appointment of an election agent for William Graham, the parliamentary candidate whom it had nominated (and whom the Labour Party had subsequently adopted). Having received an unhelpful response from Pottinger,[37] the ILP wrote again,

> requesting a joint conference of ... [the ILP] Executive and the Executive of the local Labour Party, along with Mr. Shaw, the Scottish Secretary [of the Labour Party] 'to consider Councillor Graham's candidature for the Central division and to make definite arrangements'.[38]

Pottinger's response was to point out that the ILP, as nominators, were 'responsible for 75 per cent of the expenses' of an agent, along with some other requirements, but that the appointment, control and salary of the agent would lie with the Labour Party. 'That, briefly, is the position, and a conference on the question is therefore scarcely necessary',[39] was the crisp conclusion.

If, then, we leave aside the motives of those who formulated the new constitution, and seek the motives of those who accepted it - not always enthusiastically, but without controversy - in Edinburgh, neither Clause 4 nor a need for greater union control is adequate. When Henderson argued for the new constitution at the Nottingham

Conference, he stressed the need for both 'a broader organisational basis and a more clearly defined objective' if the
party was to take advantage of the expanded electorate
after the war.[40] If the latter was not taken up in Edinburgh,
the former struck a chord. In his report, the Edinburgh
delegate concentrated on Henderson's 'very clever speech'
on

> the big question ... - The New Constitution.
> He[nderson] pled for its adoption on several
> grounds: the after-war situation, the necessity for
> broadening the base of the Party, the possibility of
> a General Election about September of this year,
> and the Executive's determination to place 400
> Parliamentary candidates in the field.[41]

These were thoroughly organisational motives: although the
delegate was an enthusiastic guild socialist, he did not even
mention the new Clause 4. Whether this reflected his own
outlook, or deference to his readers, is unimportant: in the
later war years, reorganisation in the interest of efficiency
was hard to oppose, and the advocates of the new constitution drew strength from this fact. The Edinburgh Labour
Party had believed that the 1918 Conference was 'the most
important ... yet held, owing to the discussion on draft
Constitution';[42] it largely failed to persuade the local labour
movement, however. For the latter, the new constitution
was simply uncontroversial.

THE FORMATION OF THE TRADES AND LABOUR COUNCIL

If the 1918 Labour Party constitution was given legitimacy
by the strength of notions of organisation and efficiency,
this was in an essentially negative sense: it was difficult to
oppose. But in 1917 the Labour Party was peripheral to
labour politics in Edinburgh: only the prospect of an election
(repeatedly raised by Henderson in correspondence with
local parties) kept it alive. One constitutional development
whose significance was generally accepted in these
immediate post-war years in Edinburgh's labour movement,
was the 1920 amalgamation of the Trades Council with the
local Labour Party, forming a Trades and Labour Council.
This was controversial, but its importance was widely acknowledged, even by its opponents.

We have seen that the Trades Council's political role
had been enhanced during the war years: in particular, it had
- perforce - begun to encroach on areas, such as working

175

class representation on public bodies, for which the Labour Party had been established. This raised questions about the relationship between the two organisations. Between 1917 and 1920 virtually all the trade union branches affiliated to the Edinburgh Labour Party were also affiliated to the Trades Council: the exceptions were insignificantly small.[43] It was, therefore, perhaps unsurprising that, in the course of a discussion on the new Constitution at a Labour Party meeting in December 1917,

> Mr. Wylie moved that Local Trades' Council and branches of the Labour Party amalgamate as advised [in the draft rules circulated from head office, since] ... at present there was much wasted energy and overlapping, which could be saved by amalgamation.[44]

Initially, there was little enthusiasm from the Trades Council: at least during the war, it was the Labour Party's energy which was being wasted. The party had 'hope[d] to see effected, during the coming year [1918], an amalgamation with the Trades Council'.[45] But not until August 1918 did the two executives even meet, although they did then agree (after extended discussion) to recommend amalgamation in principle.[46] Within the Trades Council, however, the proposal encountered significant opposition. The Executive's recommendation was endorsed by 37 votes to 14.[47] Another 14 months passed before plans were finalised - which suggests less than wholehearted commitment - and even then the first meeting of the new body was not to be held until April 1920.[48]

There were a number of reasons for this opposition and delay. First, there was some mistrust of the Labour Party within the trade union movement. In 1917/18 of the 80 union branches affiliated to the Trades Council, just 18 were affiliated to the local Labour Party; two years later the figures were 82 and 21 respectively.[49] Whilst the bulk of the remainders were content to be associated with the Labour Party, at least two branches withdrew from the Council on account of the amalgamation, and one was explicit about the political reason for its decision.[50] Such reservations may have been intensified by the socialist programme of 1918, for not even those unions locally affiliated to the Labour Party were unanimous about socialism. When the Rubber Workers' branch set down its reasons for affiliating, it also pointed, by omission, to possible reservations about a fully socialist programme:

> That this Branch recognising the benefit that
> Labour Representation in Parliament has been in
> securing by Act of Parliament conditions commen-
> surate with the cost of living, are of opinion that
> Labour Representation in the House of Commons is
> essential to the continuance of direct Government
> control of Wages agreements, and to this end are
> resolved to affiliate with the Locol [sic] Labour
> Party.[51]

Similarly, the Clerks affiliated to the local Labour branch in
early 1918, but their commitment did not extend to supporting a demonstration to 'save the New Democracies in
Europe' - despite its having been called by the party.[52] For
some union branches - if not necessarily for the politically
active trade unionists - political action had a meaning short
of some definitions of socialism.

Second, what was commonly referred to as an 'amalgamation' was in reality also a thorough reorganisation of
the Labour Party in line with the new rules. As the merger
took place, the Labour Party was shifting from a haphazard
structure (a series of ward committees under the aegis of
the Edinburgh branch), to a more centralised three-tier
structure, in which divisional parties in each constituency
superseded the single Edinburgh branch, but were all subject
to the authority of the Trades and Labour Council. The
Secretary of the local branch gave a lucid account of how

> in a city which is divided into several
> constituencies, a Local Labour Party must be
> formed in each constituency. Each of these Local
> Parties are entitled to five representatives on the
> Central Labour Party, which would be the control-
> ling authority for the whole area.

But he found it 'somewhat difficult to explain', and expected
to have to meet affiliated organisations' representatives in
order to do so.[53] One union branch committee thought the
Draft Constitution and Rules 'were complicated', and put
consideration off until the next meeting - where, 'after
considerable discussion it was agreed ... that the letter "lie
on the table" '.[54]

The sheer complexity of the new structure and rulebook
- 'Set D (pp.45-53) is the set of rules applicable to cities like
Edinburgh', wrote the Edinburgh Party's Secretary[55] - was
only a symptom of the view that organisational efficiency
stems from centralisation and hierarchy. In the course of
time, this structure required an increase in the resources

available at the upper levels of the party, and an acceptance of a subordinate role by the members of local Labour parties and affiliated bodies. In the event, commitment to reorganisation and the Labour idea was not adequate to carry through the original plans. Very likely, amalgamation was initially intended to allow Trades Council and Labour Party together to sustain a central organisation which was beyond each alone; as the Labour Party had it:

> Whether a scheme of amalgamation matures or not, the Party must be prepared to take its place in the forefront of the political life of the City, &, in this connection, we would emphasise the need for a full-time Secretary-Organiser with an office & the necessary clerical staff.[56]

Neither, however, appears to have been prepared for the degree of opposition - not, indeed, to the principle, but to the cost. The original proposal was for an affiliation fee to the joint council of 1s. per member per year.[57] The current Trades Council affiliation fee was based on a scale which, though far from simple, ranged from less than 1d. per member (for very large branches), to a maximum of 4d. (for the smaller branch).[58] One branch, 500 strong, paying £3 annually to the Trades Council on the old scale, feared it would have to pay £25 instead, and its 'delegates were instructed ... to question the affiliation fees, and to vote down everything higher than 6d. per member'.[59] As unions were represented on the council in proportion to their size (not to their financial contribution), we need not be surprised that a fee of 4d. per member was settled upon:[60] what is remarkable - and a testament to the strength of the belief in the need for reorganisation - is that 1s. was ever seriously suggested.

'At first the combination of the two great forces seemed to bristle with difficulties, financial and otherwise', wrote the Trades Council's executive in 1920, but after an incredible amount of work on the part of the Joint-Executives, the scheme became an accomplished fact.'[61] But even incredible amounts of work will only prevail if their purpose is seen as relevant. The great advantage of amalgamation's advocates was that there seems to have been little legitimate basis for opposition to the reorganisation - those who criticised it on financial grounds did not argue that centralisation was a mistake, for example, or that it was more important to strengthen the various affiliated unions and parties. It is almost as though the opponents were ashamed of their arguments. Conversely, the arguments for reorganisation were strong; based upon the strength of notions of administrative efficiency, and hierarchical structures. There was, for instance, an assumed congruence between the 'Amalgamation' of Edinburgh with Leith ('any measure which tends towards efficiency, economy, and the prevention of overlapping should receive ... [the workers'] heartiest support') and 'Our Own Amalgamation': the two items were juxtaposed in the Trades Council's Annual Report.[62]

As in the trade union sphere, this reflected a simplistic view of organisation: not only was efficient organisation necessarily mechanistic - highly centralised and hierarchical; efficiency was a characteristic of the organisation, and not of the relationship between the' organisation and its environment. Thus the new structure was seen as transcending the strategic differences within the movement:

> With regard to this new machine, it is unnecessary to embark on any academic disquisition regarding principles or policy. Whatever views on these may be held by the various units of the new body, we are all agreed that the need for a transformation of our system of government is becoming more insistent and more clamant than at any time in our previous history.[63]

This 'effective machine' would give 'adequate expression to the aims, the hopes, and the aspirations of the working class of this city': it was to be capable of carrying through whatever policy the movement required of it:

> Trade Unions and Socialist Societies will not come to us to be told what wants doing. They will come to get things done. They must forge the bolts: we are commissioned with the duty of firing them. For long the worker has sighed for the two-edged weapon, that would enable him to cut his way to freedom. The tool is here; we place it in your hands. Emancipation awaits you.[64]

RESTRUCTURING MARXIST ORGANISATION

As the unity of the post-war labour movement was built, in essence, on the submergence of argument about method or strategy beneath an apparent unity on organisation, so also with Marxism. The political differences which, in pre-war years, had led to the growth of a variety of organisations did not disappear; rather, having been reassessed in the light of wartime experiences, they were outweighed by a belief in the value of organisational unity. The Bolshevik revolution won widespread support within the British labour movement, but sympathy, even vicarious pride at working class achievement, did not imply acceptance of Bolshevik methods. The revolution raised questions of socialist strategy, and lent legitimacy to methods involving some 'direct action' or force. But it was perceived in the light of varying British experiences.

Some elements of Edinburgh's labour movement were predisposed to see the revolution in industrial terms by a background in syndicalism or industrial unionism. There is evidence in Edinburgh that the soviet idea had a strong impact on those who had been involved in the workers' committees of the engineering industry.[65] Inside the ILP Central branch, for instance, it was Bob Foulis, an iron-moulder and leader of the engineering and shipbuilding workers, who pressed the Bolshevik case in 1918.[66] The 'Hands Off Russia' Committee was run by a group of engineers, and seems to have been started, in early 1919, during just those months when the Forth Workers' Committee (never the strongest such body) was on the wane: it may be that the two organisations shared active members.[67] Certainly a critic found the 'Hands Off Russia' Committee 'more anxious for the formation of Soviets here than anything else'.[68] But on the railways sympathy for the revolution's methods reflected another view of what was important. It demonstrated the need for 'a General Strike to establish a dictatorship of the proletariat in this country', to 'organise our forces', to 'line up with all workers to take hold of the means of wealth production'.[69] This is the language of syndicalist industrial unionism: not of soviets or workers' committees. Where workplace organisation was not strong, the idea of soviets had little resonance. (And in those sectors where union organisation was but recently established, the revolution's relevance was unlikely to be perceived in industrial terms - it was just too remote. Neither the Clerks nor the Rubber Workers showed any real sympathy for the revolution, and certainly do not seem to have perceived it as having any relevance to their organisation.)[70]

The Russian revolution could, of course, be interpreted in another perspective: by those who, impressed by the strength of the state during the war, felt that labour's failure to win control of it was partly due to organisational factors. For such as these the lessons of October were political, rather than industrial. Through the soviets, or the Bolshevik party, the Russian working class had been more efficiently organised than its counterpart in Britain, and had been able to advance just because it had won state power. The Bolsheviks had broken with the 'compromising' and 'treacherous role' of the Mensheviks and Social-Revolution-aries.[71] Certainly, the Bolshevik experience seems to have been at least catalytic in inducing an element of Edinburgh's ILP to question the methods and organisation of labour politics: they began to press the ILP into debate with leftist organisations such as the SLP and to subscribe to their press;[72] they attacked those in the ILP who were pro-war, or who appeared in other ways to compromise with the state;[73] they attempted to promote common action between the ILP and various revolutionary organisations.[74] During 1918 and 1919, at least, they seem to have had considerable success: by mid-1919 a motion 'to arrange an immediate Conference of the Local I.L.P., B.S.P., S.L.P., B.S.I.S.L.P., and Communist Workers' League with a view of consolidating local Socialistic efforts' had been passed by 25 votes to seven.[75] (Of course, others may have seen the importance of state power and efficient organisation clearly demonstrated in Russia, and yet demurred at Bolshevik attitudes to reform and constitutional change - especially in relation to Britain.)

These perspectives on the Russian revolution did not divide Edinburgh's Marxists into two clear groups: rather, they were sources of motive and understanding. As the months passed after the Armistice, events in Britain also led to political reassessments among revolutionary socialists. On the one hand, the growth of a number of organisations, largely issue-based, brought Marxist socialists together to pursue common objectives. Defence of the revolution led to the 'Hands Off Russia' Committee. The Forth Workers' Committee, which had led the 40-hours strike in Edinburgh, involved not only those with a background in the SLP: one of its leaders was a member of the ILP, and had been a Labour parliamentary candidate in 1918.[76] The history and economics class, run by the Central Labour College for Edinburgh District of the NUR, had for several years been taught by John S. Clarke, a leading member of the SLP: it had become a focal point of the railwaymen's revolutionary industrial unionism.[77] From 1916 the Labour College (or Plebs League) grew in the city, and its interpretations of

Marxism broadened. The Railwaymen's class was opened to other occupations.[78] Other classes were started, with organisations like the Engineers and the ILP.[79] New tutors were found, by no means all of whom had backgrounds in the SLP.[80] In February 1920, what had become the Edinburgh District of the Scottish Labour College merged with the Marxian School of Economics,[81] leaving a single organisation for Marxist education in the city. Associated with this increased intercourse between the various strands of Marxist thought was a weakening of the internal cohesion of the various socialist parties. Within the ILP, for instance, a group began to identify with Marxism as well as - perhaps rather than - the party itself. It began to attack another group which identified with the aims, and sometimes the organisation, of the NSP, and more generally on the ILP's right: one such attack is revealing. Euphemia Laing, a former suffragette later to become a Communist, moved the expulsion of Thomas Drummond Shiels (who liked to be referred to as 'Captain', and was to become a Labour councillor and MP) as 'Mr. Shiels had taken office in the Edinburgh branch of the National Socialist Party, a party which had consistently opposed the policy of the I.L.P. throughout the War'.[82] Drummond Shiels did not deny the facts: only that 'he had done nothing to violate the Constitution of the ILP'. The motion was narrowly defeated (by 36 votes to 33):[83] clearly, many members did not find membership of another party improper. Similarly, a division opened within the SLP, essentially between those who had been involved in the workers' committees (and thus jointly with other Marxists in industrial conflict) and those who had remained in the older mould of SLP separatism.[84]

While the institutions of socialist politics were thus in flux, those revolutionary socialists whose outlooks were grounded in industrial experience found reasons for reassessment. These reassessments varied, however, for experiences were not uniform. In Edinburgh, Marxist views had flourished in two main settings. In engineering and shipbuilding, the shop-stewards movement, never as strong as on Clydeside, had suffered the national defeat of the early months of 1918, and had swung to political agitation when industrial methods seemed to have failed.[85] By October the Forth Workers' Committee had established an economics and industrial history class in conjunction with the Plebs League.[86] After the Armistice, the defeat of the 40-hours strike further undermined the industrial support for the shop-stewards movement; yet just for a brief period employers were able to undercut militancy by offering concessions to official union leaders. And by 1920 the depression was beginning. In these circumstances, the thinking of the revolutionary shop stewards became, as it were, political rather than industrial: from workers' committees, the movements' leaders began, for instance, to propose the formation of 'social committees'.[87] They no longer perceived industry as providing a fundamental source of social power: it was necessary to mobilise resources elsewhere.

Marxist views had also flourished among Edinburgh's railwaymen. Their wartime experiences, however, had been different from the engineers'. Government control and national negotiation had undercut the emergence of strong, unofficial, workplace organisation. During 1919 and 1920 the railwaymen moved back into the vanguard of industrial struggle. They were mobilised in national strikes. The victory of October 1919 was seen as a vindication of industrial unionism; and industrial action - solidarity action - as a realistic strategy for revolutionaries. Effort was therefore put into organising the local Triple Alliance.[88] But just as the Triple Alliance was fragile nationally, so in Edinburgh these efforts were often frustrated. At a local conference of the Alliance summoned in December 1919, 'only railwaymen turned up'.[89] Nearly three months later a Railwaymen's delegate was still reporting that 'The miners had not responded. As it stood', he continued, 'the T.A. is largely a farce'.[90] At the same time the union's revolutionary elements came deeply to mistrust their national leaders; whom they saw as unwilling, for political reasons, to exploit industrial advantages to the full. 'Thomas and his political clap-trap had done our movement great harm.'[91] Gradually, however, they began to mix the language of syndicalism with a sense that political organisation was necessary:

> That Edinburgh No. 1 branch NUR calls upon all railway workers to organise in a revolutionary political party and in one great Industrial Union of the working class in order to destroy the robber system, and to hold the means of wealth production ... [92]

During 1920 the emphasis remained on industrial organisation, especially when autumn brought the prospect of a miners' strike. The No. 1 branch demanded

> a strike of NUR members ... in support of the
> miners if the Government compel them to strike.
> Failing a settlement in three days instruction be
> sent to each locality to take possession of
> Railways, Mines, etc and work them in the interest
> of the working class.[93]

This is a classic assertion, in the syndicalist tradition, of the
political potential of industrial power. But as 1920 became
1921, the failures of the Triple Alliance multiplied. The
explanation was generally similar ('The dissension of Mr.
Thomas and his wrecking tactics'),[94] but confidence began
to wane.

Now the realisation of the need for political organisation bore fruit. In June 1921, just seven weeks after the
Triple Alliance's final fiasco ('Black Friday'), the No. 1
branch of the Edinburgh Railwaymen agreed to set up 'its
own political Committee with a view to running its own
Municipal and other Council candidates'.[95]

> The Committee is the political expression of a very
> large and active branch of railway workers. It will
> oppose other political bodies in so far as such
> bodies do not express the interests of the working-
> class, and whoes [sic] political outlook is not that
> of the class struggle. It will defend, and work for
> the Industrial development of the workers'
> organisations, and stands for the unity of all
> workers, on behalf of all workers against the
> common enemy - the capitalist class.[96]

So the need for political organisation was interwoven with
the syndicalist tradition.

The peculiarity of the revolutionary movement on the
railways should not, however, obscure the central reality:
the weakening of industrial militancy was leading to a
receptiveness, among those who regarded themselves as
revolutionaries, to political debate and action. The weakening cohesion of many parties of the left was allowing
political strategy to be considered in a new context; and
there developed, in the Labour Colleges and the 'Hands Off
Russia' Committee especially, institutions which - though
for limited purposes - regrouped Marxists within the labour
movement. Some indication of the impact of Marxism on
Edinburgh labour, and more importantly on the extent to
which intercourse developed among the Marxist left, can be
gained from the growth of the Colleges in Edinburgh.
Although in mid-1917 Edinburgh took more copies of Plebs

than any other city, there was just the single class based on
the NUR.[97] In the autumn a branch of the Plebs League was
started:[98] the District Organiser began to attend union
meetings to promote classes: another was started in
Leith.[99] Progress was still slow, however; the Leith class
enrolled only 17 members,[100] and even in April 1918 the
Edinburgh class could report an advance only 'in knowledge
not numbers'.[101] The real advance came in 1919 and 1920,
as the post-war ferment began. During 1919/20 what had
become the Edinburgh District of the Scottish Labour
College enrolled 120 students in four classes; in 1920/21 an
initial October enrolment of 490 students in 18 classes[102]
rose over the succeeding months to 617,[103] 654,[104] and
finally 'nearly 700' in 21 classes.[105] Sales of Plebs rose from
eleven, to 20 and then 30 dozen monthly.[106]

In these circumstances the Communist Party was
formed. Fred Douglas recalled being drawn into the party
almost as a natural progression, having been involved in
'Hands Off Russia' agitation, in a Marxist economics class,
and in distributing The Worker.[107] Bob Foulis, having led
the 40-hours strike and the left group within the ILP, moved
into the Communist Party, perhaps through the Red
International of Labour Unions - of which he became
Scottish organiser.[108] Arthur Woodburn, having led the
Marxian School of Economics into its merger with the
Labour College, joined the new party.[109] The common
theme was neither personal background nor agreement over
strategy: rather it was that sense, by no means limited to
the revolutionary left, that effective political (or industrial)
action required effective organisation; and that this was
best achieved through a single centralised institution after a
military model.

In the years before the Communist Party was formed,
Britain's 'marxist movement lacked any adequate
organisational theory', according to Walter Kendall, while
the shop-stewards movement allowed its critique of
bureaucracy to obscure the fact that 'long term organisation
is ... impossible without ... bureaucratic organisation'.[10]
The war simultaneously exposed these inadequacies,
demonstrated the advantages which the state possessed
through effective organisation, and provided a working
model in the organisation of the nation for the war effort. It
also showed what workers could do, given adequate
organisation, in the industrial field. In the immediate post-
war years the revolutionary movement became acutely

conscious of its organisational failings, especially in politics. Toward the end of the first year of peace, John S. Clarke expressed this view:

> The capitalist class confronts its enemy with the up-to-date organisation of capitalist high finance - the worker feebly wields the out-worn weapons of a century ago. Against the tank, Howitzer, Lewis Gun, and aeroplane, the worker hurls himself, heroically armed with - a muzzle-loader of the days of Waterloo. Is it any wonder he is ignominiously defeated?[111]

Or, as Gallacher and Campbell had it,

> Old tactics and old methods of organisation have to be overhauled and brought up to date to enable us to meet and overcome the latest developments of organisation from the employers' side. Delay spells disaster. Everywhere the organisation of the employers and their catspaw government is being improved to meet all eventualities.[112]

The formation of the Communist Party represented, above all, an organisational innovation among British revolutionaries. There was, within the labour movement, and among British Marxists, a strong sense of the need to reorganise, to unify; and the available models of organisation were hierarchical, often military. The Bolshevik experience was catalytic; it provided one unifying issue. But the demand for reorganisation had arisen within the British movement in any case; and it seems likely that any such reorganisation would have drawn on the models which underlay the contemporaneous developments in Labour and trade union organisation.

NOTES

1. TC AR 1920, p.13.
2. Graham received 7,159 votes, with a majority of 364 over his Coalition Liberal opponent, in a 45.2 per cent poll. The results were not so encouraging elsewhere in the city: in Leith and Edinburgh west, Labour candidates were at the bottom of the poll (see Appendix A).
3. All six candidates were unsuccessful at the November elections, although each polled between 850 and 1,509 votes. Labour's six sitting councillors did not face re-election.
4. TC minutes, 11 March 1919. On government news management, see K. Middlemas, Politics in Industrial

Society (London, 1979), pp.131, 145-6; M. Cowling, The Impact of Labour 1920-24 (Cambridge, 1971), esp. pp. 45-59.
5. TC AR 1920, p.10.
6. S. White, 'Ideological Hegemony and Political Control: the Sociology of Anti-Bolshevism in Britain, 1918-20', Scottish Labour History Society Journal, no.9, p.3. Cp Lloyd George's 1920 comment (quoted by Middlemas, Politics, p.152): 'Bolshevism is almost a safeguard to society, for it infects all classes with a horror of what might happen if the present organisation of society is overthrown.'
7. TC AR 1919, p.17: emphasis added.
8. See, e.g., TC AR 1917, p.15. Cp E.P. Thompson's discussion of the 'free-born Englishman', The Making of the English Working Class (London, 1963), esp. pp.77-101; see also V.G. Kiernan, 'Working Class and Nation in Nineteenth Century Britain', in M. Cornforth (ed.), Rebels and their Causes. Essays in Honour of A.L. Morton (London, 1978), pp.123-39.
9. TC AR 1917, p.15. Cp Council of Workers' and Soldiers' Delegates, What Happened at Leeds (London, 1917); S. White, 'Soviets in Britain: the Leeds Convention of 1917', International Review of Social History, vol. 19 (1974), pp.165-93.
10. SSF minutes, 10 January 1919: only on 26 January did the SSF formally declare itself a branch of the NSP.
11. NSP Edin. branch minutes, 9 March 1919.
12. Ibid., 16 March 1919.
13. Ibid., 22 June 1919.
14. The evidence for this latter suggestion is limited, and the conclusion must be tentative. A prominent member of the SSF branch (Cllr J.A. Young) was attacked at a meeting of the ILP Central branch (of which he was also a member) for being a member of the SSF and associated with the British Workers' League; it was even implied that the latter might put him forward as a parliamentary candidate for Edinburgh central. See ILP Central branch minutes, 20 September, 18 October, 15 November 1918. On the British Workers' League, see R. Douglas, 'The National Democratic Party and the British Workers' League', Historical Journal, vol. 15 (1972), pp.533-52.
15. Letter, G.J. Huckle, Secretary, Cambridge ILP to Secretary, ILP Central branch, 24 March 1918. The letter, which asked for approval and forwarding of a resolution, is endorsed 'Sent 23/4/18', which suggests support.
16. ILP Central branch minutes, 19 April, 19 July 1918.

17. Ibid., 16 August 1918, record a decision to send four delegates to a Plebs League discussion on allied intervention.

18. Ibid., undated (but 31 January 1919). It is unclear where the conference was held: a London 'Hands Off Russia' Committee was formed in January, though the national committee was only established later in the year; very likely an Edinburgh committee was also formed early in the year. Cp J. Klugmann, History of the Communist Party of Great Britain, vol. 1 (London, 1968), pp.78-9; L. MacFarlane, ' "Hands Off Russia", British Labour and the Russo-Polish War, 1920', Past & Present, no. 38 (1967), pp.126-52.

19. F. Douglas, Evening Dispatch, 9 August 1955.

20. See, e.g., TC minutes, 1 April, 6 July, 9 September 1919; NUR Edin. No. 1 branch minutes, 13 April 1919, 1 February 1920; NSP Edin. branch minutes, 23 June, 27 July, 12 December 1919, 4 April 1920; ILP Central branch minutes, 19 June 1919.

21. Douglas, Evening Dispatch, 9 August 1955.

22. The NUR Edin. No. 1 branch (minutes, 30 May 1920) agreed to affiliate; the Press and Machinemen pressed the Trades Council to send delegates to a Hands Off Russia conference (TC minutes, 18 May 1920).

23. T&LC minutes, 6 August 1920.

24. Douglas, Evening Dispatch, 9 August 1955. Cp R. Palme Dutt's comment that it was 'not essentially a revolutionary class-issue but simply an expression of war-weariness and horror at being dragged into another war' (Communist, 19 August 1920, quoted S. White, 'Labour's Council of Action 1920', Journal of Contemporary History, vol. 9 (1974), p.113).

25. T&LC minutes, 17 August 1920; Douglas, Evening Dispatch, 9 August 1955. For accounts of the visit to Moscow, see W. Gallacher, Revolt on the Clyde (London, 1936), pp.250-4, and The Rolling of the Thunder (London, 1947), pp.7-21; R. Challinor, John S. Clarke (London, 1977), pp.57-67.

26. T&LC minutes, 17 August 1920.

27. G.D.H. Cole, A History of the Labour Party from 1914 (London, 1948), p.56; see also R. Miliband, Parliamentary Socialism (London, 1973), pp.60-1; D. Coates, The Labour Party and the Struggle for Socialism (Cambridge, 1975), pp.14-15.

28. Miliband, Parliamentary Socialism, p.60; see also R. McKenzie, British Political Parties (London, 1963), p.482.

29. R. McKibbin, The Evolution of the Labour Party 1910-1924 (Oxford, 1974), p.244; see also ibid., pp. 91-106, R. Barker, Education and Politics 1900-51 (Oxford, 1974), esp. p.34.

30. R. Harrison, 'The War Emergency Workers' National Committee, 1914-1920', p.259; see also S. Beer, Modern British Politics (London, 1969), p.127.

31. ILP Central branch minutes, 17 December 1917, and passim.

32. The Trades Council's failure to comment on the Nottingham conference may reflect, in part, the timing of its annual reports, but the minutes for 1918 are also silent on the constitution.

33. LP Edin. branch AR 1917/18, p.3.

34. There is one intriguing example of the use of the language of Clause 4 in another context: a motion to include within the NUR's rules the following aim. 'To secure for Railwaymen the full fruits of their industry and the most aquiable [sic] administration and distribution thereof that my [sic] be possible, upon the basis of the common ownership of the means of production' (NUR Edin. No. 1 branch minutes, 15 September 1918). There is no indication as to whether the motion was passed. The branch's membership was aggressively socialist in its language at this time - indeed, this formulation is mild in comparison with several other motions agreed during 1918-20.

35. Letter, LP Edin. branch to Secretary, ILP Central branch, 17 December 1917.

36. When Pottinger resigned as LP Secretary, the SSF wrote 'thanking him for his work for the Federation': SSF minutes, 10 January 1919, emphasis added.

37. Letter, Pottinger to M. Marcus, Interim Secretary, ILP Central branch, 30 July 1918.

38. Letter, Pottinger to Secretary, ILP Central branch, 13 September 1918.

39. Ibid.

40. McKenzie, British Political Parties, 475-8.

41. LP Edin. branch AR 1917/18, p.3. The imminence of a general election was a constant theme of Henderson's correspondence with local Labour organisations during late 1917 and early 1918.

42. LP Edin. branch minutes, 13 December 1917.

43. Unions affiliated to the LP, Edinburgh branch, numbered 20 in 1917/18; 24 in 1919/20. Of these, those not affiliated to the TC were the Sawmillers and Workers Union

No. 1 branch (in both years), and the NUR No. 1 branch (in 1919/20). The first two were both small (the smallest unions affiliated, judging from affiliation fees); the Railwaymen disaffiliated from the TC for most unusual reasons.

44. LP Edin. branch minutes, 13 December 1917.
45. LP Edin. branch AR 1917/18, p.2.
46. TC minutes, 27 August 1918.
47. Ibid.
48. TC minutes, 14 October 1919; TC AR 1920, p.13.
49. TC ARs 1918, pp.25-8, 1920, pp.27-31; LP ARs 1917/18, p.8, 1919/20 in TC AR 1920, pp.22-3.
50. TC minutes, 23 March 1920 (ASLEF), 2 November 1920 (Amalgamated Portmanteau, Bag and Fancy Leather Workers' Trade Society).
51. NAUL No. 292 branch minutes, 21 April 1918.
52. NUC Edin. branch minutes, 4 March, 17 June, 4 November 1918, 14 July 1919.
53. Letter, Pottinger to J. McCorquodale, Secretary, ILP Central branch, 27 June 1918.
54. NAUL No. 292 branch minutes, 17 July, 7 August 1919.
55. Letter, Pottinger to McCorquodale, 27 June 1918.
56. LP Edin. branch AR 1917/18, p.2.
57. NAUL No. 292 branch minutes, 23 June 1919.
58. TC AR 1919, p.55.
59. NUC Edin. branch minutes, 23 June 1919.
60. TC AR 1920, p.55.
61. Ibid., p.13.
62. Ibid.
63. Ibid.
64. Ibid.
65. J. Hinton, The First Shop Stewards Movement (London, 1973), esp. p.307, discusses the impact of the soviet idea, especially strong in the west of Scotland.
66. ILP Central branch minutes, 19 April 1918; on Foulis, see John McArthur's recollections in I. MacDougall (ed.), Militant Miners (Edin. 1981), p.21; Douglas, Evening Dispatch, 11 August 1955; G. Brown, 'The Labour Party and Political Change in Scotland, 1918-1929', unpublished Ph.D. thesis, Edinburgh University, 1981, pp.115-16.
67. Douglas, Evening Dispatch, 9 August 1955; Hinton, First Shop Stewards Movement, pp.270-1, recounts the decline of the workers' committees from 1919.
68. NSP Edin. branch minutes, 2 May 1920: the speaker was reporting on meetings held 'some time' earlier, having been ill.

69. NUR Edin. No. 1 branch minutes, 10 November, 7 July, 29 September 1918.
70. NUC Edin. branch minutes, passim, esp. 23 September 1918; NAUL No. 292 branch minutes, passim, esp. 20 May 1920.
71. The quotations are from V.I. Lenin, 'Lessons of the Revolution', in Selected Works, vol. 2 (Moscow, 1970), pp.209-21. ILP Central branch minutes, 19 July 1918, show that this pamphlet was circulating in Edinburgh (in English) during the latter half of 1918.
72. ILP Central branch minutes, 7 March 1918 (subscription to The Socialist, an SLP newspaper), 22 March 1918 (debate with SLP 'That the ILP is worthy of working class support' proposed by R. Foulis, but rejected 11-4), 14 January 1919 (agreed 27-2 that 'it is desirable to have an open [ILP] platform for discussion from opponents', proposed by Foulis).
73. Ibid., 20 September 1918, 2, 9, 23 May 1919.
74. Ibid., 19 June 1919.
75. Ibid., 16 May, 19 June 1919. On the national context of such moves, see R. Dowse, Left in the Centre. The Independent Labour Party 1893-1940 (London, 1960), pp.47-8; A. Marwick, 'The Independent Labour Party (1918-32)', unpublished B. Litt. thesis, Oxford University, 1960, esp. pp. 84-92, 96-101; Klugmann, Communist Party, pp.25-38; W. Kendall, The Revolutionary Movement in Britain 1900-21 (London, 1969), esp. pp. 197-219, 269-70. By January 1920 the ILP in Scotland had voted for affiliation to the Third International by 151 votes to 28; this was overturned (472-206) at the April 1920 national conference.
76. Brown, 'Labour Party and Political Change', pp.115-16.
77. J.P.M. Millar, The Labour College Movement (London, n.d. [1979]), p.20.
78. J.H. Roberts, 'The National Council of Labour Colleges - An Experiment in Workers' Education', unpublished M.Sc. thesis, Edinburgh University, 1970, p.40.
79. Ibid., p.49; Plebs, November 1917.
80. E.g., Tom Drummond (ILP, formerly SLP), James Clunie (BSP), J.P.M. Millar (ILP): Plebs, December 1918, November 1920.
81. Roberts, 'The NCLC', p.55.
82. ILP Central branch minutes, 2 May 1919; the case had already been referred to the ILP's Divisional and National Advisory councils (ILP NAC minutes, 6-7 March 1919). At the following meeting (ibid., 9 May 1919) Shiels resigned, but was also declared to have ceased to be a member

'automatically' by virtue of the 'International' section of the new ILP rules; the minutes were 'not adopted' by 31 votes to 7.

83. Ibid., 2 May 1919.
84. Hinton, First Shop Stewards Movement, esp. pp.301-2; R. Challinor, The Origins of British Bolshevism (London, 1977), pp.240-4; Kendall, Revolutionary Movement, pp.196-201.
85. Hinton, First Shop Stewards Movement, p.255-69.
86. Plebs, December 1918.
87. Hinton, First Shop Stewards Movement, p.320-4.
88. NUR Edin. No. 1 branch minutes, 7, 21 December 1919.
89. Ibid., 21 December 1919.
90. Ibid., 29 February 1920.
91. Ibid., 28 March 1920.
92. Ibid., 29 February 1920.
93. Ibid., 12 September 1920.
94. Ibid., 24 October 1920; cp 24 April, 8 May 1921 (when it was recorded that the local Triple Alliance strike committee 'condemns the procrastination, and the lack of courage displayed' by the national leaders).
95. Ibid., 5 June 1921.
96. Ibid., 14 August 1921: this is the 'Platform' of the committee.
97. Plebs, June 1917.
98. Ibid., September 1917.
99. Ibid., November 1917: the Organiser was James Stobie.
100. Ibid., January 1918.
101. Ibid., April 1918.
102. Ibid., November 1920.
103. Ibid., December 1920.
104. Scottish Labour College, Edin. district minutes, 15 January 1921, quoted in Roberts, 'The NCLC', p.57.
105. Plebs, June 1921.
106. Ibid., December 1920, August 1921.
107. Douglas, Evening Dispatch, 9, 10, 11 August 1955.
108. T&LC minutes, 23 August, 6 September 1921.
109. Millar, Labour College Movement, p.186; Roberts, 'The NCLC', p.103. Woodburn's membership of the CP was only brief.
110. Kendall, Revolutionary Movement, p.294.
111. J.S. Clarke, 'Foreword' to W. Gallacher and J.R. Campbell, Direct Action. An Outline of Workshop and Social Organisation (London, 1972 [first published Glasgow, 1919]), pp.10-11.
112. Ibid., p.32.

Chapter Nine

THE STRUGGLE FOR LABOUR POLITICS

the time has arrived, if not already past, for a
general stocktaking in the Socialist movement. Our
weapons and armour have become obsolete. ... The
high hopes of 1919 are already shattered, and
pessimism is gaining ground. The tactics of
Socialism must be altered to meet an entirely new
situation.[1]

The apparent unity achieved within the labour movement
during those brief post-war years was founded on understandings and beliefs about the nature of politics, about
political and industrial action, about their relationships and
possibilities. These were grounded in the movement's pre-
war experience, but had in most cases been fundamentally
modified by the war: in addition, the war had given
legitimacy to certain principles which had an overarching
effect in the post-war reconstruction of the political
organisation of labour. Essentially, these had pointed the
way to more 'efficient' organisational structures: which
meant hierarchical, centralised structures after the military
model. 'Organisation' in this sense was attractive almost
universally, for it appeared to provide the solution - or at
least a part of the solution - to many of the problems which
the movement confronted: despite varying definitions of the
problems themselves. However, this unity did not run deep.
It could justify a need for better mechanisms, but it could
not point to how these should be used. Thus although some
of the motives which lay behind the formation of the Trades
and Labour Council and of the Communist Party were the
same, the former was not seen by Marxists as a substitute
for the latter.

At the same time, unity was enhanced in the immediate
post-war years by a number of factors. First, during 1919, to
an extent into 1920, industrial organisation could be seen as
a major source of political power for labour: it had shown
great possibilities during 1910-14 and the war; its failings

during 1919 (and earlier) could plausibly be ascribed to poor leadership (or organisation). In addition, although the 1918 Representation of the People Act had given Labour a means of constitutional advance, the General Election had been a disappointment. William Graham's victory was against the tide; Ramsay MacDonald, who lost his seat in the debacle, argued in January 1919 that 'this Parliament has no moral authority. When political organisation is crushed by fraud or force industrial organisation is the only defence that is left.'[2] Many who would normally have opposed strenuously any 'unconstitutional' action now contemplated it as a means to press a deceitful government back to responsibility. Industrial action might be used to redress the balance of the constitution.[3] In Edinburgh this seems to have been a common view: Graham for instance, (who did not share it) was strongly attacked within the ILP for, among other reasons, stating that 'he was no believer in the "ca'canny" policy'. The first Labour MP in the city, within seven months of his election, survived a vote of no confidence from one of the branches which had nominated him by just 36 votes to 25 - and at a public meeting.[4]

Third, as we have seen, the political differences within the labour movement in 1918-21 were often within, as well as between, its various parties and organisations. This had two aspects. On the one hand, it discouraged the development of clear central principles within an organisation. During 1917, the Scottish Secretary of the Labour Party expressed concern about this:

It is a little aggravating to find so many organisations cropping up and appealing to our clientele and more or less overlapping ours. It cannot be helped meantime ... when challenged those persons point to the fact that the Labour Party has no programme.[5]

But even after February 1918 Labour's programme was a very general one, which allowed both Graham and John Maclean to be official candidates in 1918. On the other hand, the structure of labour politics hindered attempts to impose any clear definition of its purpose or boundaries. The ILP - to a lesser extent the other socialist parties - and the various trade unions had members who could spread the word, or they had money, or both. The Labour Party had neither: the growth of the apparatus of individual membership after 1918 was painfully slow;[6] and many of these members seem also to have been ILPers or

Communists - their membership a matter of convenience, and their prime loyalties elsewhere. The Labour Party's main strength was its electoral role: its claim to control the movement's interventions in elections was generally acceded. But the electoral setback of 1918, followed by poor showings in municipal elections in 1920 and 1921 (Labour representation fell from six to two) eroded the perceived importance of elections. Thus the Labour Party was unable to prevent the Railwaymen from fielding, in 1921, its own municipal candidate in opposition to Labour - despite support from the national leaderships of union and party.[7] When electoral politics did not convince as a route to power, the Labour Party's ability to control the disparate elements of the movement was small. Consequently, it was unable to assert effectively any definition of what Labour politics was. During the early post-war years, Labour's political unity was based (in large part) not on agreement, but on confusion about the nature of the disagreements, and on inability to enforce any particular version on the movement.

From 1920, new allegiances, new coalitions, began to form within the labour movement. These were based on common understandings of the political world: the strength of the working class; whether this strength was primarily 'industrial' or 'political'; what these terms meant; the possibilities of parliamentary action; and so forth. Sometimes - as when reassessment reduced the contradictions within individuals' or groups' political outlooks - they could become formal alliances between political or social groups. Some of these coalitions did not last; but by the later 1920s the politics of labour were, ideologically as well as in organisation, recognisably those which persisted for half a century.

THE FAILURE OF DIRECT ACTION, 1920

If the early post-war years brought a reorganisation of labour's political institutions, for some they had promised more. 'Direct action' would bring real achievements for labour and socialism - whether revolutionary change or, as MacDonald preferred, 'Parliamentary Opposition ... from the outside'.[8] During 1920 the Labour Party, for the first and last time, initiated substantial 'extra-parliamentary' action: in the celebrated Council of Action campaign against British intervention in the Russo-Polish war.[9] The Labour leadership - so many now outside the Commons - was prepared to countenance such methods: at least, found opposing them

195

more difficult. Elections were still distant, and the parliamentary party weak, especially within the movement. 'Hands Off Russia' committees had been forcing the pace around the country. Defence of the revolution was closely bound up with defence of Russians' right to choose their own form of government, evoking memories of Belgium and labour support for war in 1914. More war and conscription threatened. The objective was clear; the method appropriate; the end achieved.

Yet by the end of 1920, confidence in direct action - at least in Edinburgh - had been dashed. The Council of Action campaign coincided with the city's own exercise in direct action: an exercise which was to occupy the local labour movement's institutions for far longer, yet which was destined to fail. The Scottish rent strike of 1920 deeply influenced perceptions of what direct action could achieve, at least for the movement's mainstream. Housing had long been an important issue for labour; the war brought rent rises, rent strikes, rent restriction legislation, the formation of the Scottish Labour Housing Association, and (in 1917) the Report of the Royal Commission on Scottish working-class housing.[10] Together these showed that successful action on housing was possible, and lent strength to arguments for drastic action. Just after the war, the government seemed ready to move: state provision of 'habitations fit for the heroes who have won the war'[11] (of superior design and in much larger numbers) was promised by the 1919 Housing Act. By late 1920 the government was playing down this commitment, as the Treasury won the battle for 'economy' and the threat of revolution receded.[12] In Edinburgh, where property owners dominated the Town Council and its committees (they made up, for instance, 69 per cent of the Housing and Town Planning Committee), official enthusiasm for the 1919 policy was ever muted.[13]

> For six months, demobilised men and civilians have been clamouring for employment, but not a stone or brick has been laid in Edinburgh. The public were assured that schemes were ready; that, as soon as labour could be found, the work would be tackled. The Town Council now blame the Local Government Board [which] ... denies responsibility,[14]

the Trades Council reported in 1919. Eventually building began, on various schemes, but they 'proceed[ed] at a painfully slow pace,' although the need became 'daily ...

more clamant'.[15]

In the summer of 1919, a rent strike occurred in Rosyth which, as we have seen, had close links with Edinburgh. Accounts of the number of householders involved differ: 700, and 1,500 to 1,600 out of 1,602 houses. But it was substantial: and despite legal action against 14 strikers, 'thanks to the amazing solidarity on the part of the workers' wives in withholding the rents for over six weeks, they were successful in compelling the Government to have their claims fully investigated'.[16] This set the labour movement thinking: the Trades Council, for instance, commended 'a novel method of dealing with the Rent Question'; 'a precedent which will not readily be lost sight of by the working class of Edinburgh'.[17] The strike reached its successful conclusion in August 1919; in October the Trades Council convened a conference on housing, and in December it agreed to call a public meeting to establish a Tenants' Defence League.[18] This was 'manned and officered by men of legal training', and was to 'keep a jealous eye on the rights of its members': within three months it had a membership of 'quite respectable proportions'.[19]

A mechanism designed to associate the labour movement with tenants, this was probably also intended to mobilise: the main activity of earlier 'Tenants' Defence Leagues', notably in Glasgow and Rosyth, had been just the prosecution of rent strikes. There had, then, been over six months' local preparation when, in May 1920, the Scottish Labour Housing Association summoned a conference in Glasgow, to consider action against rent increases under the 1920 Rent Act.[20] There was a strong difference of opinion, certainly among Edinburgh labour. The Trades Council's delegates' report was rejected by 33 votes to 10 when it became clear that they had supported a rent strike if rents were increased.[21] A Railwaymen's delegate (a strong revolutionary syndicalist) referred in particular to a suggestion that the rent strike should be associated with a stoppage of work: 'the proposed 24 hours strike discussion had been rushed'; he was not opposed to industrial action for political ends, but to the entire objective. 'He thought it was a waste of time. The real issue is not to restrict rents but to get houses damn the high rents, get this in your wages.'[22]

So in Edinburgh at least there were serious doubts about whether a rent strike, and associated industrial action, could succeed. The SLHA felt it necessary to summon another conference; the STUC called on its affiliates to attend and support the call for a 24-hour stoppage of work.[23] The Trades Council's Executive met with eight members of the Tenants' Defence League: their view was that a rent strike alone was unlikely to succeed, and that it should be associated with a stoppage of work which was more than symbolic. Recommended to support either 'no strike' or a 'complete strike', the council instructed its delegates to argue for a complete strike until the 1920 Act was withdrawn.[24] The Railwaymen, still reluctant to act on rents, nonetheless agreed to send delegates to Glasgow 'on ground that workers must be up and doing. If Glasgow workers resisted paying rents we cannot stand by without giving them help.'[25] At the conference, attended by '14 or 15 hundred delegates from all over Scotland',[26] the Trades Council's motions were ruled out of order,[27] and it became effectively committed to the resolutions agreed: a 24-hour stoppage of work on 23 August in opposition to the government's allowing rent rises; a refusal to pay the increases proposed by the new Act; and the organisation of meetings and demonstrations in support of these.[28]

Edinburgh's misgivings proved well founded. Substantial preparation took place: a manifesto, and a covenant to be signed by tenants refusing to pay, were drawn up: a public meeting was called in the Meadows to demand 'No Increase in Rents'.[29] The Trades Council's Secretary, Alexander Smith, was exceptionally paid a salary to work full-time as organiser of the campaign: he opened a 'central bureau' at the council's rooms in Bristo Port.[30] Yet although the one-day stoppage of work was judged a success (according to Forward, 10,000 attended the demonstration that Monday),[31] by 31 August the council's Executive virtually admitted defeat: only about 15 per cent of tenants were withholding payment, and 'owing to the number of people paying rent they recommended that tenants should not resist eviction'.[32] Attempts were made to resuscitate the action: a conference of union officials was summoned, advertisements were placed in the press for financial support, an effort made 'to organise for November'. But all to no avail: by late October the Rent Strike Committee was £80 in the red, and in early December it was wound up.[33]

This set-back, whilst coinciding with the apparent achievement of the 'Hands Off Russia' action, had a far more profound impact on the political thinking of labour in Edinburgh. It demonstrated the fragility of the movement: its image as an army, a machine, organised for the struggle, crumbled before a different reality. The 'unity' which could produce institutional change was not strong enough to achieve a successful mobilisation in 'direct action'. A number of institutions within the movement (from the Parliamentary Labour Party to local union branches) opposed the rent strike. A number of union branches doubted their ability to mobilise even for a 24-hour stoppage of work on the issue; two rejected the Trades Council's proposals outright.[34] But perhaps more telling, of the organisations represented at the Edinburgh conference which had given instructions to proceed with the rent strike, no less than 32 had not contributed financially over two months - the two critical months - later.[35] In short, the action failed not because the forces of the landlords, or of the state, had proved too powerful in open conflict: labour had simply proved unable to bring its battalions on to the field.

This led to widespread questioning of labour's strategy and tactics - although the movement's various currents developed different criticisms. For some syndicalists, the rent strike was 'dragging the workers into a mess'; the answer was to 'ask the working class to organise themselves to abolish the cause of rising rents and all their other problems - the capitalist system'.[36] For others on the left, although the 'only thing to cause the oppressors to think was to stop the wheels of industry', the rent strike should be supported because it was necessary to act 'on the ground of the class struggle as we found it, this on the ground of historic development'.[37] For one important element, however, the lessons of the rent agitation were lessons about direct action, and about the possibilities of any industrial action. This interpretation also drew on recent industrial experience, a sense that 'with overwhelming numbers of unemployed, with Capital armed with large reserve funds and replete with carefully prepared machinery, the power of the strike can only be effective to an uncertain degree'.[38] For this section of the movement, an alternative strategy was to 'return to political effort':[39] to concentrate on developing local Labour parties 'to carry out the necessary Parliamentary and Municipal propaganda',[40] and to shift away from direct action - now characterised as 'revolutionary industrial methods'.[41]

The failure of direct action, and the erosion of union strength, placed intolerable strains on the post-war labour coalition. This, though not deeply-rooted, had rested on two main elements. The first was the strength of notions of organisation and efficiency, which provided the basis for the restructuring of the movement's political institutions. In essence, this remained unchallenged. The second was the commonality over method which, temporarily and over a limited range of issues, had seen labour politicians prepared to take 'direct action'. Many factors were required for this, but perhaps the most basic was a belief that the methods of direct action worked. During 1920 this belief was knocked away; not, indeed, for the entire spectrum of labour thought, but for a crucial segment. From late 1920, therefore, labour politics regrouped around two new positions.

LABOUR SOCIALISM, MARXISM AND THEIR COALITIONS

In an important study, Stuart Macintyre has proposed that labour politics in the 1920s can be understood in terms of 'the opposition of two doctrines, Marxism and Labour Socialism'. The latter was 'the political perspective of the Labour activists of the period, along with the more general understanding of the social and economic processes which supported this perspective':[42] it was most clearly articulated by men such as MacDonald and Philip Snowden:

> The purpose of Labour Socialism ... was to lift the working class up from its lowly pre-occupation with wages and conditions, and to endow it with a sense of social purpose. This involved the articulation of an elaborate theoretical edifice: a historical perspective of social progress in the nineteenth century positivist tradition; an economic analysis to show that the worker was denied the full fruits of his labour; an organic view of society to indicate how this injustice ought to be corrected.[43]

This doctrine implied considerable scepticism about strikes, which threatened the concept of an organic society, and great confidence in the power of moral appeal and education. Now in the immediate aftermath of war, this doctrine was weak. MacDonald, ejected from Parliament, found a justification for direct action. William Graham, recently returned, and most prominent of Edinburgh's Labour Socialists, went some way to meet the direct actionists. He expressed doubts about the House of Commons, whose 'whole atmosphere ... was almost fatal to men who were in earnest ... Hardly any measure within recent times had gone to the roots of the social and

economic wrong.'[44] And he extended a hand to the direct
actionists, essentially inviting them to enter the Labour
Socialist fold:

> The most ardent advocate of direct action would
> not dispute that it was wrong to concentrate on
> industrial issues. After all their discussion they had
> always to come back to general well-being, to a
> real community of effort, in which sectional
> demands were subordinated to public progress, and
> to such a combination of activity in the industrial
> field and in politics as would achieve the proper
> relationship of industry to the State and the State
> to industry ... [45]

As the post-war boom passed, however, the self-confidence
of Labour Socialism increased. Direct action no longer
seemed capable of providing solutions; the Labour Socialist
commitment to progress through moral appeal was no longer
threatened. Thus we find Graham attacking 'the "Left Wing"
[and] ... the harm they were doing to the Labour Party'[46] at
a Trades and Labour Council meeting; and the council's
Executive regretting that

> The easily seen benefits and quick returns of war
> and post-war trade union activity gave an undue
> prominence to the possibilities of revolutionary
> industrial methods, and created an attractive
> school of thought, which found expression in the
> growth of some revolutionary bodies and the
> creation of others.[47]

It was a 'lamentable fact that these organisations attracted
undesirable elements', and 'the ebullient propaganda of
the[se] bodies which dub themselves revolutionary have
entirely failed to attract any substantial support from the
workers generally'.[48] This 'fact' was comforting, for it
underlined the Labour Socialists' belief that 'revolutionary
heroics do not readily accord with the temperament of the
men and women who make up the great body of our people',
and that 'the development of the local Labour Parties ... to
carry out the necessary Parliamentary and Municipal propaganda ... will put a power into our hands that cannot be
denied'.[49]

　　In practice, of course, Labour Socialism was important
as the central, justifying, doctrine of an important section
of labour. Its adherents - men and women in the mould of
William Graham - were as nothing unless they could
construct effective alliances. (In 1919 and early 1920 this

had been impossible: indeed, its isolation had been so great as to induce confusion among some of its leading exponents.) But a coalition could not require the wholesale acceptance of Labour Socialist beliefs. Rather, it required certain central notions: fragments of Labour Socialist doctrine sometimes, or the outcome (so to say) of 'negotiations' between Labour Socialism and the guiding assumptions of other groupings.

Though not static, the coalition which formed around Labour Socialism was grounded on two main principles. First, political and industrial action were seen as distinct; in particular, the latter could not be used legitimately in pursuit of the former. This formed the basis of the alliance between Labour Socialism and the more economistic, 'labourist', views of many prominent trade unionists. For while Labour Socialism was essential unsympathetic to industrial action, labourism often involved an acceptance that militant industrial action was necessary in pursuit of a 'fair day's pay'. The resolution lay in confining industrial action to a collective bargaining role. This was, of course, a notion enshrined in law: unions' entitlement to take industrial action 'in contemplation of furtherance of a trade dispute' had been hard won and not easily maintained; ardent defence of this position no doubt enhanced still further the status lent to it by statute.[50] Moreover, this formulation allowed the Labour Socialists to justify their apparent sympathy with some of the direct action of 1919 and 1920: retrospectively, it could be redefined as industrial action, pure and simple. Second, political action was constitutional action: fighting parliamentary and municipal elections, and propaganda and organisation to this end. This was not, in itself, a meeting-point with other sections of the movement; but there was a widespread agreement that this was a fundamental form of politics even among those (many, for instance, in the ILP) who did not agree that it defined the boundaries of politics. Thus it enabled Labour Socialism to adopt a clear strategy which could be pursued at all times, and which (at almost all times) could be pursued in co-operation with the Labour left.

Between Labour Socialism and its main opposition - Marxism - were at least three political trends which provided motivation for significant numbers within the labour movement: labourism, the ILP left, and syndicalism. These, the main trends whose support Labour Socialists could seek, were also objects of Marxist blandishment. Their strength waxed and waned in relation to many factors - not least, of course, their successes. Thus the objective, though not always consciously or clearly stated, of Labour Socialists and Marxists was not merely to mobilise these trends in common action, but to shift individuals' outlooks nearer to their own. Since this was but partially achieved, what we may term the Labour Socialist and Marxist coalitions[51] were inherently unstable. They were constructed around a limited range of issues, and on the basis of certain sets of legitimising principles; when the issues (or the way they were perceived) changed, the alignments might shift.

THE LABOUR SOCIALIST COALITION AND LABOURISM
The eventual success of Labour Socialism stemmed from its ability to form working relationships with trade union labourism and with the Labour left, largely grouped in the ILP. We now examine how these were achieved.

When the possibilities of direct action began to seem more remote, perhaps from the summer of 1920, Labour Socialism began to assert itself. At this stage there was no clear appreciation of future allies and adversaries. To be sure, in a paper probably written in 1921, Graham appealed to the trade unions to 'determine their attitude to political action', claiming that 'The extravagancies of some of the left-wing theorists of recent years have been costly to the trade union movement and they have in part contributed to present chaos.' At the same time, he claimed to note a 'healthy reaction in favour of reliance on the ballot box'.[52] But whilst the ideas of direct action might be wrongheaded, there was in 1920 and 1921 an attempt to win over the people who held them. Their contributions were praised. The revolutionary bodies, for instance, 'have undoubtedly generated sincere enthusiasms, and, of more importance, they have created a healthy movement for economic study, untramelled by the accepted nostrums of orthodox defenders of the system of big and easy profits'.[53] Some of the institutions created in this period were now, apparently, seen as established parts of the labour body politic - to be converted, perhaps, in due time. 'The Scottish Labour College, and like institutions,' opined the Trades and Labour Council's Executive in 1921, 'have sprung into permanent being, and when they emerge from the inevitable limitations of immature experience, they will undoubtedly contribute greatly to the real progress of Labour.'[54] Labour Socialism's electoral strategy needed, not indeed the ideas, but the effort, of syndicalism's erstwhile or temporary adherents. The 'ebullient propaganda of the bodies which dub themselves revolutionary', and their 'Enthusiasm, ability and genuine effort have undoubtedly attracted a goodly number of keen workers who would normally have been useful units in the great work of the Labour Movement'.[55]

During 1921, the hopes of syndicalism were dashed as the Triple Alliance fell apart. The syndicalists themselves were increasingly isolated: a railwayman, for instance, who attacked his union's election manifesto as 'not ... in line with revolutionary socialism' found himself in a small minority.[56] This meant, on the one hand, that direct action waned in importance, losing the direction provided by an ascendant and self-confident syndicalism. On the other hand, it became easier for Labour Socialists to establish links with those who, for several years previously, had advocated direct action. In short, syndicalism was less of a threat - and its former supporters more open to attempts to win them into alliance on other bases.

Trade union support was essential if the Labour Socialist strategy was to succeed. Union membership was the only substantial and reliable source of income for the Labour Party, particularly during the early years when membership and electoral success might prove elusive. This became especially clear after the debacle at the 1919 municipal election: for the ILP's contribution to the Election Fund in that year (£55 8s 9d) slumped to £2 7s 2½d in 1920, whilst union contributions (which had been larger anyway) fell just £7 3s 6d to £61 6s.[57] The ILP's reliance on the efforts of individual collectors[58] was far more sensitive to moods of success and failure than the institutional decisions of union organisations. Yet electoral success was expensive. In 1919, for instance, £223 18s 10d had been spent on elections in Edinburgh alone; but all six Town Council candidates were defeated, and only two Parish Council candidates were victorious.[59] The rate of return was poor; other indications from this first post-war contest were equally inauspicious. The defeats were, at least in part, due to 'a new coalition, a combination of all sections of Liberals and Unionists against collectivism in municipal affairs', The Scotsman reported:

> the electors did not ask the politics of the candidates who stood against the Labourists; in several cases it was, indeed, not known to which

party a non-Socialist candidate belonged. It was enough for the average citizen to be appraised of the man who represented the Labour ticket. That knowledge determined his choice; and by agreement between the non-Socialist parties the door of Edinburgh Town Council has been closed against preachers of the street corner gospel of extremism.[60]

If Labour was to be thus opposed, the road to electoral victory might be long, arduous, and expensive.

The onset of depression broke the liaison - always unstable and tenuous - between syndicalism and labourism. The apostles of direct action had been of some value when industrial action seemed a viable union strategy: they had various organisational and tactical skills, and their activism was dedicated to trade union (rather than 'political') organisation. But even in 1920 the liaison had been limited to a relatively narrow range of issues. When, for instance, an active Railwaymen's departmental representative applied for promotion to inspector,[61] some argued from a syndicalist position against 'active members taking official positions. It being a mere impossibility for a member to fight on both sides. Too often it meant that such members "emancipated" themselves and not the workers.'[62] But they were isolated, unable to overcome the labourist assumption that a good man could exercise managerial tasks in the interests of the workers. From 1921 the areas on which syndicalism and labourism could find common ground diminished further, leaving room for the Labour Socialists' advances. In a conscious re-evaluation of strategy in 1921, the Trades and Labour Council's Executive implicitly criticised post-war union policies.

The Strike is one of the most important rights which we possess, and your Executive would be the last authority to suggest that the Strike weapon must be abandoned or relaxed ... [But] while it is a weapon, it is only a weapon. It cannot become a policy and only foolhardy men, regardless of consequences, can be blind to its limitations.[63]

Here was labourism distancing itself from syndicalism and direct action.

Labourism, however, was never a coherent and consistent political standpoint, as Marxism and Labour Socialism were (or as syndicalism aspired to be). It had no theorists: it was, rather, an amorphous amalgam of attitudes and policies, with a more or less specific relationship to collective bargaining. Although this lent it great flexibility, it was also a limitation. For while syndicalism and the theorists of direct action might have been peddling a 'foolhardy' strategy, it was at least a strategy. Here Labour Socialism found a role. The war and its aftermath had demonstrated that

> whatever our trade ... while Governmental power is
> in the hands of Capital interests, the strength of
> the State stands armed against the worker.[64]

Labour Socialism promised that this power could be won by electoral means: it proposed a strategy in which the unions had a vital role, but not one which would jeopardise their industrial position. It did not suggest (unlike syndicalism or Marxism) that industrial action could further political ends. Rather, it allowed the unions to retain flexible, empirical, industrial attitudes: 'a positive industrial policy includes much more than the use of the Strike in every emergency', but 'should be supplemented by vigorous and sustained work by Labour in the political field.'[65]

In essence then, Labour Socialism and labourism could marry because each accepted a division between 'political' and 'industrial' issues; and because the latter were acknowledged to be the preserve of trade unions. Their relationship was not always an easy one. The labourists' economism (perhaps most explicitly expressed when the Plasterers condemned the Town Council's 'stopping the work on Housing Schemes in the City' not because of the resulting shortage of accommodation but because it was 'preventing a worker from selling his Labour in the Highest Market)'[66] lay uneasily with Labour Socialist notions of social unity and harmony. And when economism became militant, or when employers took the offensive, the axis of labourism could shift again to a point where the direct action of syndicalism or - increasingly - Communism began to seem relevant. But the liaison was underpinned by the growth of the Labour Party's apparatus. This enabled Labour Socialism to promote a definition of politics which severely restricted the left; and it provided a structure which sought to separate political from industrial action, and thus supported labourist views of trade unions' role.

The assumption of those who had formed the Trades and Labour Council was, as we have seen, that it could be turned to whatever end its members and affiliates might desire. During our period it did indeed serve as a 'council of action', as well as directing the local Labour Party apparatus. But these two roles, which typify the syndicalist (or Communist) and Labour Socialist strategies respectively, made structural demands on the entire local labour and trade union movement; these roles were incompatible.

Before the Trades and Labour Council was formed, local Labour organisation in the city was haphazard: ward committees varied in strength, but were concentrated in some - by no means all - of the working class wards. Probably they existed sporadically, being formed on a more or less ad hoc basis when an election was imminent, and fading away thereafter: they had, after all, no other function.[67] By 1920, when the amalgamation took place, there was 'the nucleus of three Divisional Labour Parties in the city - Central, West and North'[68]: a formulation which suggests there was little more than a nucleus.[69] The Labour Party, therefore, had much to gain from its organisational fusion with the trade unions, but little to offer save hope for the future: 'The remedy is obviously not to petition, but to control.'[70] Save financially, however, gains did not automatically accrue; in 1920 and 1921 the trade union delegates (a substantial majority of the new council)[71] showed little sign of concern for their new charge - clearly demonstrated in the council's unwillingness to postpone or rearrange its regular fortnightly meeting on election day in 1920.[72] Apart from agreeing election addresses and selecting candidates,[73] party organisation was not discussed until June 1921.

So for the first 18 months, or thereabouts, of the new council's existence, the Labour Party had handed over its government in Edinburgh to trade union delegates - amongst whose notions of political activity electoral strategy did not loom large. During the latter part of 1921, however, this began to change. A loose Labour Socialist grouping, centring on the Edinburgh branch of the Social Democratic Federation, took advantage of the eroding influence of direct action. A substantial number of SDF members held important positions in the local movement, and especially in the Trades and Labour Council;[74] they seemed to have realised that the Labour Party apparatus could be used to develop a strong, constitutional, political bloc within the movement. So it was William Elger, the council's President and a member of the local SDF executive committee, who in June 1921 set in train the organisation of the party machine. The council's executive heard reports from divisional Labour

Parties: Elger stressed the need for 'perfecting machinery', and insisted on statements of the 'actual position' of membership and finance from each. Each local party was to meet within three weeks, and a special sub-committee of council executive and DLP representatives would meet monthly.[75] Over the following months this detailed work was started: questions of finance, propaganda, literature, registration of voters, were tackled. Previously, it seems, the party had not even had copies of the voters' roll.[76] Then, when the 1921 municipal elections were over, a system of central funding to DLPs was agreed.[77]

All this could be achieved for three main reasons. First, the pressure from national and Scottish Labour Parties was backed by politically and organisationally able local supporters. Second, direct action was beginning to seem less and less plausible as a political strategy. And, third, the direct action coalition had never, in any event, defined political action to the exclusion of electoral methods: it had simply won a commitment to its own. In addition, it had developed no institutions which could impose, and 'police', such definitions. So there was no basis for the emergence of opposition to the Labour Socialist proposals. The strength of the Labour Socialist strategy, then, was its ability to mobilise widely held principles - essentially, those based around notions of organisation, which were non-contentious - to promote a form of political organisation; a form, moreover, which promoted a particular type of political activity. Although Labour politics were not narrow, encompassing right and left trends, they did increasingly define the strategy (as electoral) within which these trends could operate.

A critical decision was made in April 1922: the Trades and Labour Council appointed a Political Officer,[78] to 'be responsible for those duties appertaining to the activities of Local Labour Parties'.[79] This allowed a measure of autonomy to the party apparatus, and meant that one man was responsible for the party. The first Political Officer was relatively ineffectual; but he was succeeded in April 1923 by a man of considerable energy and ability, Frank Smithies. In his early forties, Smithies was a long-standing member of the SDF; he was in a position to organise his own time, earning his living after 1921 as a conjurer and Punch-and-Judy man.[80] He also had the good fortune to take on the post when the Labour vote in Edinburgh was growing most rapidly. Apart from pressing on with the development of local organisation,[81] Smithies fought to expand and consolidate the role of the Political Officer, ensuring, for instance, that he should attend all selection conferences as of right.[82]

The gradual strengthening of the divisional parties continued over the following years, helped, no doubt, by Labour's successes at the general elections of 1922, 1923 and 1924.[83] By the spring of 1924 the Trades and Labour Council was claiming that 'Ward Committees have been established in all wards of the City, and are working energetically'.[84] As a result, the status and strength of the party, in relation to other sections of the movement, improved. Of course, many ward committees were weak creatures; and the ILP continued to be the main source of active support. But the divisional Labour Party delegates were, in the main, more assiduous in their attendance at the (governing) council's meetings (as Table 9.1 shows). Thus, in large part, they determined the political direction of the movement as a whole. Increasingly, too, the DLPs began to exercise a certain autonomous authority, in relation to elections at least - and, so far as Labour Socialism was concerned, could be a counterweight to the Trades and Labour Council when the left gained a (temporary) ascendency. When, for instance, a council executive member and ILP leftist 'called Ramsay MacDonald a traitor' at a Council meeting,[85] she was forced to resign as a Town Council candidate by her ward committee and DLP, despite support from the Trades and Labour Council.[86] In addition, the various other labour political parties - above all, the ILP and the Communist Party - could be 'boxed-in' by a variety of means; prevented from gaining access to important areas. In 1924, for instance, as Table 9.1 suggests, the ILP seems to have made an effort to assert its authority within the local movement: the Trades and Labour Council made sure it did not succeed. The ILP was forbidden to ask union branches for money without the council's approval;[87] the Central ILP branch was excluded from the East Division parliamentary nomination meeting;[88] an attempt by an ILP branch to summon a parliamentary selection meeting in South Edinburgh was severely squashed.[89] The process by which Communist influence was attacked, though similar, was more protracted; we shall deal with this later in the chapter.

Table 9.1: Participation of ILP and Labour Party Delegates in Edinburgh Trades and Labour Council 1920-7

	1920/1	1921/2	1922/3	1923/4	1924/5	1925/6	1926/7
Number of Delegates:							
Labour Party	18	21	24	27	30	30	31
ILP	9	6	6	15	20	21	23
Mean Number of Meetings Attended by each Delegate (a):							
Labour Party	8.0	6.4	10.1	5.5	6.0	10.0	7.1
ILP	8.0	16.0	7.8	4.5	7.8	4.5	5.8
Mean Number of Delegates Attending each Meeting (a):							
Labour Party	5.3	5.4	9.3	5.5	5.6	8.3	7.9
ILP	2.7	3.8	1.8	2.5	4.9	2.6	4.7

Note: (a) Because the number of meetings held varied slightly from year to year, these figures are not strictly comparable between years. This applies especially to 1924/5 and 1925/6, when substantially more meetings than usual were held.

Source: Calculated from T&LC ARs, 1921-7.

THE LABOUR SOCIALIST COALITION AND THE LABOUR LEFT

The basis of Labour Socialism's coalition with the left was the ILP's missionary zeal, for most of Labour's left was grouped in the ILP in the early and mid-1920s. In essence, the ILP, and the left, were permitted, even encouraged, to indulge in propaganda; generally, no bounds were put on this. The Trades and Labour Council did not, for instance, attempt to control the ILP's public speakers, or reprimand them for unacceptable utterances. Here the ILP was very active. And because the ILP in the early 1920s had 'no conception of a disciplined and centralised party permeating the looser organisation of the Labour Party',[90] when it did wander outside its appointed area, it. tended to do so in a confused and ineffectual way. These 'frontier skirmishes' became more common from 1923, as the ILP drove to strengthen its organisation and increase its membership and number of branches; and as, in reaction to the experience of the Labour government, the ILP left attempted to change the nature of its party. But they remained the exception: in general, the achievement of the ILP was its enabling radical opinions to be expressed, but in an institutional context which minimised their effect on the direction of Labour politics. Three major areas into which the left's energies were channelled illuminate this process: the ILP's organisational and propaganda work; the socialist movement's attempts to integrate the young; and the promotion of a local labour paper, the Labour Standard.

The ILP reached a peak of membership in 1920, from which it declined over the following two years. But from 1922, under a new national leadership, and spurred by the election results of that year, it embarked on a period of furious organisational growth; Scotland made the pace.[91] The increases in the number of ILP branches in Edinburgh, and in their total membership, were dramatic; although the figures in Table 9.2 are not a wholly reliable guide (ILP branches were not obliged to affiliate to the Trades and Labour Council and there was no effective method of ensuring affiliation on full membership), the scale of the changes leaves little room for doubt.[92] The early and mid-1920s was a period of massive upheaval for the ILP in Edinburgh. New members had to be integrated, educated into its outlook and methods. Branch management was a major problem; many officials were inexperienced, and themselves needed training. And this is to leave aside the

Table 9.2: The ILP in Edinburgh, 1919-27

	Number of ILP branches:		T&LC Affiliation Fees:			
	Affiliated to T&LC	Paying Affiliation Fees to T&LC	Amount Paid £	s	d	Number of Members Paid for
1919/20	3	4	1	13	8	(a)
1920/1						
Edinburgh	4	3	5	8	4	325 (b)
Leith	1	1		19	0	76 (b)
1921/2	2	4	5	7	10	323
1922/3	2	4	4	8	4	265
1923/4	5	3	4	8	4	265
1924/5	8	5	6	12	0	396
1925/6 (c)	9	8	10	5	6	616
1926/7	10	8	9	13	2	579

Notes: (a) No record survives of affiliation fee scales for the Edin. LP before amalgamation.
(b) Affiliation fee to Edin. T&LC was 4d per member throughout; affiliation fee to Leith United TC&LP was 3d per member.
(c) Edin. Central ILP Women's section was also affiliated in 1925/6, paying 6s 8d (fee for 20 members): it has been excluded from these figures since its members were probably also members of ILP Central branch.
(General) The T&LC's financial year ran from 1 April to 31 March.

Sources: T&LC ARs, 1921-7; T&LC Rules, 1922; Leith United TC&LP Rules, 1918.

party's political work: 'doing propaganda, ... watching our interests within the Labour Party', and so forth.[93] The organisational problems were but partially surmounted, not least because all the ILP's local officials were volunteers. A special report on the ILP's Scottish organisation found that in Edinburgh 'there is not the proper spirit amongst the

Federation officials'. 'We have no co-ordinate scheme in attending to the needs of the area, and I am afraid we cannot get the best results until full time work in organising the district is established.'[94]

In late 1926 the Trades and Labour Council's Chairman spoke at a local ILP branch meeting. 'Six years' membership of the ILP, he said, had left him woefully lacking in Socialism, but it had imbued in him a taste for literature. I.L.P. literature was second to none at the present time.'[95] While the first comment is a reflection on how difficult the ILP found integrating new members in the early 1920s, the second points to a great ILP strength: its propaganda. For the author of the Special Report on the Scottish ILP, organisational inadequacies were important because they meant 'we are not getting the best service' from 'quite a number of good propagandists in Edinburgh'.[96] 'Propaganda' was evangelism: the work of able speakers at public meetings, and acknowledged to be the ILP's main task. Its purpose was 'the creation of an atmosphere in the country', among 'the great mass of non-political voters, who have little time or inclination for prolonged and intensive study of a political issue'.

> They tend to have a vague fear of new methods and ideas. They are suspicious of social changes. It is the work of the propagandist to make the new idea familiar, by explanation, discussion and repetition, until that intangible but formidable distrust, gives place to an atmosphere of confidence ... [97]

The bulk of the propagandists were local men (and some women), schooled in the cut-and-thrust of the street-corner meeting; but on occasion a nationally-renowned speaker (Maxton, for instance) would be billed. The pattern was well-established; a planned programme of winter meetings, indoors, mostly in ILP halls; and, in the summer and at election times, on street-corners.[98]

The ILP's conception of a socialist movement extended from cradle to grave. Where for adults there was propaganda, for children there were Socialist Sunday Schools, and the Guild of Youth. By a process of 'permeation', the young would grow into the movement.[99] One 'Woman's Outlook' column in the Labour Standard, explained how

> At our [Socialist Sunday] schools we try to point to the children how these things can be put right by the people owning the land, and using it for the benefit of all, instead of its being used under the

> present system of private ownership, for the
> benefit of the lucky few ... the basic aim of our
> Socialist teaching is human equality.[100]

The link between the Sunday Schools and the 'adult
organisation' was the ILP Guild of Youth, whose object was
'to give an opportunity for the physical, intellectual and
aesthetic development of young people between the ages of
fourteen and twenty-five years'.[101] Edinburgh's seven guilds
had a total membership in 1925 of 350: activities included
football, socials, whist drives, educational meetings (most
were affiliated to the Labour College), theatre visits ('a
large party of enthusiasts' saw Shaw's Saint Joan at the
King's Theatre).[102] Their Cycle Club went on 'runs
throughout the Lothians', sometimes stopping to spread the
word ('last weekend, a propaganda meeting held in Dunbar:
quite quickly a crowd gathered around the 26 cyclists').[103]

This, then, was the politics of the ILP: much effort,
much enthusiasm, but directed so as to win the hearts and
minds of the workers, rather than to intervene in the
politics of the Labour Party - and not always well-directed.
But the commitment of many ILPers to their own
conception of political method, and to their party, is
undoubted. One illustration will suffice: in early 1926, Leith
ILP moved to new premises.

> The work of adaptation [of two wooden huts into a
> hall to seat 300] cost nothing, beyond the material
> required ... Morris's 'News from Nowhere' came
> true; friends came from near and far to assist in
> the work. Only devotion to a cause could perform
> such a transformation as can today be seen at
> Bonnington Toll.[104]

Perhaps the supreme example of co-operation between
Labour Socialism and the ILP left in Edinburgh was the
formation and publishing of a weekly Labour newspaper. As
early as 1919 the Trades Council had thought a Scottish
Labour daily 'long overdue', for the 'capitalistic press ...
misrepresents the cause of the workers and is biased in the
employers' interests';[105] but this proposal had no result. In
1920 the Trades and Labour Council had made a half-
hearted attempt to set up a paper, but the scheme was ill-
founded, and came to naught.[106] It was in January 1924 that
the council became involved in discussions with members of
the ILP: this led to a committee's being formed with
representation from the council, the ILP, Labour parties and
trade unions from throughout the Lothians.[107] A business

manager-cum-editor was appointed (an ILP stalwart), a company formed, and the first issue of the Labour Standard appeared on the streets on 21 February 1925. It was, indeed, a paper in the ILP tradition: although (contrary to early fears) the newsagents did sell it, all its contributors were unpaid, and all its (£500) capital was raised from the labour movement.[108]

In many ways, the paper was a success: its journalism was of a remarkably high standard, considering that it was entirely the product of voluntary effort. Its columns were open to a wide range of views - perhaps just because, if this voluntary commitment was to be sustained, no narrow definitions could be imposed. It made an impact on local politics. But it never achieved its target circulation of 10,000; advertising revenue must have been small. Only nine months after starting, 'finance was urgently needed', and by mid-1926 it was obliged to reduce its number of pages to four.[109]

Let us summarise. When the basis of syndicalist and revolutionary influence subsided during 1920 and 1921, Labour Socialism developed a strategic vision which enabled it to build coalitions, over certain issues and within more or less limited spheres, with two vital political traditions: labourism and the ILP left. Two principles underpinned the Labour Socialist vision, and allowed these coalitions to be generated: that political action and industrial action were distinct; that political action was constitutional action. These enabled Labour Socialism to find common ground with trade union labourism and with the ILP left: in each case, it meant accepting that their efforts would be limited to certain categories of activity. In particular, trade unions were offered a path to working class power which did not put them in the front line, whilst the ILP was encouraged to continue in the strategy to which it had long adhered.

THE MARXIST COALITION AND THE SYNDICALIST TRADITION

Ultimately, the Labour Socialist coalition was victorious: but it was consistently criticised - and sometimes threatened - by Marxism. Marxism had two main institutional forms in 1920s Edinburgh: the Labour College movement and, above all, the Communist Party. These played different roles. The Labour College ensured that the city's labour movement was permeated by people who took at least some Marxist views for granted; and it successfully established a belief, even among those who were not Marxist, that 'Marx gave Socialism a scientific foundation by looking at history through working-class spectacles'.[110] The party was different. Its notion of Marxism was more specific, linking broad understandings to firm (if sometimes changing) views on strategy. It intervened politically, both in industry and elsewhere. Like the Labour Socialists, the Communists could achieve little unless they succeeded in mobilising the support of other sections of labour: again, given the fragmented nature of class consciousness, this was more likely to be achieved in relation to particular issues and legitimising principles, than in general.

There were two political tendencies with which Communism could hope to find significant common ground. One we may term syndicalism - but using this term in a wide sense, to include many forms of militant or revolutionary trade unionism. The second was the ILP left. (There might, on occasion, be ground for common action with labourism: but only in extreme circumstances, as during a strike.) With both it achieved a substantial degree of co-operation, although for different reasons this did not prove well-founded.

Marxism, and particularly Communism, very largely succeeded in weaving the various threads of revolutionary trade union theory and practice into a single strand. From 1921 or 1922 onward, the Communists set the agenda for theoretical strategic debate in this area. Unfortunately for them, each of the threads which they sought to weave had weakened markedly since the heady days of 1917-20, and the final product was decidedly frayed. Local Marxists had begun to proselytise for the Red International of Labour Unions[111] early in 1921, perhaps even before a local branch of the Communist Party was formed.[112] Their argument was a simple one. 'The Capitalist system is forcing us to the point where we will be forced to fight, and we must be prepared, nationally and internationally. Thus the need of the Red Trade Union ...'[113] But it was attractive: it offered the possibility of separate, revolutionary, unions, but it did not require individual trade unionists or union branches to move in isolation; and it stretched out an arm of international support to trade union revolutionaries who were under great pressure at home. (It is perhaps no coincidence that the No. 1 branch of the Railwaymen voted 'to affiliate to the Moscow International' just nine days after 'Black Friday'.)[114] They may have believed, or hoped, that

216

the revolutionary government in Russia would make more practical difference to the working class movement in Britain than proved to be the case. But the main problem was that the economic basis of working class strength was eroding - and, with it, the basis of revolutionary strength in industry.

Two examples illustrate this problem. Although, firstly, the shop-stewards movement in engineering and shipbuilding had never been strongest in Edinburgh, it had made some mark during 1918 and early 1919. One of its most prominent leaders was Bob Foulis, a Labour parliamentary candidate who left the ILP to join the Communists. It was he who became Scottish Organiser of the Red International in 1921.[115] Yet it was he, too, who in September of the same year was a leader of the unemployed in Edinburgh:[116] the militant shop stewards had lost their base in the workshops. Secondly, among the Railwaymen the dismissals of 1921 had undercut the syndicalists' support. The revolutionary rhetoric of 1919-20 was supplanted by a sectionalist labourism which continued to use the language of industrial unionism, but for very different purposes. It was no accident, for instance, that some of the syndicalists joined ASLEF in 1924: during the ASLEF strike, Edinburgh NUR footplatemen had voted overwhelmingly to strike with them; the No. 1 branch then voted to tell 'our Loco members to immediately return to work and thereby preserve the principle of one Union for Railwaymen'.[117] This labourism could, of course, justify solid and militant action, as in the General Strike: but the No. 1 branch's reaction to the latter is telling. At a mass meeting, it agreed 'a vote of censure on our leaders for their lack of foresight in leading us into a[n] illegal strike'.[118] This was a long way from revolutionary syndicalism.

So the coherence of the syndicalist tradition was seriously threatened. The extent to which Communism could find common ground with it was limited: often syndicalism was too weak even to confront an issue in a concerted way. With rare exceptions in Edinburgh,[119] the tradition found expression in just two areas. The first was amongst trade union activists, and especially within the Trades and Labour Council. Here it remained possible for syndicalist and Communist ideas to coincide in the pursuit of a number of objectives, especially the need for union solidarity and the more effective organisation of the council. The view was pressed, on occasion with success, that the council should be seen as, or turn itself into, a Council of Action - in effect, a general staff of the local labour and trade union movement. For example, in the period leading up to 'Red Friday' in 1925, the council agreed to establish itself as a Council of Action, appointed a special committee to organise accordingly, and summoned a conference of shop stewards.[120] But this current of thought, so strong five years before, could by this time command a majority on the Trades and Labour Council only when large-scale industrial action seemed imminent or unavoidable (as in 1925 and 1926), or (though to a lesser degree) in support of Russia when she seemed threatened by Britain (as over the Curzon ultimatum in 1923).[121]

Communism and syndicalism were permanent currents of opinion on the Trades and Labour Council. But in normal circumstances their influence was limited. Thus during 1923 and 1924 a number of trade union delegates became concerned that the 'political' role which the Council had taken on since 1920 was hindering the Council's industrial work - an expression of labourist concern. An industrial committee was appointed to consider how these problems could be overcome. Reporting, the convenor of the committee, a Communist, said that the 'work of [the] Committee had been hampered by a feeling among [union] branches that it was a Communist Com[mit]tee': this, he felt it necessary to point out, 'was not the case'.[122] But the suspicion illustrates a real limitation in Communist influence.

The second area in which the syndicalist tradition of direct industrial action continued to have an impact, and in which Communism was able to take a lead, was the organisation of the unemployed. Fred Douglas describes various tactics designed to press their demands: one, the 'irritation march'

> consisted in setting off from the Mound at an ordinary pace. Reaching the West End we wheeled round to march back along Princes Street on the other side. And at this point we brought the pace down to dead slow. With a couple of thousand men behind us this meant a traffic jam for a considerable time.

They would then speed up, and let out 'barbaric cries' while the police 'helmeted and buttoned up to the chin in blue, heavy serge, sweated to keep abreast, ... and near panic set in among pedestrians'.[123] Such demonstrations could make a considerable impact, and the Unemployed Committees also built up considerable reputations through contesting local elections, 'fighting cases', and 'propaganda'. The only surviving figures suggest that they had perhaps 1,500 members in the Edinburgh area[124] - though, if Douglas is to be believed, demonstrations could be rather larger. Yet although these methods made unemployment a major issue (it was, for instance, by a long way the matter most frequently discussed at the Trades and Labour Council in the early 1920s), the structural weakness of the unemployed prevented their having any decisive impact. And within the labour movement a coalition of Labour Socialism (which saw the Unemployed Committees as thinly-veiled Communist fronts) and labourism (for which the unemployed were primarily a threat) ensured they remained marginal: frequently listened to and discussed, but always without real power.

So both syndicalist and Communist traditions could find expression only in limited areas, and were unlikely seriously to influence the movement's direction. Their sources of industrial strength rapidly waned after 1920, re-emerging only for brief periods of militancy. They did not, therefore, have a lasting institutional source of power within the labour movement.

THE MARXIST COALITION AND THE LABOUR LEFT

In January 1926 an epigram appeared, without comment but in a manner indicating endorsement, in the Labour Standard:

Speaking as one who has broken the law, I say most deliberately that it is true what the warder said to me when I first went into Brixton Prison: 'Cheer up, Mr. Lansbury, there is never anything accomplished in England till somebody goes to prison.' Mr. GEORGE LANSBURY, M.P.[125]

This neatly, if accidently, encapsulates the motivational basis of the Labour left's relationship with Communism during the early and mid-1920s. On the one hand, the left saw a state operating in the interests of a single class, and without mercy; this had to be opposed, and not only by parliamentary means. But, on the other, appeal could be made, by exposing the inequity of such class justice, to a wider political community: at root a rationality and a justice transcended those of class - and explained society's tendency to progress toward democracy and socialism.[126] It was, of course, this latter assumption which linked the

Labour left with Labour Socialism; but the first assumption meant that the left was continually impatient, discontented, with constitutional bounds on political action. The Labour left was, therefore, always ready to consider tactics similar to the Communists'; perhaps, too, its concept of supra-class justice and rationality was, in practice, little different from the Marxist concept of proletarian justice and reason.

When the Communist Party was formed, in 1920 and 1921, a section of the ILP left had, of course, joined it. Especially at a local level, they seem to have regarded this as a realignment within the Labour movement; and, indeed, it is likely that many of those who joined the Communists also remained ILPers.[127] Many, however, seem to have drifted away from the Communist Party during the following two or three years, particularly, perhaps, after its reorganisation (on 'Bolshevik' lines) in 1923.[128] A prominent Scottish Communist recorded in 1924 that many 'old-timers ... seem to miss the resounding revolutionary speeches of the earlier movements'.[129] The close relationship between the ILP left and the Communist Party over the period up to, say, 1924 was not political only, but also personal. So when Euphemia Laing, a former ILPer, stood as Communist candidate for St Leonards ward in the 1921 Town Council election, it is likely she was popularly regarded as the Labour candidate, and received support from ILP activists in this ILP stronghold.

But the left's flirtation with Communism was dependent on a concept of the socialist movement which, from 1921 on, rapidly ceased to be real. As early as September 1921 the Trades and Labour Council's Executive decided an application for affiliation from the local branch of the Communist Party 'could not be accepted' since their party was not nationally affiliated to the Labour Party.[130] At this time, however, the council could do little to extend such a ruling - and there is little sign that it would have wished to do so. In that year just four Labour candidates stood in the Town Council elections, for instance, whilst there were also Unemployed, Railway Workers, Ex-Service, and SLP candidates.[131] No narrow definition of the socialist or labour movement could be enforced, therefore; and over a wide spectrum of the left, it is unlikely that one existed. During the years up to 1925, however, a definition of the Labour movement was developed and enforced by the alliance of labourism and Labour Socialism. This definition was initiated nationally, and transmitted to the Edinburgh

Labour Party in a series of decisions and meetings; its essence was to exclude Communism by establishing commitment to the parliamentary system as central to Labour Party membership. Ben Shaw, the party's Scottish Secretary, explained to the Trades and Labour Council's Executive in 1923 that he 'was of opinion that a fundamental difference of policy was shown when Mr. Newbold, M.P. stated in House of Commons that his [Communist] Party did not believe in Parliamentary Government'.[132] This, Shaw held, justified a requirement that all delegates to the council should sign a pledge accepting the constitution and rules of the Labour Party.

If the Labour left and the Communists had been able to consolidate their alliance, this re-orientation of Labour politics might have been resisted with more success than it was. But they were beset by a shortage of issues around which they could work successfully together. The main reason was that their strategy for political change required a scale of mobilisation which, in the economic circumstances of the 1920s, was most difficult to achieve. Apart from those discussed in the previous section (for the distinction between the Labour left and militant trade unionism was always unclear), there were just two categories of issues on which Communists and the Labour left could make common cause: international issues, and housing. Yet on neither were they able to achieve the level of action which could make their strategy a threat to the electoralism of the Labour Socialist coalition.

The Communists brought international questions into the Labour movement to an unprecedented extent. They called for a Council of Action against British sanctions against Russia in 1923;[133] they wanted 'to start a movement in support of German workers' later in the same year;[134] they drew attention in 1925 to 'recent political events' in Bulgaria and Italy, warning of the dangers of a 'seizure of power by Fascism';[135] and so forth. But whilst they could win the - virtually unanimous - support of the labour movement on these, in passing resolutions, they could achieve little else.[136] Symbolic of this was Robert Wilson's decision to make 'Imperialism the Issue' of his campaign in the 1927 Leith by-election. ' "I shall," said Mr. Wilson, "make China the acid test of this by-election." '[137] Wilson, a leading local Labour left-winger, did just that - and lost. Hew Robertson, the local Communist organiser, tacitly acknowledged the problem when calling, at a Trades and

Labour Council meeting, for 'all active workers in working class bodies ... to pledge support to German workers'. 'Asked what was meant by pledging support Mr. Robertson stated that had not been considered by his committee.'[138] The problem was precisely the meaning of 'support'. If it was to be mere rhetoric, it would be widely seen as unimportant and uncontroversial: 'unity' would be easy to achieve, but of little import. If, however, it was to require industrial or political action, the scale of action required was very great, while its effect might be small; and in any case, it would be felt only in far-away climes. It demanded too much in an adverse economic situation. United action on international issues, almost inevitably ineffectual, could generate no solid base for a lasting coalition.

After the defeat of the 1920 rent strike, the focus of labour activity on housing shifted from rents to the volume and quality of new housing provision. These were pursued through propaganda (including one excellent pamphlet),[139] deputations, and so forth: the apparatus of reasoned debate with the city authorities. No attempt was made to mobilise people in action, until in 1923 a public meeting was called 'to organise against the eviction of people for arrears of Rent arising from Unemployment or Low Wages'.[140] A Central Tenants' Defence League was re-established - soon said to be 'on a functioning basis'.[141] But although similar bodies were formed in Leith and elsewhere, led by the left and by Communists,[142] they found mass mobilisation difficult to achieve. They occupied themselves largely in processing grievances, leading deputations, fighting court cases.[143] On occasion, they expressed a desire to take more radical action: the Leith Tenants' Defence Association, for instance, criticised an attempt to raise money (£25-£50) for counsel's opinion; the money should have been used to 'fight insanitary dwellings'.[144] But there is no record (in contrast to Clydeside in the same period) of substantial popular action having occurred. Again, this meant that unity of Communists and the left was relatively ineffectual. At the same time, it prevented the Tenants' Defence League from becoming a powerful institution within the movement, and ensured that the former's left-wing leadership remained relatively isolated.

The central problems confronting attempts to develop a 'Marxist coalition', after 1921, therefore, were these. First, the tactics on which the coalition's elements could find common ground were rendered highly problematical by the prevailing economic environment: they demanded large-scale mobilisation. Second, since the tactics were rarely achieved, the institutions which might have given shape and authority to the coalition were also generally absent. (The major exception, of course, was the General Strike.) Third, the organisational developments which the left had supported in 1920-1 provided the Labour Socialist coalition with an institutional base from which to oppose the left: perhaps as important, electoral activity and 'pure-and-simple' trade unionism provided routine forms of activity for this new organisation. In an adverse political and economic situation, the Marxists were unable to develop a strategy which could offer the type of sustained and regular activity necessary to organisational development.

RESPONSES TO THE GENERAL STRIKE
Probably the supreme achievement of the Marxist coalition was organising, and legitimising, the General Strike over nine days in May 1926.[145] It was a cruel irony that it was Labour Socialism which reaped the rewards of this achievement - and crueller, perhaps, as the Labour Socialists had little enthusiasm for the Strike,[146] as the labourist union leaders appeared to have 'sold it out', and as it was the industrial militants, Communists, and so forth who bore the brunt of employers' victimisation.[147]

The Strike was experienced as an outstanding achievement of collective working class action. 'From the first our ranks were solid and disciplined.' This had been complemented by 'Splendid Organisation'.[148] Undoubtedly, it was a major achievement of mobilisation, which appears to have had important effects on working class political outlooks. But the defeat of the Strike dealt a powerful blow to strategies, industrial and political, of mass action. For the left, there was much rancour. Why was it called off?

> Were the workers showing signs of weakening? Were there holes in our ranks? So far as we heard in Edinburgh there were none. Then for why? For the sacred shibboleth 'Constitution'? For the alleged threat to the Community? Because miners, railwaymen, transport workers, printers, and a hundred other trades had struck at a community that is themselves, with but a few millions of an antagonistic class in the great minority? So it was. For that and for that alone, the General Strike,

even before it had time to reach its height, was called off.[149]

Yet, through the rancour, confidence in the method was destroyed. The despair is clear in William Elger's contribution to a Labour College weekend school on the General Strike: a

General Strike could only arise as a spontaneous movement of the rank and file of the workers, and ... therefore ... could neither be definitely predicted at any given moment, nor could it be adequately prepared for. In any case, it had only a limited value, and that mainly as a defensive weapon against the aggression of the employers and as a 'political demonstration.'[150]

Elger, of course, can hardly be counted on the left, and as secretary of the STUC no doubt felt defensive: but his speech evokes a sense of hopelessness at the ability of the movement to run so major an event. The confidence was gone.

In these circumstances, the Marxists' alliance with other elements of the left could not hold: for the latter, only the electoral strategy offered a way forward. 'Let all lip sympathy, hypocritical jejunes reckon with a conscious awakened electorate in November',[151] the Labour Standard remarked. Those who sought to 'draw political capital out of the results of the strike', and to 'discredit the strike weapon, ... point[ing] with outstretched arm to the ballotbox as the only hope of the workers'[152] - such people reaped the political harvest of the General Strike within the labour movement. Margaret Cole observed that 'what really perished in 1926 was the romantic idea, dating from before the first world war, of the power of syndicalism, "direct action", and the rest of it'.[153] In an important sense, she was right. But 1926 could only mark the end of an idea (which had been far more than merely romantic), because the electoral alternative was already strongly positioned to exploit its weakness.

NOTES

1.   John Gibson, in Labour Standard, 23 January 1926.
2.   Forward, 11 January 1919.
3.   G. Brown, 'The Labour Party and Political Change in Scotland 1918-1929', unpublished Ph.D. thesis, Edinburgh University, 1981, esp. pp. 101-9, argues this case strongly.

Cp Philip Snowden's comment (An Autobiography, vol. 2
(London 1934), p.574) that MacDonald was 'canvassing ... for
support' in these years: his Forward articles 'played up to
the Left Wing'.
4.　　ILP Edin. Central branch minutes, 9 June 1919. The
editor of the Evening News, an old friend, wrote to Graham
in 1919: 'you are getting praised so much from the capitalist
press ... [that] the rumour strongly prevails that you will be
the Liberal candidate ... at the next election. N.B. this is
not a joke.' (Quoted T.N. Graham, Willie Graham (London,
n.d. [c.1948]), p.93.)
5.　　Ben Shaw to J.S. Middleton, 3 April 1917, quoted
Brown, 'Labour Party and Political Change', p.55.
6.　　See Appendix A.
7.　　NUR Edin. No. 1 branch minutes, 14, 28 August, 11
September, 9 October, 20 November 1921; T&LC minutes,
31 August 1921.
8.　　J.R. MacDonald, Labour Leader, 2 January 1919.
9.　　S. White, 'Labour's Council of Action 1920', Journal of
Contemporary History, vol. 9 (1974), pp. 99-122.
10.　Report of the Royal Commission on the Housing of the
Industrial Population of Scotland, Rural and Urban, Cd. 8731
(1917).
11.　D. Lloyd George, The Times, 13 November 1918.
12.　M. Swenarton, 'An "Insurance against Revolution":
Ideological Objectives in the Provision and Design of Public
Housing in Britain after the First World War', Bulletin of the
Institute of Historical Research, vol. 54 (1981), pp.87-9, 95-
8.
13.　B. Elliott, D. McCrone and V. Skelton, 'Property and
Politics: Edinburgh 1875-1975', unpublished typescript,
Edinburgh University, n.d., esp. pp. 16-20, tables 1 and 2.
(The figure refers to 1925; 'property' excludes own place of
residence.) The main argument was that 'politics' and
'government departments' should be kept out of municipal
administration.
14.　TC AR 1919, p.14.
15.　TC AR 1920, p.5.
16.　Ibid.; see also TC minutes, 27 July 1919.
17.　TC AR 1920, p.5.
18.　TC minutes, 26 October, 2 December 1919.
19.　TC AR 1920, p.5.
20.　The Increase of Rent and Mortgage Interest
(Restrictions) Act 1920 allowed a rent rise of 15 per cent.
21.　T&LC minutes, 1 June 1920.

22. NUR Edin. No. 1 branch minutes, 20 June 1920.
23. Circulars from SLHA (June 1920) and STUC (15 July 1920) cited in I. MacDougall (ed.), A Catalogue of Some Labour Records in Scotland and some Scots Records outside Scotland (Edinburgh, 1978), pp.157, 214.
24. T&LC minutes, 18, 27 July 1920.
25. NUR Edin. No. 1 branch minutes, 18 July 1920.
26. Ibid., 4 August 1920.
27. T&LC minutes, 3 August 1920.
28. NUR Edin. No. 1 branch minutes, 4 August 1920.
29. T&LC minutes, 3, 6, 10 August 1920: the meeting was cancelled when the 'Hands Off Russia' campaign intervened.
30. Ibid., 15, 27 August 1920.
31. Forward, 28 August 1920.
32. T&LC minutes, 31 August 1920.
33. Ibid., 31 August, 12 September, 24 October, 5 December 1920.
34. Ibid., 10 August 1920.
35. Ibid., 24 October 1920. There is no record of how many organisations attended the 14 August Conference; 95 organisations were affiliated to the T&LC in 1920/1.
36. NUR Edin. No. 1 branch minutes, 4 August 1920.
37. Ibid.
38. T&LC AR 1921, p.2.
39. Ibid.
40. Ibid., p.5.
41. Ibid., p.2.
42. S. Macintyre, A Proletarian Science. Marxism in Britain 1917-33 (Cambridge, 1980), p.47.
43. Ibid., p.55.
44. Graham, Willie Graham, p.100.
45. Ibid.
46. T&LC minutes, 29 May 1920.
47. T&LC AR 1921, p.2.
48. Ibid.
49. Ibid., p.5.
50. Cp K.W. Wedderburn, The Worker and the Law (Harmondsworth, 1971), pp.305-27; J. Saville, 'Trade Unions and Free Labour: the Background to the Taff Vale Decision' in A. Briggs and J. Saville (eds.), Essays in Labour History (London, 1967), pp.317-50.
51. These terms imply only that Labour Socialists and Marxists formed the core of these coalitions, not that all their members were (or became) Labour Socialists or Marxists.

52.   W. Graham, 'Effective Trade Unionism' (n.d.), Webb Trade Union Collection, BLPES.
53.   T&LC AR 1921, p.2.
54.   Ibid.
55.   Ibid.
56.   NUR Edin. No. 1 branch minutes, 9 October 1921: the vote was 42 to 11.
57.   See Appendix A.
58.   TC AR 1920, pp.24-5, lists 28 individual ILP collectors.
59.   Another three were returned unopposed: TC AR 1920, p.18; Scotsman, 5 November 1919.
60.   Ibid., 6 November 1919.
61.   'Departmental representative' was a union post; 'inspector' was a junior managerial grade.
62.   NUR Edin. No. 1 branch minutes, 23 May 1920: the vote was 31 to 2, but the debate was coloured by claims that the representative concerned was being accused of 'belly crawling' and being a 'traitor to the NUR'.
63.   T&LC AR 1921, p.6.
64.   Ibid.
65.   Ibid.
66.   T&LC minutes, 8 August 1922.
67.   E.g., a 'strong committee' was formed in George Square ward in late 1917; a committee was formed in Dalry ward in 1918. But Dalry, at least, had been fought successfully by Labour before the war. Only two ward committees, Gorgie and St Leonards, paid dues to the Labour Party's Edinburgh branch in 1917/18. LP, Edin. branch minutes, 22 November 1917, 13 June 1918; R. Fox, 'Members of the Labour Party Elected to Edinburgh Town Council', unpublished typescript, Edin. City Library, 1971, pp.1-2.
68.   Edin. branch LP AR 1919/20 in TC AR 1920, p.18. This excludes Leith, which had a separate burgh LP.
69.   Only four ward committees paid dues to the LP, Edin. branch in 1919/20: George Square, St Leonards and St Giles (in the Central division) and Gorgie (in West division). A Dalry committee is recorded as existing, but paid no dues; a West division Women's Section also existed. LP, Edin. branch AR 1919/20 in TC AR 1920, p.22.
70.   T&LC AR 1922, p.8.
71.   In 1920/1 there were 32 delegates from political bodies, and 282 from trade union branches. There was at this time no restriction on who could vote on 'political issues'.

See T&LC AR 1921, pp.21-6.
72.   T&LC minutes, 19 October 1920 the meeting in
question was held on 2 November 1920.
73.   T&LC minutes, 18 May, 18 August, 14, 15 September,
12 October 1920. All these discussions, except the first,
were in the T&LC's executive, rather than the full council.
74.   The following T&LC officers and executive committee
members can be firmly identified as SDF members: T.A.
Cairns (T&LC Treasurer 1922-4, President 1925, EC 1926-9);
W. Elger (T&LC EC 1920, President 1921-2 (Secretary,
STUC 1922-46)); A. Eunson (TC President 1916-18); G. Hogg
(Leith United TC and LP President 1920, T & LC Vice-
President 1921, President 1922-4, EC 1925-7); R. Martin
(T&LC Librarian 1921); T.E. McDonald (T&LC EC 1921-2);
R. McKenzie (T&LC Librarian 1920); J.J. Pottinger (TC
Assistant Secretary 1918); F. Smithies (T&LC Librarian
1922, Political Officer 1923-35); G. Williamson (T&LC
Treasurer 1920-2). Other prominent Edin. SDF members
were: T. Drummond Shiels (Councillor 1919-20, MP for Edin.
East 1924-31); A. Young (Councillor 1922-4, 1926-32, MP for
Glasgow Partick 1923-4); J.A. Young (Councillor 1909-20).
75.   T&LC minutes, 1 June 1921.
76.   Ibid., 5, 6 July, 2 August 1921.
77.   Ibid., 9, 22 November 1921.
78.   Ibid., 21 March, 4 April 1922.
79.   T&LC Constitution and Rules (Edinburgh, 1922), p.8.
80.   I am grateful to Dr F. Smithies, of Cambridge, for
biographical information concerning his father.
81.   On the growth of Labour organisation and voting, see
Appendix A.
82.   T&LC minutes, 18 December 1923.
83.   Although nationally 1924 was a small setback for
Labour, in Edinburgh the party captured its second seat.
84.   T&LC AR 1924, p.7.
85.   T&LC minutes, 18 August 1925.
86.   Ibid., 1, 8, 25 September 1925.
87.   Ibid., 25 March 1924; Appendix A suggests this
prohibition may not always have been effective.
88.   Ibid., 8 July 1924. ILP branches were not delineated by
ward or parliamentary divisional boundaries; the Central
branch would have had a number of members resident in the
East division.
89.   Ibid., 14 October 1924.
90.   R. Dowse, Left in the Centre. The Independent Labour
Party 1893-1940 (London, 1960), p.71.

91. Ibid., esp. Chapter 7; A. Marwick, 'The Independent Labour Party (1918-32)', unpublished B. Litt. thesis, Oxford University, 1960, esp. pp.222-9.
92. This picture is supported by surviving records of affiliation fees to ILP head office ('Affiliation Fees ... Year Ending February 1927', ILP papers, BLPES), and by Marwick, 'The ILP', p.228.
93. 'Special Report, Division 1: Scotland', ILP papers, BLPES: this was prepared for the ILP NAC, probably in 1927.
94. Ibid.
95. Labour Standard, 9 October 1926.
96. 'Special Report'.
97. M. Pallister, The Orange Box. Thoughts of a Socialist Propagandist (London, 1924), pp.8-9. This short volume is an excellent introduction to the ILP's propaganda methods, by a celebrated exponent.
98. See Labour Standard, 3 October 1925, 2 October, 25 December 1926, for accounts of local propaganda. Pallister, Orange Box, pp.47-51, argues that the growing number of women voters needed a different approach: her advice does not seem to have been followed in Edinburgh.
99. Pallister, Orange Box, p.52.
100. Labour Standard, 19 September 1925. Cp F. Reid, 'Socialist Sunday Schools in Britain, 1892-1939', International Review of Social History, vol. 11 (1966), pp. 18-47.
101. Labour Standard, 24 October 1925.
102. Ibid., 24 October 1925, 6 June 1926.
103. Ibid., 17 July 1926.
104. Ibid., 1 May 1926.
105. TC minutes, 11 March 1919.
106. T&LC minutes, 7, 14 September, 12 October 1920.
107. Ibid., 6, 8, 13, 22 January, 10 February 1924. The committee was composed of representatives of ILP branches (5), LP branches from outside Edin. (3), CPGB (1), University LP (1), trade union branches (5), T&LC (3), together with the business manager. The Labour Standard was thus not an 'ILP paper', though its editorial policy was that of the ILP left. Cp R. Harrison, G. Woolven, R. Duncan, The Warwick Guide to British Labour Periodicals 1790-1970 (Hassocks, 1977), p.268.
108. T&LC minutes, 10, 19 February, 19 August, 7, 14 October 1924; Labour Standard advertising leaflet.
109. T&LC minutes, 20 October 1925; Labour Standard, 2 June 1926.

110. Michael Marcus, B.L., 'Leaders of Modern Democracy I - Karl Marx', Labour Standard, 17 April 1926. Marcus, an ILPer and MP for Dundee from 1929, was described (Anon., The Scottish Socialists. A Gallery of Contemporary Portraits (London, 1931), p.237) as one of the 'safe men' of MacDonald's PLP.

111. Until the late summer of 1921, the Provisional International Council of Trade and Industrial Unions - but even then, colloquially, the Red International. Cp NUR Edin. No. 1 branch minutes, 24 April 1921; T&LC minutes, 5, 12 July, 2, 23 August 1921; J. Klugmann, History of the Communist Party of Great Britain, vol. 1 (London, 1968), pp.108-11.

112. There is no firm evidence of when a CP branch was first formed in Edinburgh. Fred Douglas (Evening Dispatch, 11 August 1955) recalls attending 'the rules conference' in Manchester as an Edinburgh delegate: this was held on 23/24 April 1921.

113. NUR Edin. No. 1 branch minutes, 24 April 1921.

114. Ibid.

115. T&LC minutes, 23 August, 6 September 1921.

116. Ibid., 20 September 1921. This was the common lot throughout the country: see, e.g., W. Hannington, Unemployed Struggles 1919-1936 (London, 1936), esp. pp.1-11.

117. NUR Edin. No. 1 branch minutes, 27 January 1924. One man who left the NUR in 1924 was James Stobie. The ill-feeling between groups within the NUR led, in July 1924, to the establishment of a special branch for Edinburgh's locomen; this was explained in the No. 1 branch Jubilee Souvenir, p.33, as 'a means to combat the many calumnies of the A.S.L.E. & F. which is largely their stock-in-trade'.

118. NUR Edin. No. 1 branch minutes, 23 May 1926: only four votes were cast against this motion.

119. E.g., Communists made significant headway in the St Margarets railway workshops.

120. T&LC minutes, 3 March 1925. These moves were initiated by a Communist. Over 100 delegates attended the conference, held two days after 'Red Friday' (ibid., 4 August 1925).

121. Ibid., 8, 15 May, 5, 12, 19 June 1923: although a Council of Action was agreed (after Communist pressure) on this occasion, its preparations give an impression of half-heartedness when compared with 1920 or 1925. See also Klugmann, Communist Party, vol. 1, pp. 148-57.

122. T&LC minutes, 8 July 1924.
123. Evening Dispatch, 12 August 1955.
124. T&LC minutes, 28 January 1927. The figures were: Leith, 400; Edinburgh, 450; Portobello, 360; Mussleburgh, 250.
125. Labour Standard, 23 January 1926.
126. Cp Macintyre's assertion, Proletarian Science, p.63, that the Labour left's 'crucial characteristic was the commitment to parliamentary action': in Edinburgh, at least, the left was often highly critical of, and sceptical about, parliament.
127. See ILP NAC minutes, 28-30 August 1924, on the problem of Communists in the ILP: in reply to enquiries from branches, the NAC held 'it is difficult to understand how a member of the Communist Party could accept the constitution of the ILP'.
128. For estimates of CP membership, see Macintyre, Proletarian Science, pp. 27-8.
129. W. Joss in Communist Review, November 1924, quoted Klugmann, Communist Party, vol. I, p.332.
130. T&LC minutes, 13 September 1921.
131. Scotsman, 2 November 1921.
132. T&LC minutes, 11 September 1923.
133. Ibid., 8 May 1923.
134. Ibid., 24 October 1923.
135. Ibid., 7 July 1925.
136. Except support for the Workers' International Relief (which yet had to deny it was a Communist organisation: ibid., 17 June 1924), and like bodies.
137. Labour Standard, 12 February 1927.
138. T&LC minutes, 24 October 1923.
139. T&LC, Our Unseen City Revealed. A Tale of Housing Atrocities (Edin. n.d. [1922]).
140. T&LC minutes, 6 February 1923.
141. Ibid., 13, 27 February 1923.
142. Labour Standard, 31 October 1925.
143. See, e.g., T&LC minutes, 22 August 1923.
144. Ibid., 19 September 1923.
145. The General Strike in Edinburgh is very fully covered by I. MacDougall, 'Edinburgh', in J. Skelley (ed.), The General Strike 1926 (London, 1976), 140-59.
146. Cp G. Phillips, 'The Labour Party and the General Strike', Llafur, vol. 2, no. 2 (1977), pp.44-58.
147. MacDougall, 'Edinburgh', esp. pp.153-4; Labour Standard, 29 May 1926; NUR Edin. No. 1 branch minutes, 16,

231

23 May 1926.
148. Labour Standard, 22 May 1926.
149. Ibid.
150. Ibid., 9 October 1926.
151. Ibid., 19 June 1926.
152. Ibid., 12 June 1926.
153. Letter in BSSLH, no. 34 (1977), p.14.

Chapter Ten

CONCLUSION

The truth is that one cannot choose the form of
war one wants, unless from the start one has a
crushing superiority over the enemy.[1]

In the decade or so which began in the midst of the Great
War, the politics of labour were reformed. When war broke
out neither parliamentary nor direct action strategies held
uncontested sway. The war did not destroy these political
traditions, but it changed their environment, and overlaid
them with new (or at least newly strengthened) bases of
allegiance associated with patriotism. The traditions
evolved; were strengthed, weakened, or altered by such
factors as the growth in union strength or Labour's
participation in government. But certain aspects of these
evolutions became, as it were, recessive, emerging only
when patriotic impulses waned after the Armistice.

During these brief years the essential contours of the
modern labour movement were mapped. By the later 1920s
labour politics were dominated by a coalition centred on an
electoral, parliamentary strategy which was bolstered
institutionally. Trade unions had developed structures and
methods which assumed they could intervene in 'politics'
only through the Labour Party, and which defined unions'
roles in a close relationship to collective bargaining. The
element which advocated extra-parliamentary political
methods (especially industrial action for political purposes)
had not been eliminated, but it was confined to a subsidiary
role: of criticising what had become the mainstream of
labour, of motivating industrial militants, and so forth.

We have examined the processes of labour's reformation
in Edinburgh. First, we briefly surveyed the structure of the
working class, and its relationship to the city's bourgeoisie.
The social distance between classes was reinforced (from
the mid-nineteenth century) by greater spatial segregation,
and may have encouraged the growth of more independent
working class values. Especially during the war, inequalities

within the working class - particularly in relation to housing - were compressed: this eroded groupings such as the 'labour aristocracy'. Nevertheless, the post-war working class remained fragmented, due to the city's industrial and occupational diversity, the economic performance of the various industries, unemployment, and similar factors. But the overlapping of various sources of fragmentation reduced the significance of any single grouping: a labour aristocracy could hardly persist when income differentials within industries were often less than those between skilled workers in different industries (especially in so industrially diverse a city). So whilst Edinburgh's working class was by no means uniform (indeed, it remained more fragmented than the working class of many other towns and cities), the intensity of its internal divisions seems to have lessened somewhat.

As a result, a common vocabulary of motivation could be more widely held and effective. Of course, this cut two ways. Certainly in wartime notions of patriotism were extremely effective on behalf of the state. But after the war no similarly effective language replaced it. The strength of (and the existence of a legitimate role for) labour appears to have been accepted; neither the state nor the non-labour political parties (at least after the fall of Lloyd George) seems to have tried actively to mobilise working class opinion. Rather, they relied on the contradictions between theoretical and practical consciousness engendering 'moral and political passivity'[2] - or, as the Labour Standard had it, 'Apathy! Apathy! Apathy!'[3] In Edinburgh, the diversity of the city's bourgeoisie may have made an effective anti-labour strategy at this level the more difficult to achieve.

During the war, two main short-term developments occurred whose effects were felt throughout industry. First, with the need for high levels of production, and buoyant demand for labour, the balance of power in industry shifted in favour of workers. But, second (and equally important), a number of factors combined to enable this power to be exercised: not only was labour stronger; it felt its strength - and the justice of its actions - more. Chiefly, the factors stemmed from the war: the central role of the state in industry, the importance of 'profiteering', working people's sacrifice in France, and so forth. Such notions as 'efficiency' and 'organisation' became distanced from commonly associated notions (above all, 'profit'); increasingly, they became effective in legitimising action in the labour interest. By the same token, of course, they became less effective as principles legitimising action by employers. In a number of respects, too, the law became less unfavourable to unions; while the state was less concerned with employers' rights and profits than ensuring continuity of production. Finally, the problems of war - rising prices, above all - could link general principles to workplace action. During 1919 and early 1920 these factors continued to hold sway; they were compounded by the loss of self-confidence which occurred among important elements of capital and the state. When revolution was apparently on the agenda, material concessions seemed a cheap insurance.

So, in effect, the motivational basis of trade union advance during and immediately after the war was a fortuitous consequence of the international conflict. To be sure, those notions to which the war lent strength were interpreted in the light of workers' experiences: but at root they were available because of the changes in the meaning of the 'nation' and in the operation of state and economy entailed by total war. Sustained and active working class support for the war effort required justification by principles acceptable to workers; yet for dominant political institutions to deploy such a vocabulary was, ipso facto, to strengthen it, and to open it to more effective use by labour in its own interest. In Gramsci's terms, the contradiction between theoretical and practical consciousness had been reduced by the ruling class's having shifted the former more into line with the latter: the working class was more likely to act, but also to act in its own interests.

The war's influence on labour politics was less unambiguously positive than it was for the unions. Whether or not the war was justified split virtually every section of the labour movement. United action became more difficult to achieve. Wartime events led to the development of two conceptions of political action within the movement. One drew strength from the power of the wartime state, and saw labour's task as the winning of control over the state. The second drew strength from the power of the wartime trade union movement. But these images of politics developed in a period when nationalism, patriotism, was the fundamental determinant of allegiance within the labour movement: during the war, they did not structure coherent political groupings or coalitions.

During 1919 and 1920 patriotism ceased to be very

effective as a principle legitimising action within the working class: or, rather, having formed the foundation of a coalition supportive of a national effort, it now became, if anything, supportive of a general working class self-confidence and self-assertion. But among the working class the images of political action which had been developing (but secondary and ineffective) during the war, remained indistinct. Trade union action continued to seem an important path to political power, particularly since electoral methods (which had in any case become less prominent during the war) seemed unlikely to be effective after the 1918 general election, and the municipal contest of 1919. At the same time, both 'right' and 'left' continued to stress the power of the state: many had experience of it during the war; for many, this was the lesson of the Bolshevik revolution. In short, during this immediate post-war period of ferment, confusion reigned over labour's political strategy; no clear allegiances had developed.

In this situation, a broad coalition formed, based on some of the motives which had become available to labour during the war: primarily, those associated with 'efficiency' and 'organisation'. This coalition was limited to the restructuring of the labour movement: it carried through the amalgamation of the Trades Council and the Labour Party, and, at another level, brought most of the city's Marxists into the Communist Party. It was based on the assumption that efficiency was an inherent attribute of certain organisational structures; all could concur on organisational change, for the structure thus created would be appropriate to any political task. The organisational form seen as efficient was centralised and hierarchical, not only drawing on managerial images (and to some extent, practice), but also drawing strength from military organisation, and from how the state controlled the wartime economy. Such structures promised unity in action: disagreements would be settled in a central, representative forum (the Trades and Labour Council in Edinburgh; but by analogy the TUC, Labour Party Conference, or whatever); thereafter, all elements of the movement would act in concert, directed by central organs and supported by a central administration. The virtues of such a structure were acknowledged at once in both political and industrial spheres.

Yet the structures thus developed were not universally efficient; and when combined with a number of other factors, their effect, over the following years, was to enable

236

the right of the movement to establish an ascendancy. Such mechanistic structures are effective chiefly when their environment is stable, and when the commitment of their constituent individuals and institutions is assured. These conditions were largely fulfilled in the actual prosecution of industrial (and other 'direct') action during 1919 and 1920: the action was relatively brief, so the environment was quite stable; the objectives and methods were (more or less) clear; attitudes were militant. Nevertheless, many of the wartime and immediate post-war advances were in fact achieved not by such structures, but despite them. The enormous expansion of union membership, for instance, depended upon the ability of groups of workers to act on their own initiative – it required an acceptance of common aims and attitudes, but not strong, centralised resources. But this went largely unrecognised. The expansion was perceived as achievement despite a lack of organisation, rather than as being the product of a distinct, looser, type of organisation, albeit in embryonic form: it was consequently taken to indicate how much greater the advances might be if all were properly 'co-ordinated'.

Moreover, to see but a single, and universally efficient, form of organisation was artificially to divorce technical structures from their moral, their motivational, context. Thus organisation and propaganda were widely seen as distinct: certain organisations were zealous propagandists, to be sure, but organisation itself was not seen as intimately associated with the moral climate in which it existed. Though unions developed strong, centralised, structures, they saw propaganda as a task which belonged elsewhere, and did not develop strong central propagandist institutions; the Trades and Labour Council's attempts to forge unity in political outlook among its constituent elements were desultory.

Whether the labour movement could have developed strong, mobilising, institutions during 1917-20 must be doubtful: even coping with the administrative burdens of growth stretched its resources to their limits. Whether such institutions could have weathered the rigours of depression is still more uncertain. From 1920 the balance of power in industry turned against labour. Unions were weakened, sometimes eliminated. At the same time, the balance of legitimation shifted against the working class: press support evaporated; state recognition was increasingly restricted to very narrow definitions of union activity; working class

237

purchase on notions of 'efficiency', 'organisation', and so forth, was reduced as wartime understandings became more distant; above all, few problems were now soluble within the workplace - even where issues did exist, unions might be unable to mobilise around them. As a result, the degree of unity of purpose within the trade union movement deteriorated: its central aims became less widely powerful; sectional and self-interested motives became more pronounced; it became more difficult to achieve united action around common principles.

Similar problems beset labour politics. Industrial action seemed less and less a realistic path to political power; 'direct action' of other kinds also began to fail for lack of mass support. And in these circumstances the strategic 'bias' inherent in the movement's images and structures of organisation began to reveal itself. The prevalence of mechanistic structures and images encouraged unions - at every level - to respond to their new environment in certain ways. First, they came to see propaganda as important (though they did not link it with a radical critique of organisation). Second, when propaganda brought no success, they took steps to strengthen their structures: in particular, internal discipline was strengthened. Third, they attempted to stabilise their external environment: unable to control it, they could only minimise its unpredictability. In industrial relations this meant supporting national bargaining, 'procedure', and so forth. In politics, it implied supporting a strategy which encouraged the construction of stable institutions, and minimised the exposure of union institutions to weakening through political conflict.

So union opinion shifted away from support for 'revolutionary industrial methods'. At the same time, a coherent Labour Socialist grouping began to form, criticising the policies of direct action increasingly vociferously as the latter's successes became rarer. Under these pressures, the shallow foundations of labour's post-war coalition were undermined. The electoral strategy now became the foundation of a new coalition, in which Labour Socialism was able to unite the Labour left with trade union labourism. Based on a clear distinction between political and industrial action (and a definition of the former in constitutional-electoral terms), this permitted the development of routinised forms of political activity, and institutions, which were a vital counterweight to the development of a leftist (what we have termed 'Marxist') coalition. Initially unstable, because based around a limited range of issues, the Labour Socialist coalition was, by the later 1920s, possessed of a strong institutional base which could resist the lure of more radical conceptions of politics even (say) after the debacle of 1931. For its competitor, the current based around revolutionary socialism and industrial militancy, and now led by the Communist Party, was unable to develop countervailing institutions; it could win widespread support only in situations of militant industrial action - and these were neither lasting enough, nor successful enough, to enable it to consolidate.

The labour movement which was reshaped in these few short years during and just after the Great War has been at the centre of twentieth-century British politics. Labour's subsequent achievements - and limitations - have been underpinned by political and organisational assumptions and alliances cemented over little more than a decade. The electoral focus of Labour; the definition of politics in electoral terms; the acceptance that, for trade unions, political action must be conducted through the Labour Party (and might in the end be reducible to the payment of the 'political levy'); the exclusion of industrial action for political ends; trade union concern for order in industrial relations - all these attitudes marked the labour movement by the end of the 1920s, and have marked it since. Of course, such attitudes were by no means unknown before 1914. But during the war and the early 1920s they were firmly buttressed by the growth of centralised organisational structures in both unions and political parties.

In these structures, although authority was formally vested in the members at large, in practice a few hands held the reins of power. It was through conferences, committees, routines, rules - the apparatus of bureaucracy, albeit writ small - that workers were to express their solidarity, their unity. Democracy to be sure: but centralised democracy, in which initiative, change, response to local developments, were secondary to consistency, conformity, universality, as perceived centrally. In which the influence of those close to the seats of power - who had the ears of national or local officers, committee members, and so forth - often weighed more heavily than the formal authority, not to say the opinion, of members. And in which the maintenance of rules, of organisational integrity, might bring disciplinary action for those who sought change.

The political bloc cemented in the years after the

239

Conclusion

Great War was well-adapted to certain tasks: in its various aspects, to fighting elections, to collective bargaining and so forth, particularly in the context of a predominantly manual working class. In these areas its subsequent achievement was remarkable. But ideology, ideas, have always been at a discount. Gramsci has emphasised the importance - if a class or social group is to achieve a leading or hegemonic role - of creating strata of intellectuals, who will not merely generate ideas, but disseminate them, organise the rising class: 'give it homogeneity and an awareness of its own function not only in the economic but also in the social and political fields'.[4] In the British labour movement, theory, philosophy - the mainsprings of the moral element - have been received rather than created, defined rather than developed, policed rather than regenerated. The result has been a movement which, in the main - on both left and right - responds to change, to developing social movements, by exclusion and intensified internal dispute rather than by attempting to ally, to give moral and political direction, to lead.

It was when the social base of Labour's strength began to erode - after the second World War, but especially from the 1960s - that its limitations began to be exposed. The movement was, as it were, set tasks which it found difficult to recognise or acknowledge, let alone tackle: immigration and racism, the decline of the manual working class, increasing white-collar employment, women's claim for an equal role in society, and so forth. Having failed (or not attempted) to create a genuine socialist consensus within the movement or more widely, the movement's response to these developments was marked by suspicion, by fear, by internal dissent; and with reason, for these developments threatened both the stability on which labour's organisational edifice depended, and an already eroding electoral coalition.

These are large claims based on a small study; and perhaps they smack uncomfortably of original sin. But this study was founded on a belief in the importance of detailed local research in analysing the growth of labour. If it provokes further investigations of the complex inter-play of motives and organisation which reformed British labour during and after the Great War, it may in some modest way contribute to the movement's renewal.

NOTES

1. A. Gramsci, Selection from the Prison Notebooks (London, 1971), p.234.
2. Ibid., p.333.
3. Labour Standard, 21 March 1925; cp S. Macintyre, A Proletarian Science. Marxism in Britain 1917-1933 (Cambridge, 1980), esp. pp.198-218.
4. Gramsci, Prison Notebooks, p.5.

Appendix

LABOUR PARTY ORGANISATION IN EDINBURGH 1917-27

Few studies exist of the growth of local Labour Party organisation.[1] As there is but a single surviving item produced by an Edinburgh divisional party or ward committee during these years (and that not very useful),[2] this account is gleaned from other sources.

Divisional and Ward Organisation. Before 1918 Labour Party ward committees were few in number and fleeting in existence. Only two were strong enough to pay dues to the Edinburgh branch in 1917/18; only four in 1919/20.[3] At the time of amalgamation, confidence was expressed about the progress of party organisation,[4] but this was premature. Table A.1 summarises the surviving evidence on when DLPs and ward committees were formed (or first known to exist). Although some ward committees may not be recorded, this is more likely in the later years, after their care was delegated to DLPs and the Political Officer. In several cases DLPs were not formed until four or more years after the 1918 constitution decreed their existence.

At the 1918 general election, union and ILP branches seem to have co-operated on an essentially ad hoc basis to fight it: they sent delegates to the selection conferences (held under the Edinburgh branch's auspices); very likely their commitment to the resulting electoral effort depended in part on whether their favoured candidate was selected. Election agents were appointed by the branch, though largely financed by the organisations nominating the successful candidates. Municipal election organisation was similar; but although elections provided the catalyst for organisation, it is far from clear that the organisation thus created always outlived the election. The West division, for instance, was fought in December 1918; in early 1920 a DLP was only in the process of formation.[5] And while Canongate ward, where a Labour candidate had been victorious in 1913, was contested in 1919, 1920 and 1922,[6] the T&LC was endeavouring to form a ward committee as late as 1923.[7]

Table A.1: The Growth of Labour Party Institutions in Edinburgh 1917-24

	Central	North	South	East	West	Leith
1917	George Sq (F) St Leonards (E)				Gorgie (E)	
1918	Women's Section (F)				Dalry (F)	Burgh LP (E)
1919	St Giles (E)				Women's Section (E)	
1920	'Nucleus' of DLP (E)	DLP (F)			'Nucleus' of DLP (E)	
1921						DLP (F)(a)
1922			DLP (F?)			Ward committees (F)
1923		DLP (E) Calton (F)		Canongate (F) Portobello (F)		
1924	DLP (E)	Committees in four wards (F)		DLP (F)		

Notes: (E) Institution recorded as being in existence in this year; this does not imply it was not also formed in this year.
(F) Institution recorded as formed in this year.
(a) Probably just a consequence of amalgamation of Leith UTC&LP with Edin. T&LC.

Source: Edinburgh trade union and labour records.

Appendix

Table A.2: Divisional Labour Parties in Edinburgh: Affiliation Fees 1924–8

	DLP	Fee Paid	Members Represented
1924/5	West	30s	180 or less
	North	30s	180 or less
1925/6	West	30s	180 or less
	North	30s	180 or less
1926/7	West	55s (a, b)	330
	North	30s (a)	180 or less
	South	30s	180 or less
1927/8	West	53s (c)	318
	North	30s	180 or less
	South	30s	180 or less
1928/9	West	70s 4d (c)	422
	North	30s	180 or less

Notes: (a) In 1926 DLPs were called upon to pay a double affiliation fee: North and West DLPs each paid an extra 30s, which is excluded here.

(b) Including 17s 8d not paid until the following year.

(c) West DLP's 1927/8 payment is marked 'part 1927': the figures for 1927/8 may thus understate fees and membership whilst those for 1928/9 may be correspondingly overstated.

Source: T&LC ARs, 1925–9.

Even when formed, local Labour Party organisation seems often to have been less than vibrant. We know little of ward committees, but DLPs were required to pay an affiliation fee to the T&LC, with a minimum of 30s.[8] Until the year 1924/5, no DLP did so; Table A.2 shows progress over 1924–8. Two points stand out. First, in neither the two divisions won by Labour during these years (Central and East), nor in Leith where Labour's challenge otherwise came closest to victory, was there a divisional party. Probably the strength of the ILP accounts for this in Central Edinburgh and Leith, while the three areas of Labour strength in East Edinburgh (Canongate, Portobello and Musselburgh) were widely scattered: a DLP was only formed in early 1924.[9] Second, two of those DLPs which were strong enough to affiliate had less than 180 members throughout the period - both, of course, were in barren Labour territory. Only one built up a membership greater than 180: West Edinburgh, a division with a pocket of long-standing Labour strength (Dalry and Gorgie wards had been won in the Town Council elections of 1909 and 1911 respectively) - yet even here the DLP probably never had more than 400 members.[10]

In these circumstances, the role of the T&LC and the DLPs was chiefly the mobilisation and co-ordination of other bodies (especially the ILP, but also trade unions) in electoral work: the DLPs lacked adequate strength of themselves. We have no full description of electoral work in the early 1920s, but after the 1925 municipal elections a re-assessment took place which reveals some of the perceived weaknesses of earlier practice. (Although set in train early in 1926, most of the reassessment took place after the General Strike, which strengthened centralist notions of organisation.) A Political Committee of the T&LC was to take charge as a 'Central Election Committee' (CEC): this was to organise and allocate speakers 'in the same manner as was being done by the Strike Com[mi]tt[ee] for the Miners meetings'; it would control all press advertising on the basis of information supplied by ward committees; rather than granting money to wards, it would itself incur expenses (up to a maximum of £20 per contested ward); no ward committee would be empowered to issue publicity material without prior approval of the CEC; a 'motor cycle corps' would ensure 'rapid distribution of messages and information' from the CEC, which would be in constant session each evening for the four weeks preceding polling day 'to ensure 100% efficiency'.[11] In fact, political control of Labour candidates at election time was centralised at least from the time of the T&LC's formation: in 1925, for instance, wards had to get the Council's permission to issue an extra handbill, or whether to include a statement of their candidates' 'bonafides' in their publicity.[12] If centralisation had weaknesses, the solutions lay in lessons learnt in 1926 about how centralised structures could work efficiently.

Table A.3: Edinburgh Trades and Labour Council: Political Income and Expenditure 1919-28

Values shown as £ s d (per cent figures in parentheses).

	1919/20 (a)	1920/1 (a)	1921/2	1922/3	1923/4	1924/5	1925/6	1926/7	1927/8
Affiliation fee income:									
Total		365 17 3	358 5 8	322 10 10	322 16 0	437 4 11	456 19 0	472 17 1	366 9 6
From political bodies		5 17 0	6 7 10	6 10 8	5 15 8	11 2 4	11 2 2	13 3 8	13 1 2
(per cent)		(1.59)	(1.79)	(2.03)	(1.74)	(2.53)	(2.43)	(2.78)	(3.56)
Edinburgh Labour Party special election fund:									
Total sum raised	154 19 3	93 19 2	37 1 10	57 11 4	139 12 0	178 15 4	123 11 3	150 19 4	84 2 6
- of which for:									
Municipal election fund			31 9 10	57 11 4	86 4 0	95 12 0	123 11 3(d)	108 5 7	73 15 6
Parliamentary election fund			(5 12 0)(c)		53 8 0	83 3 4		42 13 9(e)	10 7 0(e)
- of which from:									
Trade union bodies	68 9 6	61 6 0	22 6 10	49 4 10	137 1 6	172 10 10	120 6 3	134 12 6	73 12 6
(per cent)	(44.2)	(65.2)	(60.2)	(85.5)	(98.2)	(96.5)	(97.4)	(89.2)	(87.5)
ILP bodies	55 8 9(b)	2 17 0	3 10 0	6 4 0	2 0 0	5 2 6	3 5 0	5 18 0	4 5 0
(per cent)	(35.8)	(3.0)	(9.4)	(10.8)	(1.4)	(2.9)	(2.6)	(3.9)	(5.0)
Local Labour Party bodies	25 0 0	23 7 2	3 6 6	1 10 0				6 11 0	1 0 0
(per cent)	(16.1)	(24.9)	(9.0)	(2.6)				(4.3)	(1.2)
Other sources (f)	6 11 0	5 19 6	7 18 6	12 6	12 6	1 2 0		3 17 10	5 5 0
(per cent)	(4.2)	(6.4)	(21.4)	(1.1)	(0.4)	(0.6)		(2.6)	(6.2)
Edinburgh Labour Party election expenditure									
Total	228 11 10	160 11 11	112 13 5	137 16 2	188 3 10	252 1 9	148 16 2	303 10 4	246 11 7
- of which:									
Town and Parish Council	171 19 1	160 11 11	83 15 8	125 15 2	99 15 2	100 0 0	128 16 2	235 16 7	231 4 7
Parliamentary	51 19 9		8 17 9	4 11 0	53 8 8	83 3 4		42 13 9	10 7 0
Education Authority						38 18 5			
Donations to local Labour parties for organisation, etc.	4 13 0	20 0 0	20 0 0	7 10 0	30 0 0	30 0 0	20 0 0	25 0 0	5 0 0

Notes:
(a) Excluding Leith.
(b) Includes many collections by individuals, listed under 'ILP' and presumably members.
(c) Education Authority election.
(d) Municipal and Parish Council election.
(e) Leith by-election fund.
(f) Chiefly donations by individuals.

Source: T& LC ARs, 1920-8, and calculations thence.

Finance. The centrality of trade union finance to electoral strategy is clear from the T&LC's income and expenditure (see Table A.3). Political bodies' contribution to routine income was insignificant - only rising above 3 per cent of affiliation fee income in 1927/8. For election income, the story is similar. Although the ILP and Labour Party made significant contributions in 1919/20 and 1920/1, and individual donations grew the following year, thereafter contributions from both these categories declined both relatively and absolutely. Union contributions, however, grew rapidly in both respects, and for the four years from 1923 constituted 90 per cent or more of election income. Of course, these figures must be treated with some caution: we might expect, in particular, local Labour Party organisations to retain income for their own purposes, rather than contribute it to a central fund, whilst this would be the natural route for union contributions. Yet bodies which found difficulty in meeting minimal - and obligatory - affiliation fees can hardly have been wealthy, and the scale of union electoral contributions from 1923 onward is beyond anything the political bodies had managed, even in the 'affluent' years just after the war.

Control. Union opinion was vital to the Labour Party not only for financial reasons. From 1920, union delegates at the T&LC could, in theory, control the policy of Labour in Edinburgh. Table A.4 shows that, even at the end of our period, delegates from DLPs and other political organisations made up less than one-fifth of the T&LC's delegates; nor could they gain effective control by more assiduous attendance. Indeed, if anything (save during 1921-3) they attended the Council's meetings less frequently than their trade union comrades. They did, it is true, achieve generally better representation on the T&LC's executive committee, which was important: but they remained in a minority throughout (see Table A.5). Of course, many union delegates - especially, perhaps, those on the executive committee - had political affiliations. Save in 1920/1, for instance, we know that there was always at least one, sometimes two (and possibly more), SDF members on the executive who were union delegates.[13]

Elections. Labour's performance in parliamentary elections is summarised in Table A.6. Not until October 1924 did Labour contest more than three of the city's six divisions; in

Table A.4: Edinburgh Trades and Labour Council: Participation of Political Delegates 1920-7

	1915/6	1916/7	1917/8	1918/9	1919/20	1920/1	1921/2	1922/3	1923/4	1924/5	1925/6	1926/7
Meetings held	26	27	26	25	28	27	25	26	27	32	36	28
Organisations affiliated												
Trade union	83	79	80	84	82	95	70	79	82	86	92	93
Political						12	10	11	16	19	23	25
of which:												
- DLPs						5	5	5	6	7	7	7
- ILP						4	2	2	5	8	9	10
- Other						3	3	4	5	4	7	8
Delegates (per cent of total)												
Trade union	201	209	213	217	282	308	229	245	276	278	278	281
						(90.6)	(87.4)	(86.6)	(84.4)	(82.7)	(81.3)	(80.3)
Political						32	33	38	51	58	64	69
						(9.4)	(12.6)	(13.4)	(15.6)	(17.3)	(18.7)	(19.7)
of whom:												
- DLP						18	21	24	27	30	30	31
- ILP						9	6	6	15	20	21	23
- Other						5	6	8	10	8	13	5
Mean attendance per meeting (per cent of total)												
Union delegates	71.5	66.8	80.7	71.4	66.6	71.7	64.2	70.1	81.3	77.6	76.0	82.6
						(90.2)	(86.1)	(83.3)	(88.8)	(85.4)	(86.5)	(84.5)
Political delegates						7.8	10.4	14.0	10.2	13.3	11.9	15.1
						(9.8)	(13.9)	(16.7)	(11.2)	(14.6)	(13.5)	(15.5)
of whom:												
- DLP						5.3	5.4	9.3	5.5	5.6	8.3	7.9
- ILP						2.7	3.8	1.8	2.5	4.9	2.6	4.7
Mean number of meetings attended												
by union delegates	9.9	8.9	10.5	9.1	6.5	6.5	7.8	7.9	8.2	7.7	7.6	8.2
by Political delegates						6.8	8.7	10.2	5.6	6.4	5.2	6.1
of whom:												
- from DLPs						8.2	7.1	10.8	5.7	5.2	7.7	7.1
- from ILP						8.2	17.8	8.4	4.6	6.8	3.4	5.7

Note: (a) Adjusted for varying number of meetings in each year to permit comparison between years.

Source: Calculated from TC and T&LC ARs, 1916-28.

Table A.5: Edinburgh Trades and Labour Council: Organisational Background of Executive Committee Members 1920–8

	1920/1	1921/2	1922/3	1923/4	1924/5	1925/6	1926/7	1927/8
Delegates from:								
Trade unions (per cent)	12 (71)	11 (65)	11 (65)	10 (59)	11 (65)	11 (65)	15 (75)	14 (70)
Political bodies	5 (29)	5 (29)	6 (35)	7 (41)	6 (35)	6 (35)	5 (25)	6 (30)
of whom:								
- DLP	3	3	5	3	3	4	4	5
- ILP	2	2	0	1	1	1	0	0
- SDF	0	0	1	2	1	1	1	1
- Guild Socialist Soc	0	0	0	1	1	0	0	0
Unidentified		1						
Total Membership of Executive Committee	17	17	17	17	17	17	20	20

Source: T&LC ARs, 1920-7.

Appendix

1922, it could manage only two. Contests seem to have occurred where Labour organisation was strongest, rather than where the prospects of success were greatest. The two were not always identical. East division was won on the first occasion Labour entered the field, and just eight months after a DLP was formed; West division was consistently fought, though the prospects were poor. On three occasions (once in 1924, twice in 1929) Labour won because other parties were unable to come to an agreement; Leith, however, might well have been captured in both 1924 and 1929 had the Conservatives not stood down in favour of the Liberals. It is clear from those constituencies contested by Labour throughout the period that the main advance in electoral support came between the 1922 and 1923 elections.

Table A.6: Labour Party: Parliamentary Election Performance, Edinburgh 1918-29

	December 1918	November 1922	December 1923	October 1924	May 1929
Central					
(a)	7,161*	12,876*	13,186*	13,628*	16,762*
(b)	51.8	57.9	67.9	60.5	59.0
(c)	1	1	1	1	2
East					
(a)				9,330*	13,933*
(b)				44.3	47.3
(c)				2	2
North					
(a)				8,192	11,340
(b)				27.9	32.2
(c)				2	2
South					
(a)					5,050
(b)					14.7
(c)					2

Table A.6 Continued

	December 1918	November 1922	December 1923	October 1924	May 1929
West					
(a)	2,642		6,836	9,603	15,795*
(b)	14.7		25.7	33.1	38.6
(c)	2		2	2	2
Leith					
(a)	4,251	6,567	8,267	11,250	15,715
(b)	19.1	23.5	35.5	40.4	43.3
(c)	2	2	1	1	1

Total Labour vote

	14,054	19,443	28,289	52,003	78,595

Labour percentage of poll:

All constituencies with
Labour Candidate

	25.9	38.8	40.8	37.3	38.4

Central and Leith

	31.5	38.8	50.3	49.4	50.2

Notes: (a) Labour vote.
(b) Labour percentage of poll.
(c) Number of other candidates.
Asterisk indicates Labour candidate elected.
Two by-elections were held during this period:
April 1920 (North): Labour vote, 3,808 (17.1 per
cent of poll), two other candidates; March 1927
(Leith), 12,350 (42 per cent of poll), one other
candidate.

Source: Calculated from F.W.S. Craig, British Parliamentary Election Results 1918-1949 (London,
1969).

Appendix

Labour's municipal election performance is surveyed in Table A.8. After the war, the record was initially poor. In 1919 there was, according to the <u>Scotsman</u>, a 'Heavy Defeat for Labour';[14] in 1920 'Labour received a severe setback'[15] when only two of its 19 candidates were victorious. Whereas Labour had a significant presence on Leith Town Council before amalgamation,[16] 'not a single Labour Municipal or parish Council nominee was returned for the Port' in 1920.[17] In 1921 the number of Labour candidates slumped to four, only one of whom was returned. Over the following years, as Party organisation improved, the number of candidates increased rapidly: this apparently allowed Labour to expand in favourable areas, for the mean vote obtained per opposed candidate also rose.

Finally, we should briefly look at candidates of other labour bodies. The Socialist Labour party made a virtue of opposing Labour and Communist candidates (in the latter case, often adopting the 'Communist' label); their votes rarely rose above the derisory. Communist Party candidates fared somewhat better, in the main (see Table A.9), yet where there was no official Labour candidate, they could not win the support of all Labour voters, whilst on the single occasion the party fought an official Labour candidate, its vote slumped. Contests by other organisations are shown in Table A.10. On no occasion were these opposed by official Labour candidates. The St Giles Unemployed candidature was <u>de facto</u> (and in 1922, <u>de jure</u>) recognised as a Labour contest in all but name; even by 1921 the ex-service vote was of declining importance; whilst the Railway Workers learnt their lesson in 1921, and their candidate stood for Labour the following year.

Table A.7: Socialist Labour Party Votes in Edinburgh Municipal Elections 1919-27

		SLP	Labour
1919	Canongate	155	1,509
	St Leonards	27	1,117
	Dalry	29	1,036
	Gorgie	44	1,051
	George Sq	27	872
1920	Calton	54	1,249
	Canongate	52	1,499
	Gorgie	33	1,492
	Dalry (two seats)	47	2,061
		41	1,349
	St Leonards	36	1,304
	Leith South (three seats)	157	1,748
		123	1,330
		93	1,317
	Leith Central (three seats)	41	829
		32	753
		22	706
1921	Gorgie	34	2,192
	Dalry	151	-
	Leith South	295	-
	Leith North	141	-
1923	St Giles	46	(1,072 (u))
	St Leonards	61	(865 (c))
	Leith South	154	(408 (c))

Notes: (c) Communist.
(u) Unemployed.

Source: Scotsman, 5 November 1919, 3 November 1920, 2 November 1921, 8 November 1922, 7 November 1923, 5 November 1924, 4 November 1925, 3 November 1926; T&LC AR 1928, p.10; R.A. Fox, 'Members of the Labour Party Elected to Edinburgh Town Council', unpublished typescript, 1971, pp.1-5.

Table A.8: Labour Votes in Edinburgh Municipal Elections 1919-27

	1919	1920	1921	1922	1923	1924	1925	1926	1927
Calton	1,509	1,249	1,154	1,290	1,776	1,757	2,357	2,882	2,533
Canongate		1,499	(1,042 r)		1,910	2,075	2,289	3,734	3,169
Newington									1,134
Morningside									
Merchiston									
Gorgie	1,051	1,492	2,192*	2,398*	364 / 3,458*		2,304	3,095	3,233
Haymarket		486							868
St Bernards						1,006	1,156	1,112	
Broughton							1,139	1,407	1,479
St Stephens						787			
St Andrews									
St Giles	850	2,061*	(877 u)	849	(1,072 u)	1,854	2,544	2,839	2,451
Dalry	1,036	1,349		(b)	1,953	1,906	2,631	3,362	2,902 / 2,836
George Square	872	890	1,255	1,179	1,392		1,641	1,878	2,213
St Leonards	1,117	1,304	(930 c)	866		3,373*	3,177*	3,444*	3,907
Portobello						1,380	1,544	2,703	2,373
South Leith	(a)	1,748 / 1,330 / 1,317		1,260			1,570		2,426
North Leith	(a)	1,123 / 942 / 852				1,953*	1,731	2,114	2,580
West Leith	(a)	798					755	1,189	
Central Leith	(a)	829 / 753 / 706		768	1,417	900	1,034	1,596	1,693
Liberton	(a)	608*	719	1,126		693		1,370	1,064
Colinton									
Corstorphine & Cramond									

Table A.8 Continued

	1919	1920	1921	1922	1923	1924	1925	1926	1927
Official Labour Candidates:									
Number	6	19	4	9	7	11	14	14	16
Wards contested	6	12	4	9	7	11	14	14	15
Total vote	6,435	21,336	5,320	9,736	12,270	17,684	25,872	32,725	36,861
Mean vote per opposed candidate	1,072	1,123	1,330	1,217	1,753	1,608	1,848	2,337	2,304
Number of Labour councillors after election	6	4	2	3	3	5	6	14	15

Notes: (a) Not within Edinburgh until 1920.
(b) Labour candidate returned unopposed.
(c) A Communist candidate stood in St Leonards in 1921 against a retiring Labour councillor standing as an independent.
(r) Candidate of NUR No. 1 branch Political Committee; he stood as Labour candidate in the same ward in 1922.
(u) Unemployed candidates: T&LC AR 1928, p.10, retrospectively includes the 1923 vote as 'Labour', perhaps because the candidate was by then T&LC President.

(General) Figures exclude by-elections: refer only to elections held on first Tuesday of November each year. Where more than one vote appears, a corresponding number of seats was contested.

Sources: Scotsman, as Table A.7.

Appendix

Table A.9: Communist Party Votes in Edinburgh Municipal Elections 1919-27

	Ward	Communist	Labour
1921	St Leonards	930	–
1923	St Leonards	865	(61 (s))
	Leith South	408	(154 (s))
1924	St Leonards	172	3,373

Note: (s) Socialist Labour Party.

Source: <u>Scotsman</u>, as Table A.7.

Table A.10: Municipal Election Performance of Miscellaneous Labour Bodies, Edinburgh 1919-27

1921	Canongate	Railway Workers	1,042
	Broughton	Ex-Service	503
	St Giles	Unemployed	877
1922	St Giles	Labour and Unemployed	849
1923	St Giles	Unemployed	1,072

Source: <u>Scotsman</u>, as Table A.7.

NOTES

1.   The most important is R. McKibbin, The Evolution of the Labour Party 1910-1924 (Oxford, 1974), although this is largely based on national evidence.

2.   An account book, almost certainly of Edin. South DLP; its most complete sections relate to 1929/30.

3.   LP Edin. branch ARs 1917/18, p.8, 1919/20 (in TC AR 1920), p.22.

4.   Ibid., 1919/20, pp.18-21.

5.   Ibid.

6.   In 1921 it was contested by the NUR Edin. No. 1 branch.

7.   T&LC minutes, 28 August 1923; only five people attended its first meeting (ibid., 26 September 1923).

8.   T&LC Constitution and Rules (Edin., 1922), p.5: the fee was then forwarded to Labour Party head office.

9.   T&LC minutes, 19 February 1924.

10.   DLP members' primary loyalties were, of course, often to other organisations, especially the ILP. Cp Labour Standard, 25 December 1926: 'The people of St Leonards ... have built up an organisation, an arm of the Labour Movement, and they are represented now by three Labour Councillors. No wonder St Leonards ILP grows by leaps and bounds.'

11.   T&LC minutes, 10 September 1926: these proposals were watered down somewhat under DLP and ward committee pressure (ibid., 22, 28 September 1926).

12.   Ibid., 6 October 1925.

13.   Not always the same people from year to year: delegates' organisations changed.

14.   Scotsman, 5 November 1919.

15.   Ibid., 3 November 1920.

16.   In 1919 three Labour candidates were successful in the Leith Town Council election (ibid., 5 November 1919); the wards were redrawn on amalgamation.

17.   Ibid., 3 November 1920.

SELECT BIBLIOGRAPHY

I. MANUSCRIPT AND TYPESCRIPT SOURCES

At Edinburgh Trades Council
Edinburgh Trades Council, Minutes 1918-20.
Edinburgh Trades and Labour Council, Minutes 1920-39.
Edinburgh Trades and Labour Council, Political Committee Minutes 1926-7.
Miscellaneous Correspndence.

At the National Library of Scotland
Crawford, Gerald W., Personal Papers.
Dott, George, Personal Papers.
East of Scotland Association of Engineers and Iron Founders and Amalgamated Society of Engineers, Conference Proceedings:
    18 January 1918: 'Recognition of Shop Stewards';
    19 September 1918: 'in re Engineers Working Rules';
    30 April 1920: 'Marine Repairs - Shore and Marine Engineers'.
East of Scotland Association of Engineers and Ironfounders and The Brassfinishers' Society, Local Conference Proceedings:
    29 October 1920: 'Brassfinishers Piecework Rates - Application for Advance of 20 per cent'.
East of Scotland Association of Engineers and Ironfounders and Amalgamated Engineering Union and Scottish Brassmoulders' Union, Local Conference Proceedings:
    4 April 1921: 'Brassmoulders' Rates - Levelling Up to Ironmoulders';
    19 December 1922: 'in re Outworking Allowances, Edinburgh District';
    22 January 1923: 'in re Outworking Allowances'.
East of Scotland Engineers and Iron Founders Employers' Association and Amalgamated Engineering Union, Conference Proceedings:
    20 July 1922: 'Proposed Reduction of 12½ per cent on

258

Piecework Prices of Brass Finishers and Brass Moulders, in Gas Meter Making Works'.

Edinburgh Fabian Society, Minutes 1926-34.

Engineering and Allied Employers (East of Scotland) and Amalgamated Engineering Union, Local Conference Proceedings:
23 October 1925: 'in re Allowances for Repair Work on Diesel, Semi-Diesel and Oil Internal Combustion Engines'.

Engineering and Allied Employers (East of Scotland) Association, Executive Committee, and Amalgamated Engineering Union, Local Conference Proceedings:
22 April 1926: 'in re Local Application for 20/- per week Increase in Wages'.

Guild of Insurance Officials, Edinburgh branch, Minutes 1923-9.

Independent Labour Party, Edinburgh Central branch:
Correspondence 1917-18; Minutes 1918-19; List of Officials and Standing Committees 1917-18.

Johnston, Thomas, Personal Papers.

Labour Party, Edinburgh branch, Minutes 1911-20.

Labour Party (probably South Edinburgh DLP), Account Book 1922-9.

National Amalgamated Union of Labour, No. 292 branch, Minutes 1917-20.

National Union of Clerks, Edinburgh branch, Minutes 1918-27.

At the Edinburgh Public Library

Scottish Socialist Federation, Minutes 1919.

National Socialist Party, Edinburgh branch, Minutes 1919-20.

Social Democratic Federation, Edinburgh branch, Minutes 1920-7.

At the Labour Party Library

Correspondence with and regarding Edinburgh Labour Party, Trades Council, and Trades and Labour Council.

At the TUC Library

Correspondence with and regarding Edinburgh Trades Council and Trades and Labour Council.

At the British Library of Political and Economic Science

Graham, W., 'Effective Trade Unionism', n.d. (c.1921: Webb

Trade Union Collection).
Independent Labour Party, National Administrative Council:
 Minutes 1917-27; Papers 1917-27.

II.   PRINTED LABOUR AND TRADE UNION REPORTS

At Edinburgh Trades Council
Edinburgh May Day Committee, Programme, 2 May 1926.
Edinburgh Trades Council, Annual Reports, 1908, 1916-20.
Edinburgh Trades and Labour Council, Annual Reports 1921-
 39.
Edinburgh Trades and Labour Council, Constitution and
 Rules 1922; 1928.
Edinburgh Trades and Labour Council, Our Unseen City
 Revealed. A Tale of Housing Atrocities, Edin. n.d.
 (c.1922).
Edinburgh Trades and Labour Council, Souvenirs of Trades
 Union Congresses at Edinburgh, 1927, 1941.
Edinburgh Trades and Labour Council, Souvenir of Labour
 Party Conference at Edinburgh, 1936.
Leith United Trades Council and Labour Party, Rules 1918.
National Union of Drug and Chemical Workers, Fair Houses
 List and Manifesto, 1928.

At the National Library of Scotland
Labour Party, Edinburgh branch, Annual Reports and
 Balance Sheets, 1911/12; 1917/18.
National Guilds League, leaflets.
National Union of Railwaymen, Edinburgh No. 1 branch
 Political Committee, Election Address, Canongate
 Ward, 1921.
National Union of Railwaymen, National Shop Workers'
 Council:
 Circulars 2 April, 6 May 1924; Agenda 8 July 1924;
 Decisions of Conference 30 July 1924.

At the Edinburgh Public Library
National Union of Railwaymen, Edinburgh No. 1 branch,
 Jubilee Souvenir 1876-1926 (1926).

III.   OTHER PRINTED REPORTS

Astor, J.J. et al., Unemployment Insurance in Great Britain;
 a Critical Examination, London 1925.
Barclay, I.T. and Perry, E.E., Behind Princes Street: A

Contrast. Report on Survey of Housing Conditions of 443 Families Situated in St Andrews Ward, Edinburgh, Edinburgh 1931.

Censuses of Scotland, 1911, 1921, 1931.

Chief Inspector of Factories and Workshops, Annual Reports 1914-29: Cd. 8051, Cd. 8276, Cd. 8570, Cd. 9108, Cmd. 340, Cmd. 941, Cmd. 1403, Cmd. 1920, Cmd. 2165, Cmd. 2437, Cmd. 2714, Cmd. 2903, Cmd. 3144, Cmd. 3360, Cmd. 3633.

Commission of Enquiry into the Industrial Unrest, No. 8 Division, Scotland, Report, Cd. 8669, 1917.

Edinburgh Public Health Department, Annual Reports, 1914-30.

Joiont-Committee of the Presbytery of Edinburgh and of the United Free Church Presbytery of Edinburgh. The Housing of the Poor in Edinburgh, Edinburgh 1922.

Medical Officer of Health and Chief Sanitary Inspector, City and Royal Burgh of Edinburgh, Report on Overcrowding (as Required by the Housing (Scotland) Act 1935), Edinburgh 1936.

Ritchie, A.W. (Chief Sanitary Inspector, Edinburgh), Housing; Improvement and Clearance Schemes in Populous Areas, Edinburgh n.d. (c.1930).

Royal Commission of the Distribution of the Industrial Population, Report, Cmd. 6153, 1940.

Royal Commission of the Housing of the Industrial Population of Scotland, Rural and Urban, Report, Cd. 8731, 1917.

Scottish Chamber of Commerce, Trade and Commerce between Scotland and the Empire, Glasgow 1934.

Stephenson, T. (ed.) for Edinburgh Society for the Promotion of Trade and Edinburgh Chamber of Commerce and Manufacturers, Industrial Edinburgh, Edinburgh 1921.

Williamson, A.M. (Medical Officer of Health, Edinburgh), The Influence of Housing on Health, Scottish Labour Housing Association, Galsgow 1917.

IV. NEWSPAPERS AND PERIODICALS

Edinburgh Strike Bulletin.
Evening Dispatch.
Labour Standard.
Plebs.
Red Flag.
Scotsman.

V. UNPUBLISHED THESES AND DISSERTATIONS

Brown, G., 'The Labour Party and Political Change in Scotland 1918-1929. The Politics of Five Elections', Ph.D., University of Edinburgh, 1981.

Cox, D., 'The Rise of the Labour Party in Leicester', M.A., University of Leicester, 1959.

Gordon, G., 'The Status Areas of Edinburgh: a Historical Analysis', Ph.D, University of Edinburgh, 1971.

Holford, J.A.K., 'Consciousness, Organisation and the Growth of Labour c. 1917-c.1927. A Study in Political and Industrial Motivation', Ph.D., University of Edinburgh, 1983.

Huq, M., 'The Urban Geography of the Heart of a City: with Special Reference to Edinburgh', Ph.D., University of Edinburgh, 1960.

Marwick, A., 'The Independent Labour Party (1918-32)', B. Litt., University ofOxford, 1960.

Oldfield, A., 'The Growth of the Concept of Economic Planning in the Doctrine of the British Labour Party', Ph.D., University of Sheffield, 1973.

Roberts, J.H., 'The National Council of Labour Colleges -An Experiment in Workers' Education. A Study of the Growth of the Labour Colleges with Particular Reference to Independent Working Class Adult Education in Scotland', M.Sc., University of Edinburgh, 1970.

Thomas, P.R., 'The Attitude of the Labour Party to Reform of Parliament, with Particular Reference to the House of Commons 1919-1951', Ph.D., Univertsity of Keele, 1974.

VI. OTHER WORKS

Abrams, P., 'The Failure of Social Reform 1918-1920', Past and Present 24, 1963.

Allen, V.L. The Sociology of Industrial Relations, London 1971.

Anderson, P., 'The Antinomies of Antonio Gramsci', New Left Review 100, 1976-7.

Anon., The Scottish Socialists. A Gallery of Contemporary Portraits, London 1931.

Armstrong, P.J., Goodman, J.F.B., and Hyman, J.D., Ideology and Shop Floor Industrial Relations, London

1981.

Bagwell, P.S., The Railwaymen. The History of the National Union of Railwaymen, London 1963.

Bain, G.S., The Growth of White Collar Unionism, Oxford 1970.

Batstone, E., Boraston, I., and Frenkel, S., Shop Stewards in Action, London 1977.

Beer, S., Modern British Politics, London 1969.

Bowley, A.L., Some Economic Consequences of the Great War, London 1930.

Braverman, H., Labor and Monopoly Capital, New York 1974.

Brown, G., Sabotage. A Study in Industrial Conflict, Nottingham 1977.

Burawoy, M., Manufacturing Consent, Chicago 1979.

Burns, T. (ed.), Industrial Man, Hardmondsworth 1969.

—— and Stalker, G.M., The Management of Innovation, London 1966.

Butt, J., 'Working Class Housing in Glasgow, 1900-39' in I. MacDougall (ed.), Essays in Scottish Labour History, Edinburgh n.d. (c.1978).

Buxton, N.K., 'Economic Growth in Scotland between the Wars: the Role of Production Structure and Rationalisation', Economic History Review 33, 1980.

Challinor, R., The Origins of British Bolshevism, London 1977.

Chamberlain, C., 'The Growth of Support for the Labour Party in Britain', British Journal of Sociology 24, 1973.

Child, J., Industrial Relations in the British Printing Industry, London 1967.

Coates, D., The Labour Party and the Struggle for Socialism, Cambridge 1975.

Cole, G.D.H., Workshop Organisation, Oxford 1923.

—— A History of the Labour Party from 1914, London 1948.

Cowling, M., The Impact of Labour 1920-1924, Cambridge 1971.

Deacon, A., In Search of the Scrounger. The Administration of Unemployment Insurance in Britain 1920-1931, London 1976.

Dickson, T. et al., Scottish Capitalism, London 1980.

Dowse, R., Left in the Centre. The Independent Labour Party 1893-1940, London 1960.

Elliott, B. and McCrone, D., 'Urban Development in Edinburgh. A Contribution to the Political Economy of Place', Scottish Journal of Sociology 4, 1980.

Bibliography

Elliott, B., McCrone, D. and Skelton, V., 'Property and Politics; Edinburgh 1875-1975', mimeo, University of Edinburgh, n.d. (c.1978).

Foster, J., 'British Imperialism and the Labour Aristocracy' in J. Skelley (ed.), The General Strike 1926, London 1976.

Fox, A., Beyond Contract. Work, Power and Trust Relations, London 1974.

Friedman, A.L., Industry and Labour, London 1977.

Goodrich, C.L., The Frontier of Control, New York 1921.

Graham, T.N., Willie Graham, London n.d. (c.1948).

Graham, W., The Wages of Labour, London 1924.

Gramsci, A., Selections from the Prison Notebooks, London 1971.

Gray, R.Q., The Labour Aristocracy in Victorian Edinburgh, Oxford 1976.

Hannington, W., Unemployed Struggles 1919-1936, London 1936.

Harrison, R., 'The War Emergency Workers' National Committee 1914-1920' in A. Briggs and J. Saville (eds.), Essays in Labour History 1886-1923, London 1971.

Harvie, C., No Gods and Precious Few Heroes, Scotland 1914-1980, London 1981.

Hinton, J., The First Shop Stewards Movement, London 1973.

—— and Hyman, R., Trade Unions and Revolution, London 1975.

Hobsbawn, E.J. Industry and Empire, Harmondsworth 1976.

—— Labouring Men, London 1964.

Holton, R., British Syndicalism 1900-14, London 1970.

Keir, D. (ed.), The Third Statistical Account of Scotland. The City of Edinburgh, Glasgow 1966.

Kendall, W., The Revolutionary Movement in Britain 1900-21, London 1969.

Landes, D., The Unbound Prometheus, Cambridge 1969.

Lenman, B., An Economic History of Modern Scotland 1660-1976, London 1977.

Leser, C.E.V. and Silvey, A.H., 'Scottish Industries during the Inter-War Period', The Manchester School 18, 1950.

Lowe, R., 'The Erosion of State Intervention in Britain 1917-24', Economic History Review 31, 1978.

MacDougall, I., 'Edinburgh, with Some Notes on the Lothians and Fife' in J. Skelley (ed.), The General Strike, London 1976.

—— (ed.), A Catalogue of Some Labour Records in

Scotland and some Scots Records outside Scotland, Edinburgh 1978.

—— (ed.), Militant Miners, Edinburgh 1981.

Macintyre, S., Little Moscows, London 1980.

—— A Proletarian Science, Cambridge 1980.

Mackinven, H., 'Edinburgh and District Trades Council —— Centenary 1859-1959' in Edinburgh TC Annual Report 1959.

Mann, M., 'The Social Cohesion of Liberal Democracy', American Sociological Review 35, 1970.

Marwick, A., The Deluge, Harmondsworth 1967.

Marwick, W.H., A Short History of Labour in Scotland, Edinburgh 1967.

Matthew, H.C.G., McKibbin, R.I. and Kay, J.A., 'The Franchise Factor in the Rise of the Labour Party', English Historical Review 91, 1976.

McKenzie, R., British Political Parties, London 1963.

McKibben, R., The Evolution of the Labour Party 1910-1924, Oxford 1974.

Middlemas, K., Politics in Industrial Society, London 1979.

Miliband, R., Parliamentary Socialism, London 1973.

Milnes, N., A Study of Industrial Edinburgh and the Surrounding Area 1923-1934, Volume I, London 1936.

Nairn, T., 'The Nature of the Labour Party', New Left Review 27 and 28, 1964.

Oakley, C.A. Scottish Industry Today, Edinburgh 1937.

Palmer, B., 'Class, Conception and Conflict: the Thrust for Efficiency, Managerial Views of Labor, and the Working Class Rebellion 1903-1922', Review of Radical Political Economics 7, 1975.

Panitch, L.V., 'Ideology and Integration: the Case of the British Labour Party', Political Studies 19, 1971.

Parkin, F., Class Inequality and Political Order, St Albans 1973.

Proud, E.D., Welfare Work, London 1916.

Ramsay, H., 'Cycles of Control: Worker Participation in Sociological and Historical Perspective', Sociology 11, 1977.

Richardson, H., Vipond, J., and Furbey, R., Housing and Urban Spatial Structure: a Case Study, Farnborough, Hants. 1975.

Rowntree, B.S., The Human Factor in Business, London 1921.

Roy, D., 'Efficiency and "the Fix": Informal Intergroup Relations in a Piecework Machine Shop', in T. Burns

Bibliography

(ed.), Industrial Man, Harmondsworth 1969.

—— 'Quota Restriction and Goldbricking in a Machine Shop', American Journal of Sociology 57, 1952.

Saville, J., 'The Ideology of Labourism', in R. Benewick, R.N. Berki and B. Parekh (eds.), Knowledge and Belief in Politics, London 1973.

Scott, J. and Hughes, M., The Anatomy of Scottish Capital, London 1980.

Swenarton, M., Homes fit for Heroes, London 1981.

Tawney, R.H., 'The Abolition of Economic Controls 1918-1921', Economic History Review 13, 1943.

White, S., 'Labour's Council of Action 1920', Journal of Comtemporary History 9, 1974.

—— 'Soviets in Britain: the Leeds Convention of 1917', International Review of Social History 19, 1974.

Whiteford, J.F., Factory Management Wastes, London 1919.

Whiteside, N., 'Industrial Welfare and Labour Regulation in Britain at the Time of the First World War', International Review of Social History 25, 1980.

Winter, J.M., Socialism and the Challenge of War, London 1974.

Woodward, J., Management and Technology, London 1958.

INDEX

Index

Index

at T&LC, compared with DLPs 209-10; Bolshevism and 180-1; Central branch 159, 170, 180, 194; Communist Party and 220; dispute with Labour Party over Graham candidature 174; Drummond Shiels and 182; ethos 148, 211-15 passim; formation in Edinburgh 147; Guild of Youth 213-4; in wartime 159-60; Leith, new premises 214; Marxism and 202; organisation 211-3; propaganda 150, 211, 213; role in early Labour Party 148-9; St Leonards 253; T&LC restrictions on 209

industrial unionism 162; and 1919 railway strike 183; and union organisation 131; and views of 1917 180; government policy on 120; language used by labourism 217; SLP and 149-50

Industrial Workers of the World (IWW) 149

industry 55-6

infant mortality 11

intellectuals, and British labour movement 240

Invergordon 82

Italy, danger of Fascism in 221

justices of the peace, trade union 115, 120, 139n86, 141n22

Labour, National Amalgamated Union of (NAUL: Rubber Workers) 78, 79, 102, 180; affiliation to Labour Party 176; and Armistice 110; and shorter working week 111; competition with Clerks in rubber industry 116-7; growth in rubber

industry 116, 95n109; organisation at wire mills 105; organisation of rubber workers 104-5

labour aristocracy 5, 46, 47, 147, 234

labour college movement 150, 182; and ILP Guild of Youth 214; and Marxism 184, 215-6; growth in Edinburgh 181-2, 184-5; Plebs League 182; school on General Strike 224; see also Central Labour College - Scottish Labour College

Labour councillors 152

labour leaders 152-3, 195-6

labour movement 198-9, 220

Labour Party 3, 4, 5; 1918 constitution 1, 172-5, 174, 176; 1918 Nottingham Conference 172, 174-5; 1936 Edinburgh Conference 12; and NUR election campaign 195; and rent strike 1920 199; and union organisational thought 132; conference, supposed role of 236; control, and trade unions 245; councillors and dressmakers' strike 108; divisional and ward organisation 208, 209-10, 242-5; early development 148-51; Edinburgh branch 148, 155, 157-8, 189n43; electoral performance 247-52; exclusion of Communists 221; finance 204, 247; growth of organisation in Edinburgh 207-10; importance of electoral role 194-5; Labour Socialist coalition and organisation 207-10; town and parish council representation 153-4

labour politics 235, 236, 238

Labour Representation

Index

Mound 12, 150
Munitions of War Acts 77-8, 105, 161
Munitions Tribunals 79
Musselburgh 77, 105, 245
mutuality principle, in printing 73

'nation' 161, 168-9, 235
national bargaining 132-5
National Industrial Conference 110-11, 120
national interest 2, 103, 111, 113; impact of peace on views of 168-9
National Socialist Party 182
nationalism 2
Nelson, Thomas, and Sons, publishers and printers 71
New Craighall 77
New Town 8, 41, 45
North British Railway Company 66, 80
North British Rubber Company 16, 75, 78, 135; Castle Mills 75, 116, 135; employment exchange 77; internal labour market 77; Munitions of War Acts 77-8; welfare department 80

oil, grease and soap manufacture 16
Old Town 8, 9, 12, 150
organisation 2, 3, 6, 172; administrative efficiency and 179; and General Strike 223; and machines 56; and profit 234-5; and trade union development, and administration 118; and war effort 103; and wartime politics 160-1; bureaucracy 56; centralisation and 177; efficiency and 177, 193; hierarchy and 56, 131, 177, 179; in postwar coalition 236;

limitations of concepts 236-7; managerial images, and union organisation 131-2; mechanistic images 117-18, 128, 179, 236; mechanistic structures 57, 179; military images of 56-7, 81-2, 117-18, 185, 236, 238; organic structures 57-8; political implications of 146; trade union discussions on 128-35
Out-of-Work Donation 21, 38, 41
outworking 65
overtime 36

Painters 126
paper industry 16, 18, 64
Parish Council, Edinburgh 39, 40-1
parish relief, and 'Mond Scale' 40
parliamentary strategy 3
parliamentary system, central to Labour Party 221
patriotism 2, 168, 234
payment systems; bonus systems 59; 'mixed system' in printing 73; payment by results 59, 66; piecework 33, 51n17, 68, 77, 86; shop steward organisation in engineering and 67
Pensions Committees, local 105
planning 2, 3
Plasterers and Town Council housing schemes 206
Poor Law 38
population, of Edinburgh 8, 9, 10
Portobello 151, 245
Portsmouth 170
Pottinger, James J. 174, 189n36, 228n74
press 84, 119-20; and dressmakers' strike 108; and ex-servicemen 114; and waste 121; anti-trade union

Index

Index